*All Praises to
the Most High Elohim Yahuah!*

*This Entire Book is Because of
His Revelatory Power!*

Table of Contents

Part I: The Truth

Introduction: Tell the Children the Truth 4

Chapter 1: Finding Eden 9

Chapter 2: Finding Yahshar-el 25

Chapter 3: The Palestine Lie 48

Chapter 4: Evidence From Hidden Scriptures 62

Part II: The Conspiracy

Chapter 5: How Could This Happen? 80

Chapter 6: The Conspirators 92

Chapter 7: The Edomite Religion 108

Chapter 8: The Real Yahshar-el 147

Chapter 9: The First Jewish State 154

Chapter 10: The Dispersion 176

Chapter 11: Into Captivity 185

Chapter 12: Where the Children of Yahshar-el Went 200

Conclusion: Rebel 222

Photo Gallery 227

Part I: The Truth

Introduction: Tell the Children the Truth

"Babylon system is the vampire,
Sucking the children day by day,
I say, the Babylon system is the vampire, falling empire
Sucking the blood of the sufferers,
Building church and university,
Deceiving the people continually,
I say they are graduating thieves and murderers
Look out now, they are sucking the blood of the sufferers

Tell the children the truth
Tell the children the truth
Tell the children the truth right now
Come on and tell the children the truth
Tell the children the truth
Tell the children the truth
Tell the children the truth
Come on and tell the children the truth

'Cause, we've been trodding on ya winepress much too long
Rebel, rebel!
And we've been takin' for granted much too long
Rebel, rebel!"

~ Bob Marley, Babylon System

The world is not as it seems. As I write, the state of Israel is laying siege to the Gaza Strip, killing thousands of mostly innocent civilians, purportedly as retribution for the Hamas terrorist attack on October 7, 2023. The primarily Jewish Israel Defense Force is committing war crimes no other country would be permitted to engage in, no matter the context, including cutting off food, water and fuel to the people and using bullets and bombs with a kind of recklessness and intentionality that has led numerous international human rights organizations to label the siege a genocide, or at minimal an ethnic cleansing. All the while, Christian Zionists are openly defending Israel, no matter the horrific nature of the war crimes. They have chosen not to apply their Messiah's creed: "You have heard that it was said, 'You shall love your neighbor and hate your enemy.' But I say to you, love your enemies and pray for those who persecute you."[1] Instead, many are misapplying scripture to justify mass killings, such as, "Ashkelon will see it and be afraid. Gaza too will writhe in great pain."[2]

It's not just the Zionists. Much of the secular international community, who are constantly reminded of the horrors of the Holocaust, are peddling a narrative that the Israeli occupation of Palestine is necessary, as the Jewish people require a homeland given their history of persecution, and Palestine, as their ancestral home is that natural location. This justification relies on two preconditions: 1) the people in Israel are the descendants of the ancient Hebrews of the Bible, and 2) Palestine is the location where ancient Yashar'el (Israel)[3] ruled. If either of these prerequisites are false then the entire world has been deceived into allowing mass extermination based on tall tales and fantasy. In this book, we will show how both of these preconditions are, in fact, false.

This book is about an ancient conspiracy and coverup that will be extremely difficult for most of the world to believe. After all, believing the major world powers, despite their differences, could orchestrate a massive deception without leaving an apparent trace warrants heightened scrutiny. For both prerequisites to be false, it would necessitate a 2000-year-long conspiracy to hide the truth where all three major competing Abrahamic religions are complicit.

The reader is 100% justified in being skeptical. I strongly encourage the reader to crosscheck every scripture, source, and map referenced. As Paul the Apostle writes, we are to prove *everything*.[4]

---

[1] Matthew 5:43; All Bible verses are in the New American Standard Version.
[2] Zechariah 9:5.
[3] I have chosen to use certain Hebrew words in this work where the words or meanings are of significance to the faith.
[4] 1 Thessalonians 5:21: "Prove all things; hold fast that which is good."

Beyond crosschecking this work, the reader is encouraged to do their own research, and where truth is uncovered, reveal it to the body of believers in Yahusha (Jesus).

However, suppose the reader insists on blind reliance on the opinions of "scholars" and "experts," even when those opinions contradict scripture. In that case, this book will be useless to you. Reading a book like this takes objectivity, and most people, who are all victims of indoctrination, do not possess the capacity to be objective, especially when these prejudices have become a part of a cultural, religious and political identity.

That being said, I want to acknowledge my limitations in this effort: time, location and resources. The first is time. I first decided to do this work as a video for my YouTube Channel, Afrikan Exodus. However, The Most High Yahuah (God) strongly impressed on my heart that a video was insufficient and it needed to be put into a book. This is my second time writing a book; the first time took me over a year to complete. I knew, given the research and writing necessary for this type of bold project, that this book would likely take twice as long. However, as I began to write, Yah impressed on my heart to finish the book in 6 months. In obedience, I reorganized my life to do what was necessary to finish this book in that timeframe.

The second limitation is location. I have never been to the State of Israel. Most debilitating, however, is I have never been to East Africa, the location where the Bible mostly takes place. I write this book from the country of Ghana, West Africa, so I at least feel closer to the subject of this book than I have ever in my life. That being said, extensive work is encouraged for those on the ground in the locations that will be mentioned in this book, whether by expert archeologists or lay persons led by the Ruach HaKodesh (Holy Spirit) to do the work.

The third limitation is resources. I wrote this book alone and with what was available to me. Most of my sources are secondary sources and are limited to those which can be uncovered from the internet. The breadth of this work, of course, is deserving of an entire team of historians, archeologists, researchers and even an entire academic discipline given the nature of what has been hidden for so long.

While these are my limitations, I do not believe this work is my own. I suppose a fourth limitation would be qualification, as by most standards, I, a lawyer by training with no formal Bible education, am not qualified in the eyes of mainstream Christianity to make these assessments. However, I understand and am fully aware that it is not man or his institutions that qualify us for the call of Yahuah over our lives. I Corinthians 3:5-6 states:

> Not that we are adequate in ourselves so as to consider anything as having come from ourselves, but our adequacy is from God, 6 who also made us adequate as servants of a new covenant, not of the letter but of the Spirit; for the letter kills, but the Spirit gives life.

I know I have been chosen by Yah for this exact work, as confirmed by His Ruach. Two years ago, as I sat in my son's bedroom doing our nightly prayers, I had a clear vision that shocked me, and I saw it twice in this one setting. I saw the continent of Africa with the label "Holy Land." I was extremely confused. Never had I ever questioned where the Holy Land was. It was Palestine for the stint of my Christian faith. Even though as a Pan-Afrikanist I had discontent with Zionism, I never questioned that Palestine was Yahshar-el.

I had occasionally heard people assert that the Holy Land was in Africa. I denied such conclusions as Black people trying to claim a history that was not ours (as I am sure some of you will label this work). Similarly, when Hebrew Israelites would present arguments that we were the children of Yahshar-el, I again denied this as being attempts to distance ourselves from our "Afrikanness," which I had grown very proud of. However, I was clear on what I saw in the vision. I prayed to Yahuah to reveal the meaning of the vision in His time and left it at that. A few months later, while carefully reading the Book of Jubilees, I was shocked by what I saw, a complete confirmation of the vision Yah gave me. We will get into that later.

I thus encourage the reader to allow the Ruach HaKodesh to lead them through this reading journey, leaning on the words of Yahuah and not on the opinions of man. Without belaboring this point, we should begin.

Chapter 1: Finding Eden

"God must prove to be true, though every person be found a liar."

~ Romans 3:4

Finding the Garden of Eden is the untold gateway to finding Biblical Yahshar-el (Israel). Although in the imagination of most believers, these two locations are distinct and unrelated, in truth, you cannot find one without roughly identifying the other. But first, it is essential for the reader to know the mainstream view on what the Bible says about where the land is that Yahuah (God) promised Jacob.

Greater Israel

Scripturally speaking, where is the land Yahuah (God) promised to Abraham? Genesis 15:18 tells us of Yah's promise to Abraham:

> On that day the Lord made a covenant with Abram, saying,
> "To your descendants I have given this land,
> From the river of Egypt as far as the great river, the river Euphrates:
> [19] the (land of the) Kenite, the Kenizzite, the Kadmonite, [20] the Hittite, the Perizzite, the Rephaim, [21] the Amorite, the Canaanite, the Girgashite, and the Jebusite."

Abraham's descendants are promised a territory where two rivers act as the geographical markers of where the territory begins, and where it ends. The Promised Land starts at the "river of Egypt" and ends at "the river Euphrates." The "river of Egypt" is, of course, the Nile River, the longest river in the world that runs directly through Egypt, flowing from south to north. However, some advocates of the theory of "Greater Israel" have chosen to apply "river of Egypt" to the Wadi El-Arish, which is not a river but a seasonal stream in the Sinai Peninsula that empties into the Mediterranean Sea.[5]

Regardless of which, at face value, if Yahshar-el (Israel) were located in Palestine, this would mean the Promised Land extends far beyond the borders of Palestine today. Essentially, the Promised Land encompasses an eastern portion of Egypt and goes east into ancient Mesopotamia. This Promised Land would encompass not just Palestine but also Egypt, Israel, Saudi Arabia, Lebanon, Syria, Jordan, Turkey, and Iraq. Historically and archeologically, we know that this land mass was not occupied by a single kingdom, as the Bible describes Yahshar-el.

To explain this apparent discrepancy, some Zionists invented a concept not found in the scriptures, known as, "Greater Israel." (See Map 1) This is the idea that the land between the "river of Egypt" and the Euphrates River was promised to Abraham's descendants, but the promise has not yet been fulfilled. According to the website Christians for Israel International:

> The only correct conclusion that can be drawn from the cited Bible verses is that God has promised Israel the land from the Wadi El-Arish to the Euphrates and from the Mediterranean to the Amorite region beyond Jordan (kingdoms of Sihon and Og). That does not mean that Israel already has the right to annex all these areas. Greater Israel is still the Promised Land! When during the Kingdom of Peace Messiah intervenes, then and only then, according to Ezekiel 47 and 48, God will hand over this area to Israel. Not before![6]

However, this understanding that the borders would not be fulfilled until the Messiah's return directly contradict scripture. In Joshua 1:1-4 it reads:

---

[5]Hubert Luns, Greater Israel – From the Nile to the Euphrates, Christians for Israel International, (Nov. 24, 2020) https://www.c4israel.org/news/greater-israel-from-the-nile-to-the-euphrates/; Wadi Al-ʿArīsh, Britannica, https://www.britannica.com/place/Wadi-Al-Arish (*last visited* Dec. 25, 2023).
[6] *Supra* note 5.

> Now it came about after the death of Moses the servant of the Lord, that the Lord spoke to Joshua the son of Nun, Moses' servant, saying, 2 "Moses My servant is dead; so now arise, cross this Jordan, you and all this people, to the land which I am giving to them, to the sons of Israel. 3 **Every place on which the sole of your footsteps, I have given it to you, just as I spoke to Moses. 4 From the wilderness and this Lebanon, even as far as the great river, the river Euphrates, all the land of the Hittites, and as far as the Great Sea toward the setting of the sun will be your territory.**

When Joshua ends his military campaign in Joshua 11:23, it records:

> So Joshua took the **whole land**, in accordance with everything that the LORD had spoken to Moses; and Joshua gave it as an inheritance to Israel according to their divisions by their tribes. **So the land was at rest from war**.

As the previous scriptures state, Joshua took the *whole* land Yahuah promised to Moses, which is the land "even as far as the great river, the river Euphrates." We know this is the same land promised to Abraham, as stated in Exodus 33:1-2:

> Then the Lord spoke to Moses, "Depart, go up from here, you and the people whom you have brought up from the land of Egypt, to the land of which I swore to Abraham, Isaac, and Jacob, saying, 'To your descendants I will give it.' 2 And I will send an angel before you and I will drive out the Canaanite, the Amorite, the Hittite, the Perizzite, the Hivite, and the Jebusite.

We can confirm Yahshar-el's dominion in this region was at the "Euphrates," as King David would conquer neighboring kingdoms, as stated in 1 Chronicles 18:1-4:

> Now after this it came to pass, that David smote the Philistines, and subdued them, and took Gath and her towns out of the hand of the Philistines.[2] And he smote Moab; and the Moabites became David's servants, and brought gifts.[3] And David smote Hadarezer king of Zobah unto Hamath, **as he went to stablish his dominion by the river Euphrates**.

This dominion of Yahshar-el by the "Euphrates" is confirmed in 2 Chronicles 9:25-26:

Solomon had four thousand stalls for horses and chariots, and twelve thousand horses, which he kept in the chariot cities and also with him in Jerusalem. **26 He ruled over all the kings from the Euphrates River to the land of the Philistines, as far as the border of Egypt.**

It should be emphasized that these tributary kingdoms that Yahshar-el conquered, if we go by Bible archeology maps, are nowhere close to the Euphrates River.(See Map 2) Further confirmation of the "Euphrates'" close proximity to Yahshar-el is in Jeremiah 13:1-7, where Yah orders Jeremiah the prophet to make a trip to the "Euphrates:"

> This is what the Lord said to me: "Go and buy yourself a linen undergarment and put it around your waist, but do not put it in water."² So I bought the undergarment in accordance with the word of the Lord, and put it around my waist. ³ Then the word of the Lord came to me a second time, saying, ⁴ "Take the undergarment that you bought, which is around your waist, and arise, **go to the Euphrates and hide it there in a crevice of the rock."** ⁵ **So I went and hid it by the Euphrates, as the Lord had commanded me.** ⁶ **After many days the Lord said to me, "Arise, go to the Euphrates and take from there the undergarment which I commanded you to hide there."** ⁷ Then I went to the Euphrates and dug, and I took the undergarment from the place where I had hidden it; and behold, the undergarment was ruined, it was completely useless.

Here, Yahuah told Jeremiah to go to the river "Euphrates" to bury his undergarment, then return days later to retrieve it. There is no mention of an intense journey nor of Jeremiah having to enter another country's borders to complete his journey. This infers that the river was within a reasonable distance from Yahshar-el, or within Yahshar-el's domain. We also see this in Genesis 2:10-14 in the description of the rivers of Eden. Three out of the four rivers are given a geographical description detailing foreign lands, except the "Euphrates:"

> Now a river flowed out of Eden to water the garden; and from there it divided and became four rivers. 11 The name of the first is Pishon; it flows around the whole land of Havilah, where there is gold. 12 The

gold of that land is good; the bdellium and the onyx stone are there as well. 13 The name of the second river is Gihon; it flows around the whole land of Cush. 14 The name of the third river is Tigris; it flows east of Assyria. **And the fourth river is the Euphrates.**

The fact the "Euphrates" is simply mentioned by name with no geographical description infers familiarity of the writers and their audience with this river.

Here, the Bible believer is faced with a hard issue. We know scripturally that Yahuah promised land from the "Euphrates" to the "river of Egypt," and Yahshar-el actually conquered that land by the "Euphrates." That geography does not comport with reality. Does the Bible believer take the position that Yahuah would promise land to Yahshar-el and represent in His scripture that the promise was fulfilled, but not actually fulfill the promise? Prayerfully, the answer is no. But there is more to this story.

The river most Bible translations call the "Euphrates," a Greek word that did not even exist at the time Yahuah proclaimed His promise to Abraham, is actually the Hebrew word *Perath*. Thus, a proper reading of Yah's promise to Abraham is: "To your descendants I have given this land, from the river of Egypt as far as the great river, the river *Perath*."

If you are a believer in the perfection and accuracy of Yahuah and his promise to Abraham, the river Perath cannot be the Euphrates River. It has to be a river that either borders Biblical Yahshar-el or is encompassed by it.

The Real Perath

If the Euphrates River, which is east of the Nile River, is not the Perath, then there are two other possibilities. Either the Perath is west of the Nile River or south of the Nile River, as north would go into the Mediterranean Sea. It should be mentioned some in the Hebrew Israelite movement have advanced a theory that the Perath is the Niger River, and thus the kingdom of Yahshar-el (Israel) was in

West Africa.⁷ As evidence, some have pointed to the word "Euphrates" showing up on some historical maps in West Africa.

The author rejects this conclusion for multiple reasons. Firstly, there is no evidence of a single nation ever inhabiting such a wide breadth of territory. Second, the geography does not match Yahshar-el as is explained in scripture. The mere fact the word "Euphrates" appears in West Africa does not mean the river is the Perath. Again, the word "Euphrates" is a Greek word that did not exist at the time of Abraham.

If we look south of the Nile River, however, we do see a separate river that connects to the Nile known as the Blue Nile, which originates from natural springs above Lake Tana. While not well known in the world for its importance, the Blue Nile is a river regarded by many Ethiopians as holy. This river is also of great importance to the entire region, as it supplies most of the waters of the Nile River.⁸

The fact the Blue Nile River actually connects to the Nile River is significant as well, as we are told in the description of Eden that all four rivers that flow out of Eden were connected. As stated in Genesis, "The name of the second river is Gihon; it flows around the whole land of Cush." This major river that flows throughout the land of Cush is, of course, the Nile River. If the Perath is the Blue Nile and the Gihon the Nile, then Yahshar-el would be the land between these two great rivers in East Africa, not the "Middle East." However, we will continue to test this hypothesis.

---

⁷ Nairaland Forum, Abraham's Promised Land Is Sub-saharan Africa, With Proof, https://www.nairaland.com/6421559/abrahams-promised-land-sub-saharan-africa (*last visited* Jan. 8, 2024).
⁸ Blue Nile, New World Encyclopedia, https://www.newworldencyclopedia.org/entry/Blue_Nile (*last visited* Jan. 8, 2024).

The Rivers of Garden of Eden

If we can now identify the Perath River as the Blue Nile, that means we know one of the four rivers the Bible identifies as flowing from the Garden of Eden. Again, according to Genesis 2:10-14:

> Now a river flowed out of Eden to water the garden; and from there it divided and became four rivers. ¹¹ The name of the first is Pishon; it flows around the whole land of Havilah, where there is gold. ¹² The gold of that land is good; the bdellium and the onyx stone are there as well. ¹³ The name of the second river is Gihon; it flows around the whole land of Cush. ¹⁴ The name of the third river is [Hiddekel]; it flows east of Assyria. And the fourth river is the [Perath].

Bible scholars have long struggled to make sense of these four rivers of Eden, principally because they were attached to the idea that the Perath River was the Euphrates River. This error has also led to the *Hiddekel River* being designated the Tigris River. As for the two other rivers, the Gihon and the Pishon, they have remained the object of shrewd debate despite the fact that both rivers have geographical descriptions that should make their locations discoverable.

The Gihon River

The Gihon River is the Nile River, based on the description, "it flows around the whole land of Cush." It is important to take a moment to deal with a commonly held belief that is as ignorant as it is racist, but is taught in many congregations. That is when the Bible mentions "Cush," or as some translations state, "Ethiopia," that the scriptures are referring to all of Africa or all of Africa south of Egypt.[9]

Ethiopia, the country, did not exist at the time of the Bible. The word "Ethiopia" originates from the Greek word "Aithiops," which

---

[9] "Although some believe that, in this passage, *Cush* could be a reference to Mesopotamia, other biblical scholars believe that it is more consistent to identify it as a general term for the African lands south of Egypt." What is the significance of Cush in the Bible?, Got Questions, https://www.gotquestions.org/Cush-in-the-Bible.html, (*last visited* Dec. 15, 2023).

means burnt faces.[10] The actual Hebrew word for Cush in the Bible is *Kūš*.[11] Kūš is mentioned as a nation and not a continent or conglomerate of nations.[12] More to the point, 2 Kings 19:8-11 tells an account of the king of Kūš Tirhakah, who most scholars agree is Pharaoh Taharqa of the 25th Nubian or Kushite Dynasty,[13] aiding Yahudah (Judah) against the Assyrians:

> Then Rabshakeh returned and found the king of Assyria fighting against Libnah, for he had heard that the king had left Lachish. 9 When he heard them say about Tirhakah king of Cush, "Behold, he has come out to fight you," he sent messengers again to Hezekiah, saying, 10 "This is what you shall say to Hezekiah king of Judah: 'Do not let your God in whom you trust deceive you by saying, "Jerusalem will not be handed over to the king of Assyria." 11 Behold, you yourself have heard what the kings of Assyria have done to all the lands, destroying them completely. So will you be saved?

This would mean Biblical Kūš is the ancient kingdom Kush. The kingdom of Kush one time ruled the Nile Valley, but was later pushed to Upper Egypt (southern Egypt). This nation's history extends back to 2400 BCE, and it rose to its greatest prominence from 1069 BCE-350 CE.[14] Kush was a political and military rival to ancient Egypt, with a commanding gold industry and architecture, which included 200 pyramids.[15] Treating this powerful kingdom as an afterthought or a general designation for Africa south of Egypt is, thus, careless.

---

[10] Ethiopia, Online Etymology Dictionary, https://www.etymonline.com/word/Ethiopia, (*last visited* Sept. 22, 2023).
[11] 3568. kūš, Bible Hub, https://biblehub.com/hebrew/kush_3568.htm (*last visited* Jan. 8, 2024).
[12] Examples: 1 Chronicles 1:8, 2 Kings 19:9, Ezekiel 29:10.
[13] Bryan Windle, Tirhakah: An Archaeological Biography, Bible Archeology Report, (Mar. 18, 2022) https://biblearchaeologyreport.com/2022/03/18/tirhakah-an-archaeological-biography/.
[14] Joshua J. Mark, The Kingdom of Kush, World History Encyclopedia, (Feb. 6, 2018) https://www.worldhistory.org/Kush/.
[15] Nuria Castellano, Rival to Egypt, the Nubian kingdom of Kush exuded power and gold, National Geographic, https://www.nationalgeographic.com/history/history-magazine/article/ancient-egypt-nubian-kingdom-pyramids-sudan (*last visited* Sept. 22, 2023).

The fact that Kūš is Kush means the Gihon River is the Nile River. However, some Jewish and Bible scholars have taken an anti-historical approach to locating Kūš and the Gihon, pointing to alternative locations. According to the Jewish Encyclopedia, the Gihon is:

> The second river of Eden, surrounding the whole land cf Cush or Ethiopia (Gen. ii. 13). Its identification has been a matter of dispute among Biblical exegetes and critics. Josephus (" Ant. " i. 1, § 3) identifies Gihon with the Nile, and the Septuagint renders "Sihor" (the Nile; Jer. li. 18) by Γηών. But the Midrash and later commentators, as Saadia and Rashi, think Pison, the first river of Eden, to be the Nile. The Arabs call the Oxus "Jaihun," and it has been assumed by certain critics to be the "Gihon" of the Bible. The fact is that the identification of Gihon depends on that of Cush. Huet identifies Cush with Chusistan, and Bochart identifies it with Susiana; apparently, therefore, Gihon must be sought among Asiatic rivers, and it may be the Oxus, the Orontes, or the Ganges... Placing Eden in the region of the Mountains of the Moon, Farissol removes the difficulty presented by the fact that the Euphrates and Tigris are in Asia by declaring that these rivers, though taking their rise in Africa, actually run underground till they reappear in Assyria.[16]

These mental gymnastics of ignoring the Pharaoh Taharqa connection and instead suggesting the Gihon is an Asiatic river, or even hypothesizing an underground river system that the Bible neglected to mention in its description, are being done for a reason. If *Kūš* is the empire Kush, and if the Gihon is the Nile, the Garden of Eden would have to be located in Africa. The Nile River begins in Lake Victoria located in Uganda, Tanzania and Kenya. This river is nowhere close to the Euphrates or Tigris Rivers. Thus, not only is the Perath not the Euphrates River, but also the Hiddekel is not the Tigris River.

---

[16] Emil G. Hirsch, M. Seligsohn, Gihon, (Jewish Encyclopedia, https://www.jewishencyclopedia.com/articles/6668-gihon (*last visited* Aug. 1, 2023)

The Pishon

Having located two of the rivers of Eden we turn to the Pishon. As the four rivers of Eden start from a single source before flowing out of the garden, theoretically, we should be able to locate the final two rivers.

We are told about the Pishon that it flows "around the whole land of Havilah, where there is gold. The gold of that land is good; the bdellium and the onyx stone are there as well." However, the Hebrew translation of "bdellium" is *bedolach* and "onyx stone" is *shoham*, both of which are of uncertain derivation.[17] In the Septuagint, the Greek translation of Hebrew scripture that predates the Jewish Masoretic translation used in most Bibles by over 1,000 years, the description of the Havilah differs.

According to the Septuagint, in the land of Havilah, "there is gold. And the gold of that land is good, there also is carbuncle and emerald." This is not an insignificant difference. While bdellium is found in both Africa and Asia, onyx stone is not as plentiful in Africa as it is in Asia and South America. However, carbuncle, a garnet stone, and emerald are both found plentifully in South Eastern African countries, such as Zambia, Zimbabwe, Tanzania and South Africa.[18]

---

[17] 7718. Shoham, Bible Hub, https://biblehub.com/hebrew/7718.htm (*last visited* Jan. 9, 2024); 916. Bedolach, Bible Hub, https://biblehub.com/hebrew/916.htm (*last visited* Jan. 9, 2024).

[18] A List of Gemstones Found in Africa, Chromagems, https://chromagems.com/blog/gemstone-information/a-list-of-gemstones-found-in-africa/ (*last visited* Jan. 9, 2024); David Bressan, One Of World's Largest Emeralds Was Unearthed In Africa, Forbes, (Nov. 2, 2018) https://www.forbes.com/sites/davidbressan/2018/11/02/one-of-worlds-largest-emeralds-unearthed-in-africa/?sh=4c5d4b957ec4; Deborah Dzifa Makafui This is how Zambia became home to emeralds, Face to Face Africa, (Dec. 8, 2022) https://face2faceafrica.com/article/this-is-how-zambia-became-home-to-emeralds. The Hidden Treasures of Africa: Exploring the World's Most Valuable Gemstones, MRCSL, https://mrcsl.org/african-stones/ (*last visited* Jan. 9, 2024).

The Zambezi and the Congo River that are located in this region run so close together that it seems highly possible that they were once connected. The proximity of the Congo River to the Nile River may similarly show that they were once connected as well. In fact, the Congo River runs so close to Lake Victoria and the Nile River that the Egyptian government is considering connecting the Nile River to the Congo River to assist with water shortages.[19] Thus, the Pishon River would be the Congo River or the Zambezi River, or both rivers as one which together ran throughout Southern Africa.

This region matches what the land of Havilah was described as, a place where "the land is good," as Africa is the most minerally rich continent on earth. As stated by World Atlas.com:

> Africa has the richest concentration of natural resources, such as oil, copper, diamonds, bauxite, lithium, gold, hardwood forests, and tropical fruits. It is estimated that 30% of the earth's mineral resources are found in the African continent. Additionally, Africa has the world's biggest precious metal reserves on earth.[20]

Southern Africa, in particular, being the land of Havilah is right in line with scripture. Geography professor Royal Berglee's description of the region paints this picture vividly:

> Southern Africa is set apart from other Sub-Saharan African regions because of its mineral resources, including copper, diamonds, gold, zinc, chromium, platinum, manganese, iron ore, and coal. Countries in Southern Africa are larger in geographic area, except three smaller landlocked states: Lesotho, Swaziland, and Malawi. The larger states-South Africa, Botswana, Mozambique, Zimbabwe, Zambia, Namibia, and Angola—all have extensive mineral deposits.

---

[19] Mahmoud Sakr, Can Egypt consider diverting water from the Congo to the Nile?, (April 15, 2020), https://www.leaders-mena.com/can-egypt-consider-diverting-water-from-the-congo-to-the-nile/.

[20] Which Continent Is The Richest In Natural Resources?, World Atlas, https://www.worldatlas.com/articles/which-continent-is-the-richest-in-natural-resources.html (*last visited* Sept. 22, 2023).

These widespread mineral resources make this one of the wealthiest regions of Africa with the greatest potential for economic growth. A chain of mineral resources in Southern Africa stretches from the rich oil fields in northwest Angola, east through the central diamond-mining region in Huambo Province, and into the Copper Belt region of Zambia and Congo. A region of rich mineral deposits continues to the south called the Great Dyke in central Zimbabwe, through the Bushveld basin into South Africa. This extends southwest through the Witwatersrand and Northern Cape of South Africa toward the southern coast. Mining activity exists across the eastern region. Diamond mining is found in parts of Botswana and along the Namibian coast. Coal can also be found in central Mozambique, Zimbabwe and northeast South Africa.[21]

The Hiddekel

There is one river remaining, the Hiddekel. Genesis 2:14 details that the Hiddekel "flows east of Assyria." The word frequently translated as "Assyria" is the Hebrew word *'aš šūr* or *Assur*.[22] It is commonly assumed this is in reference to the Assyrian Empire. However, in Saudi Arabia there is an Asir province, which includes a mountain region known as the Asir Mountains, the highest mountain chain in Arabia.[23] This location seems more probable, as the word for "flow" here is actually *halak* which means "to go, come, walk."[24] Thus, when the scripture states that the river "flows east of 'Aš šūr," it is not saying the Hiddekel is flowing on the east side of Assyria as commonly thought, but that it *goes* east from 'Aš šūr.

Certainly, no modern river could fit this geographical location and be connected to the African River system of the Nile, Blue Nile, and

---

[21] Royal Berglee, World Regional Geography: People, Places, and Globalization, Flatworld Knowledge, (2012) https://open.lib.umn.edu/worldgeography/chapter/7-6-southern-africa/.
[22] 804. 'aš·šūr, Bible Hub, https://biblehub.com/hebrew/ashshur_804.htm (*last visited* Jan. 9, 2024).
[23] Arabian Peninsula: Yemen and Saudi Arabia, World Wild Life, https://www.worldwildlife.org/ecoregions/at1321 (*last visited* Dec. 9, 2023).
[24] 1980. Halak, Bible Hub, https://biblehub.com/hebrew/1980.htm (*last visited* Jan. 9, 2024).

Congo-Zambezi rivers. However, there is a recently discovered ancient river that meets that criterion, and it has been named "the Kuwait River." (See Map 3) In 1993, the New York Times reported a discovery of an ancient river that shocked the scientific community:

> Close examination of images from earth satellites has revealed traces of an ancient river under the sands of Arabia, which originated in the Hijaz Mountains of western Saudi Arabia and flowed eastward more than 500 miles across the desert to the Arabian Gulf.
>
> There it formed a delta that once covered much of Kuwait, according to Dr. Farouk El- Baz, director of the Center for Remote Sensing at Boston University, who reported the finding last week. He believes this explains the gravel found in much of Kuwait, formed from granite and volcanic basalt unrelated to local rocks. It now appears to have been carried across Arabia from the distant mountains. [25]

As reported in the New Scientist, scientists believe this river to have existed at a time that correlates to the Genesis account:

> Arabia has had wet periods at times over the past 200000 years. Water last flowed in what El-Baz calls the 'Kuwait River' between 5000 and 11000 years ago; some stretches of the river may have been up to 5 kilometres wide. Then as the region became one of the driest in the world, blowing sands covered the channel…[26]

What is even more interesting about the Kuwait River is its origin in the Hijaz Mountains, as the Asir Mountains are slightly south of the Hijaz Mountains. In the Book of Jubilees 8:12, a mysterious river called the River *Tina* originates from a mountain range called *Rafa* and empties into a gulf called the Me'at, which then empties into a great sea:

---

[25] Walter Sullivan, SCIENCE WATCH; Signs of Ancient River, New York Times, (Mar. 30 1993), https://www.nytimes.com/1993/03/30/science/science-watch-signs-of-ancient-river.html.
[26] Satellite uncovers ancient Arabian river, New Scientists, (Apr. 3, 1993) https://www.newscientist.com/article/mg13818671-100-satellite-uncovers-ancient-arabian-river/.

> ...[F]rom the middle of the mountain range of Rafa, from the mouth of the water from the river Tina...out of which this river goes forth and pours its waters into the sea Me'at, and this river flows into the great sea.

The Kuwait River in Arabia originated in the Hijaz Mountains and emptied into the Arabian Gulf. The parallels are obvious; the Kuwait River is the River Tina from Jubilees, which appears is a portion of the Hiddekel from Genesis. This conclusion is further supported by the fact the Kuwait River is in reasonable proximity to the Nile River. The Kuwait River is known to have come out from the Hijaz Mountains, which borders the Red Sea. Whether through the water of the Red Sea or through some other means, at some point, the Kuwait River would have been joined to the Nile River.

Thus, we can conclude the following identifications of the four rivers of Eden:

- **The Perath: the Blue Nile**
- **The Gihon: the Nile**
- **The Pishon: Congo-Zambezi**
- **The Hiddekel: the Kuwait River**

With this information, we can roughly identify the Garden of Eden's original location. The Nile River is the beginning of the river system, as all three other rivers are connected to the Nile. This means the river of Eden likely originates from the White Nile, the southern area of the Nile River where the Nile River begins. Thus, the Garden of Eden was located in or around what we know today as Uganda, if not a neighboring nation such as Tanzania or Kenya.

An East African Garden of Eden is further supported through the fossil records. Regardless of adherence to the dating of ancient human fossils, it is worth noting the overwhelming fossil evidence has long led scientists to the conclusion that humanity originated in Africa. As written in an article on Science.com:

> For more than a century, scientists have wondered when and where modern humans arose—and what they looked like. Genetic evidence

has pointed firmly to Africa in the past 200,000 years, but there have been few fossils from the right time and place to back that up.

Now three partial skulls from Ethiopia are putting a face on the earliest modern humans. These ancestors were African, with big brains, robust features, and a taste for hippopotamus and buffalo meat. Dated to 154,000 to 160,000 years ago, the skulls are the first strong fossil evidence that modern humans originated in Africa. "This is the oldest clear example of an early modern human we have found," says paleoanthropologist Chris Stringer of the Natural History Museum in London…Geneticists have consistently traced the oldest types of modern human DNA to ancestors who lived in Africa in the past 200,000 years. Most recently, population geneticist Sarah Tishkoff of the University of Maryland, College Park, reported at a meeting in April that the oldest versions of maternally inherited DNA arose 170,000 years ago and are found in the Sandawe people of Tanzania and the Kung San of the Kalahari desert, who both may have roots in northeastern Africa.[27]

Another article by IFL Science makes the outright claim that while the Bible has been understood to read that the Garden of Eden would be in Arabia, due to the Tigris and Euphrates Rivers, human remains say otherwise:

The so-called Cradle of Humankind can be found in South Africa around 50 kilometers (31 miles) northwest of Johannesburg. This site is home to the largest concentration of human ancestral remains anywhere in the world…So, if we're looking for a scientific Garden of Eden, it looks like South Africa and Ethiopia are our best bet.[28]

Then, of course, African wildlife is abundant, as one would image Eden as having. Although significantly depleted from colonial exploits, Africa still has the most iconic wildlife scene in the world. As Britannica notes:

---

[27] Ann Gibbons, Oldest Members of Homo sapiens Discovered in Africa, Science, (June 13, 2003), https://www.science.org/doi/10.1126/science.300.5626.1641.
[28] Tom Hale, Where Is The Garden Of Eden? And Where Would It Be Located Today? IFL Science, (Jan. 3, 2023) https://www.iflscience.com/where-is-the-garden-of-eden-and-where-would-it-be-located-today-66925.

> Africa is best known for the enormous diversity and richness of its wildlife. It has a greater variety of large ungulates, or hoofed mammals (some 90 species), and freshwater fish (2,000 species) than any other continent.[29]

The Garden of Eden being in Africa should not be controversial. Still, some will be so wedded to the Hiddekel and the Perath being the Tigris and Euphrates that they are willing to discard scientific evidence and, most importantly, scriptural evidence to maintain their understanding of a world where Africa is in the shadows, and not the centerpiece of the greatest phases of human history.

---

[29] Animal Life, Britannica, https://www.britannica.com/place/Africa/Birds (*last visited* Sept 26, 2023).

Chapter 2: Finding Yahshar-el

"How can you say, "We are wise, and the Law of the Lord is with us"? But behold, the lying pen of the scribes has made it into a lie."

~ Jeremiah 8:8

Most Bible believers pay little to no attention to geography when reading the scriptures. Many churches, after all, put emphasis on understanding the spiritual principles of the Bible as opposed to focusing on historical details. Even more so, most readers of the Bible rarely, if ever, check for the Hebrew or Greek meaning of terms they are reading, instead trusting the judgment of the translator. This is unfortunate because, in the realm of geography, Bible translators have frequently played the role of mis-translators.

The Bible's True Geography

In this section, we will focus simply on the Hebrew meaning of words in the Old Testament that point to places and locations in and around Yahshar-el (Israel). What these words reveal is that we have been sold a narrative completely contrary to that which the Bible says.

Abraham Went Down

Genesis 12:4-9 details the promise Yahuah (God) gave to Abraham about a land to be inherited by his descendants. The scripture reads:

> So Abram went away as the Lord had spoken to him; and Lot went with him. Now Abram was seventy-five years old when he departed from Haran. 5 Abram took his wife Sarai and his nephew Lot, and all their possessions which they had accumulated, and the people which they had acquired in Haran, and they set out for the land of Canaan; so they came to the land of Canaan. 6 Abram passed through the land as far as the site of Shechem, to the oak of Moreh. Now the Canaanites were in the land at that time. 7 And the Lord appeared to Abram and said, "To your descendants I will give this land." So he built an altar there to the Lord who had appeared to him. 8 Then he proceeded from there to the mountain on the east of Bethel, and

pitched his tent with Bethel on the west and Ai on the east; and there he built an altar to the Lord and called upon the name of the Lord. 9 Then Abram journeyed on, continuing toward the Negev. Now there was a famine in the land; so Abram went down to Egypt to live there for a time, because the famine was severe in the land.

Notice, when detailing Abraham's journey to Egypt, the scripture makes no reference to Abraham moving westward along the Sinai Peninsula. Instead, we read that Abraham built an altar at Bethel, then continued towards "the Negev" before heading to Egypt. The "Negev" or *han neḡ ·bāh* or *Negeb* has been translated as "south."[30] However, the actual meaning of Negeb is desert.

We then read of Abraham going "down" to Egypt, or *way yê reḏ*.[31] In ancient times in this region, the sense of direction was determined by the flow of the Nile River, which flowed from southern Africa to Egypt. As Bible researcher Avner Ramu writes in his book *Canaan? Opps Wrong Country*, "When coming out of Egypt, one may experience a sensation of "going up" only in a southward direction, if not by any other method than by watching the flow of the Nile river."[32] This is why Upper Egypt is southern Egypt, and Lower Egypt is northern Egypt.[33]

Abraham going "down" to Egypt would not mean him going from Arabia to Egypt (which is an east-to-west-to-south journey to begin with), but it could only mean him going from southern Africa to the north. This would mean not only Canaan but even the land of Ur,

---

[30] 5045. Negeb, Bible Hub, https://biblehub.com/hebrew/5045.htm (*last visited* Sept. 27, 2024).
[31] way·yê·reḏ, https://biblehub.com/hebrew/vaiyered_3381.htm (*last visited* Sept. 27, 2023).
[32] Avner Ramu, Canaan? Opps Wrong Country, Isgav Publishing LLC, (2003) 19.
[33] Egypt and the Nile, Carnegie Museum, https://carnegiemnh.org/egypt-and-the-nile/ (*last visited* Sept. 27, 2023): "The Egyptian word Tawy, means "Two Lands" – this refers to the two main regions of ancient Egypt, Upper and Lower Egypt. Lower Egypt is in the north and contains the Nile Delta, while Upper Egypt contains areas to the South. These two designations may seem counterintuitive to their physical locations, but they reflect the flow of the Nile River, from South to North."

where Abraham originates, is actually south of Egypt. One could argue mistaking north for "up" or south for "down" is an innocent mistake, given our modern sense of direction comporting with an opposite outlook. However, this is far from the only mistake in translation.

Correcting the Record

Mistranslated Keywords	
Original Word	**Usage Example**
Acharon: The word "western" is mistranslated. The actual word means "coming after or behind" [34]	**Deuteronomy 11:24** Every place on which the sole of your foot steps shall be yours; your border will be from the wilderness to Lebanon, and from the river, the river Euphrates, as far as the **western** sea.
Qedem: The word "eastward" is mistranslated. The actual word means "front" or "from the front."[35]	**Numbers 34:3** Your southern region shall extend from the wilderness of Zin along the side of Edom, and your southern border shall extend from the end of the Salt Sea **eastward.**
Mabo: The word "setting" is mistranslated. The actual word means "entrance, a coming in, entering," meaning the "entrance" of the sun (so the East)[36]	**Joshua 1:3-4** Every place on which the sole of your foot steps, I have given it to you, just as I spoke to Moses. 4 From the wilderness and this Lebanon, even as far as the great river, the river [Perath], all the land of the Hittites, and as far as the Great Sea

---

[34] 314. Acharon, Bible Hub, https://biblehub.com/hebrew/314.htm (*last visited* Aug. 7, 2023).
[35] 6924. Qedem, Bible Hub, https://biblehub.com/hebrew/6924.htm (*last visited* Aug. 9, 2023).
[36] 3996. Mabo, Bible Hub, https://biblehub.com/hebrew/3996.htm (*last visited* Jan. 9, 2024).

	toward the **setting of the sun** will be your territory.
Teman: The words "extreme south" are mistranslated. The actual word comes from "yamin," which means "right hand"[37]	**Joshua 15:1** Now, the lot for the tribe of the sons of Judah, according to their families, reached the border of Edom, southward to the wilderness of Zin at the **extreme south**.
Negeb: The words "southern" or "southward" are mistranslated. The actual word refers to a country or desert region.[38]	**Joshua 15:2-4** Their **southern** border was from the end of the Salt Sea, from the bay that turns to the south. 3 Then it proceeded southward to the ascent of Akrabbim and continued to Zin, then went up by the south of Kadesh-barnea and continued to Hezron, and went up to Addar and turned to Karka. 4 It continued to Azmon and proceeded to the brook of Egypt, and the border ended at the sea. This shall be your southern border.
Yam: The word "western" is mistranslated. The actual word means "sea" or refers to a body of water.[39]	**Numbers 34:6** As for the **western** border, you shall have the Great Sea, that is, its coastline; this shall be your western border.
Tsaphon: The word "northern" is mistranslated. The actual root word means	**Numbers 34:7** And this shall be your **northern** border: you shall draw your boundary from the Great Sea to Mount Hor.

---

[37] 8486. Teman, Bible Hub https://biblehub.com/hebrew/8486.htm (*last visited* Sept. 30, 2023); 3225. Yamin, Bible Hub https://biblehub.com/hebrew/3225.htm (*last visited* Sept. 30, 2023).
[38] 5045. Negeb, Bible Hub, https://biblehub.com/hebrew/5045.htm (*last visited* Aug. 7, 2023).
[39] 3220. Yam, Bible Hub, https://biblehub.com/hebrew/3220.htm (*last visited* Aug. 9, 2023).

"hidden" or "concealed."[40]	
Hay·'ōr: The word "stream" is mistranslated. The actual word means the "Nile River."[41]	**Daniel 12:5-7** Then I, Daniel, looked, and behold, two others were standing, one on this bank of the **stream** and the other on that bank of the **stream**. [6] And someone said to the man dressed in linen, who was above the waters of the **stream**, "How long will it be until the end of these wonders?" [7] And I heard the man dressed in linen, who was above the waters of the **stream**…

In the chart above, the disconnect is demonstrated between what Bible translators have written and the Hebrew meanings. If translators were not relying solely on Hebrew in their translation of Hebrew words, what other information could have possibly led them to interpret things that are simply not there?

Probably the most insidious of these mistranslations is the word *mabo*, translated as the "setting of the sun" when it literally means the opposite, as "entrance, a coming in, entering," would entail the rising of the sun. As the sun rises in the east and sets in the west, this term clearly means east. However, this interpretation would carry heavy consequences if interpreted literally, as the "Great Sea" being towards the east would mean Biblical Yahshar-el (Israel) would have to have a "great" sea on its eastern border. The Meciterranean Sea that borders Palestine is on the west.

---

[40] 6828. Tsaphon, https://biblehub.com/hebrew/6828.htm (*last visited* Aug. 9, 2024);6845. Tsaphan, Bible Hub, https://biblehub.ccm/hebrew/6845.htm (*last visited* Aug. 9, 2024).
[41] 2975 hay·'ōr, Bible Hub, https://biblehub.com/hebrew/hayor_2975.htm (*last visited* Jan. 10, 2023.

Another plainly deceptive mistranslation is in Numbers 34:6, where the word *yam* which means "sea" or body of water is mistranslated as "western." Again, this is another attempt to put the "Great Sea" to the west of Yahshar-el instead of the east.

There is also the mistranslation of *Negeb*, which carries wide implications. Negeb has frequently been translated as south and understood to be a country to the south of Yahshar-el. This interpretation, which favors Palestinian geography, is undoubtedly incorrect and takes away from the reading of scripture. *Negeb* in Hebrew literally means "dry land." In the Septuagint, the term refers not to one direction or even a specific location; rather, *Negeb* is a term broadly applied to mean "desert."[42] Thus, when we read about Yahshar-el's *Negeb* border in Joshua 15:2-4, the scripture actually refers to a desert border. Again, this mistranslation is not inconsequential.

Together, the correct translation of scripture reveals a geography and land mass significantly different from Palestine. Just from the aforementioned corrections, we can take away the following:

1. Yahshar-el had a "great" sea on its eastern border.
2. Yahshar-el was bordered by a desert (the Negeb)
3. Yahshar-el was bordered by the Perath River
4. Yahshar-el was bordered by a wilderness ("Wilderness of Zin")

We know, at least for Palestine, numbers 1) and 3) do not match this description. However, applying this information to an East African landscape around the Blue Nile, we can reach different outcomes:

1. The "great" sea that acts as the eastern border of Yahshar-el would be the Red Sea.

---

[42] Negev, Net Bible, https://classic.net.bible.org/dictionary.php?word=Negev, (*last visited* Sept. 30, 2023).

2. The *Negeb* or desert border of Yahshar-el is the Nubian Desert, which runs along its western side.
3. The "Wilderness of Zin," where Yahshar-el sojourned after entering Egypt, would be within the Nubian Desert to the north.
4. The *Perath*, or Blue Nile would run alongside the western border of Yahshar-el.

The Nubian Desert

If Negeb were translated correctly, Joshua 15:2-4 would read:

> Their [desert] border was from the end of the Salt Sea, from the bay that turns to the south. 3 Then it proceeded [to the desert] to the ascent of Akrabbim and continued to Zin, then went up by the [desert] of Kadesh-barnea and continued to Hezron, and went up to Addar and turned to Karka. ⁴ It continued to Azmon and proceeded to the brook of Egypt, and the border ended at the sea. This shall be your [desert] border.

According to Encylopedia.com, the Nubian Desert, which is the east region of the Sahara Desert and spans between northern Eritrea and Sudan, is an "arid region, largely a sandstone plateau, has numerous wadis flowing toward (but never reaching) the Nile, whose great bends are entrenched in the western part of the region."[43] The desert extends south and ends roughly around the same area where the Blue Nile begins. Interestingly enough, there does seem to be evidence of a time when parts of the Nubian desert were once a wilderness, with the Sabu-Jaddi rock carvings:

> Hidden amongst rock outcrops between the third and fourth cataracts of the Nile River, the archaeological site of Sabu-Jaddi (or simply "Sabu") contains more than 1,500 rock drawings spanning 10,000 years of human history in the region. Archaeologists have yet to determine when, exactly, the ancient Nubians who lived here first

---

[43] Nubian Desert, Enclyopedia.com, https://www.encyclopedia.com/reference/encyclopedias-almanacs-transcripts-and-maps/nubian-desert (*last visited* Oct. 3, 2023).

chiseled these images, but one thing is for sure: the remarkably well-preserved etchings of hippos, crocodiles and papyrus boats depict a vastly different world than the parched desert landscape that now covers much of northern Africa, and offer a glimpse into the Sahara's verdant past.[44]

The Wilderness of Zin, between Egypt and the Promised Land, would have been within the Nubian Desert. This gives us a rough idea of the northern borders of Yahshar-el. Significantly, Yahudah (Judah), which we know from Joshua 15:2 borders the "Brook of Egypt" and the Wilderness of Zin, was not, as is commonly held, a southern kingdom of Yahshar-el, but rather a northern kingdom. This means the 11 tribes that defected from the Davidic dynasty would have been the southern kingdom of the united monarchy of Yahshar-el.

The Great Sea, the Salt Sea, the Sea of Chinneroth, and the Arabah

Yahshar-el had a great sea on its eastern border. The "great sea" in scripture is the Red Sea. Joshua 15:2 also describes a "bay" that acts as Yahshar-el's border on the Red Sea, "from the end of the Salt Sea, from **the bay** that turns to the [desert]." The word here for "bay" is actually *lashon*,[45] which means tongue, often used in Hebrew writings to describe protruding land masses in the sea. On the Red Sea, we see this land mass exists in what we know as ancient Adulis, or modern-day Zula, which protrudes and points toward the Nubian Desert to the north. Thus, the northern border of Yahshar-el (more specifically, Yahudah) would end somewhere before Adulis.

As far as the southern border, we are told from scripture that the borders of Yahshar-el extended to the east of a water body described

---

[44] Matt Stirn, Sabu-Jaddi: The site revealing the Sahara's verdant past, (June 7, 2020) BBC, https://www.bbc.com/travel/article/20200607-sabu-jaddi-the-site-revealing-the-saharas-verdant-past

[45] Lashon, Bible Hub, https://biblehub.com/hebrew/3956.htm (last visited Sept 28, 2023); Got Questions, What is the significance of the Negev in the Bible?, https://www.gotquestions.org/Negev-in-the-Bible.html (last visited Sept 28, 2023)

as the "Salt Sea" or the *Yam Melach*.[46] Numbers 34:3 states, "Your **southern** region shall extend from the wilderness of Zin along the side of Edom, and your **southern** border shall extend from the end of the **Salt Sea eastward**." Again, the word here for "east" is *qedem*, which means "front," and *negeb* means "desert." Thus, the corrected form would read: "Your *desert* region shall extend from the wilderness of Zin along the side of Edom, and your *desert* border shall extend from the end of the Salt Sea to *the front*." The Salt Sea, has been identified by Bible scholars as a lake bordering Palestine and Jordan known as the Dead Sea.[47]

According to scripture, the Salt Sea is associated with a landmass known as the *Arabah*. The Hebrew meaning for *Arabah* is "a steppe or desert plain."[48] As said in Joshua 3:14-17, the Arabah is where the Jordan River meets it's end:

> 14 So when the people set out from their tents to cross the Jordan with the priests carrying the ark of the covenant before the people, 15 and when those who carried the ark came into the Jordan, and the feet of the priests carrying the ark were dipped in the edge of the water (for the Jordan overflows all its banks all the days of harvest), 16 the waters which were flowing down from above stood and rose up in one heap, a great distance away at **Adam**, the city that is beside Zarethan; **and those which were flowing down toward the sea of the Arabah, the Salt Sea, were completely cut off.** So the people crossed opposite Jericho. 17 And the priests who carried the ark of the covenant of the Lord stood firm on dry ground in the middle of the Jordan while all Israel crossed on dry ground, until all the nation had finished crossing the Jordan.

Thus, the geography of the Arabah includes a river that runs into a body of water, or *yam*, in a steepe desert plain. This description matches a location inside of Oromia, Ethiopia where the Awash River

---

[46] 4417. Melach, https://biblehub.com/hebrew/4417.htm (last visited May 28, 2024); 3220. Yam, https://biblehub.com/hebrew/3220.htm (last visited May 28, 2024).
[47] Bible Hub, Sea of the Arabah (Salt Sea), https://bibleatlas.org/sea_of_the_arabah.htm (last visited Sept. 29, 2023)
[48] Bible Hub, 6160. arabah, https://biblehub.com/hebrew/6160.htm (last visited May 28, 2024).

flows into a lake known as Lake Abbe, located in the Afar Triangle or Afar Depression. The Afar Triangle perfectly matches the description of the Arabah as a steep or desert plain. (See Addendum Map A) According to World Atlas:

> The Afar Triangle exhibits extremities in topography, having towering active volcanoes and depressions. The Erta Ale is a towering shield volcano found in the Afar Triangle, which rises 2,011 feet in elevation. The region is also home to Africa's lowest point, Lake Asal which lies 509 feet below sea level. The Awash River is the main river that flows through the Afar Triangle, and it ends up as a chain of salt lakes found about 80 miles from the Red Sea. The region's vegetation is adapted for its desert-like climatic conditions and is primarily made up of shrubs and grasses. Small trees can also be found in the region, albeit in small concentrations.[49]

Lake Abbe is a lake known for it's high-saline content which sits on the border between Ethiopia and Djibouti. It is surrounded by sand dunes and harsh desert climate, making it one of the most remote places in the world. Accord to World Atlas:

> Lake Abbe is found within the salt flats of northern Ethiopia and Djibouti. The lake is found in the lowlands of East Africa and is surrounded by salt flats in each direction for miles. Nomadic peoples herd flocks of goats and camels over the region's vast, flat landscape as they have for centuries, but outsiders rarely visit the area due to its unforgiving climate.
>
> The lake is the endpoint for Ethiopia's Awash River, which originates in the Ethiopian Highland Plateau, though it empties into a chain of interconnected lakes throughout the region. Lake Abbe is a no-drain lake. Instead, pure water evaporates from the lake's surface, leaving behind highly salinated water. The landscape around Lake Abbe is almost entirely desert except for the naturally occurring limestone chimneys. Some of these geological formations can reach 50 meters in

---

[49] World Atlas, The Afar Triangle - Unique Places In Africa, https://www.worldatlas.com/articles/the-afar-triangle-unique-places-in-africa.html, (last visited May 28, 2024).

height and are known to erupt with steaming sulfur, the result of geothermal fluid mixing with lake water underground.[50]

Lake Abbe is also known as Lake *Abhe Bad*. *Abhe Bad* carries great semblance to the word *Arabah*. Even more interesting is Joshua 3:16 states, regarding the stopping of the waters of the Jordan for Yahshrel to cross, that "the waters which were flowing down from above stood and rose up in one heap, a great distance away at **Adam**, the city that is beside Zarethan." Not far from the Awash River exists a city called Adama, whose name is believed to derive from the Oromo word *Adaamii*, a clear confirmation that this is the correct location of the Jordan River.[51] (See Addendum Map B) Thus, the Arabah is the Afar Triangle, the Jordan River is the Awash River and Lake Abbe is the Salt Sea.

The sea of the Arabah, as described in Joshua 12:1-3 runs adjacent to the "Sea of Chinneroth:"

> Now these are the kings of the land whom the sons of Israel defeated, and they took possession of their land beyond the Jordan toward the sunrise, from the Valley of the Arnon as far as Mount Hermon, and all the Arabah to the east: 2 Sihon king of the Amorites, who lived in Heshbon and ruled from Aroer, which is on the edge of the Valley of the Arnon, both the middle of the valley and half of Gilead, even as far as the brook Jabbok, the border of the sons of Ammon; 3 and the Arabah as far as the Sea of Chinneroth toward the east, and as far as the Sea of the Arabah, that is, the Salt Sea.

The Sea of Chinneroth, or *Kinaroth* or *Kinnereth* in Hebrew, is named the Sea of Galilee in the New Testament. This location has been identified by Biblical archeologists as a lake in Palestine, north of the

---

[50] World Atlas, Lake Abbe, https://www.worldatlas.com/lakes/lake-abbe.html (last visited May 28, 2024).
[51] Wakuma Kudama, Ethiopia: Adama - a Suitable Town for Investment, All Africa, (Jan. 17, 2017) https://allafrica.com/stories/201701130476.html.

Dead Sea. [52] In Ethiopia, however, to the east of Lake Abbe is the Gulf of Tadjoura, a gulf coastline at the extreme western end of the Gulf of Aden of the Red Sea. This shows that the Gulf of Tadjoura is in fact the Sea of Galilee, and the surrounding area of Djibouti is the region of Galilee. This fact is confirmed by a city named *Galîlé* located just south of the gulf.[53] (See Addendum Map C)

Biblical Geography

Perath River – The Blue Nile
Great Sea – Red Sea
Negeb – Nubian Desert
Arabah Sea or Salt Sea – Lake Abbe
Sea of Chinneroth – Gulf of Tadjoura

Thus, a more modern and literal reading of Numbers 34:3-12 would state the following:

> Your *desert region* shall extend from the *Nubian Desert* along the side of Edom, and your *desert border* shall extend from the end of the *Lake Abbe* to *the front*.
> [4] Then your border shall change direction from *the desert* to the ascent of Akrabbim and continue to the *Nubian desert*, and its termination shall be to the *desert* of Kadesh-barnea; and it shall reach Hazaraddar and continue to Azmon. [5] Then the border shall change direction from Azmon to the brook of Egypt, and its termination shall be at the sea.
> [6] 'As for the *sea/water border*, you shall have the *Red Sea*, that is, its coastline; this shall be your *western border*.
> [7] 'And this shall be your *hidden border*: you shall draw your boundary from the *Red Sea* to Mount Hor. [8] You shall draw a boundary from Mount Hor to the Lebo-hamath, and the termination of the border shall be at Zedad; [9] and the border shall proceed to Ziphron, and its termination shall be at Hazar-enan. This shall be your *hidden border*.
> [10] 'For your *front border* you shall also draw a boundary from Hazar-enan to Shepham, [11] and the border shall go *down* from Shepham

---

[52] Bible Hub, Sea of Chinnereth (Sea of Galilee), https://bibleatlas.org/sea_of_chinnereth.htm (last visited Sept. 29. 2023)
[53] Map Carta, https://mapcarta.com/12792364, (last visited May 28, 2024)

to Riblah on the *front side* of Ain; and the border shall go *down* and reach to the slope on the *front* side of the *Gulf of Tadjoura* ¹² And the border shall go *down* to the Jordan, and its termination shall be at *Lake Abbe*. This shall be your land according to its borders on all sides.'" (See Addendum Map D)

Yahshar-el's True Borders

Based on the aforementioned information, the borders of Yahshar-el would be as follows: the Red Sea was the eastern border starting from modern-day Zula then proceeding south; the Nubian Desert was the northern border which extended towards the western side along with the Blue Nile; the southern border was where both the Nubian Desert and Blue Nile ends, at which point the border moves east through the Afar Triangle to the area of the Gulf of Tadjoura. The countries that would encompass this region include Sudan, Eritrea, Ethiopia, Djibouti. The Eritrea, Northern Ethiopia and Northern Sudan region would encompass the Kingdom of Yahudah, while the rest of the land to the south encompasses the southern Kingdom of Yahshar-el. In addition, Edom, who we know bordered Yahudah, would have been left of Yahudah, within Sudan.

The Real "Jerusalem"

The goal of this book is not to determine the location of every single Biblical site. However, given the importance of Yerusalem (Jerusalem), it is worth the effort to identify this Holy City. All thanks to Yahuah, there are essential clues given to us in scripture that make this location clearly determinable.

Scriptures give us two important geographical indicators of where Yerusalem is located. Psalms 125:2 says: "As the mountains surround Jerusalem, so the Lord surrounds His people, from this time and forever." It is important to note that the city of Jerusalem, located in Palestine, although in a very hilly and low-level mountainous area, is by no means surrounded by mountains. In fact, this Jerusalem sits on a mountain itself, something never mentioned in scripture.[54]

The second geographical indicator is the Gihon. 2 Chronicles 32:30 states, "It was Hezekiah who stopped the upper outlet of the waters of Gihon and directed them to the west side of the city of David..." Then 2 Chronicles 33:14 states of King Manasseh:

> Now after this he built the outer wall of the city of David on the west side of Gihon, in the valley, up to the entrance of the Fish Gate; and he encircled the Ophel with it and made it very high. Then he put army commanders in all the fortified cities in Judah.

In 1 Kings 1:32-33 and 38, the scripture reads:

> Then King David said: "Summon to me Zadok the priest, Nathan the prophet, and Benaiah the son of Jehoiada." And they came into the king's presence.[33] And the king said to them, "Take with you the servants of your lord, and have my son Solomon ride on my own mule, and bring him down to Gihon...[38] So Zadok the priest, Nathan the prophet, Benaiah the son of Jehoiada, the Cherethites, and the Pelethites went down and had Solomon ride on King David's mule, and brought him to Gihon.

Some Bible translators, to support Palestine as being ancient Yahshar-el, have literally added a word to the original scripture, something scripture condemns.[55] The word they have added to Gihon is "spring" thus changing the Gihon from the river described in Genesis 2 to a mere spring. For example, when one reads the NIV translation, you see in 2 Chronicles 33:14: "Afterward he rebuilt the outer wall of the City of David, west of the Gihon spring in the valley..." Similarly, 2 Chronicles 32:30 of the NIV reads, "It was Hezekiah who blocked the upper outlet of the Gihon spring and channeled the water down to the west side of the City of David..."

---

[54] About Jerusalem: The City, its Geographical Site, and its location, Alquds Jerusalem, https://alqudsjerusalem.com/geography/jerusalem-city-site/ (*last visited* Sept. 28, 2023).
[55] Revelation 22:18-19.

The Jewish Encyclopedia echoes this interpretation of the Gihon as a spring, describing it as:

> A fountain near Jerusalem where the anointing and proclamation of Solomon as king took place (I Kings i. 33, 38, 45). According to one passage, it was on low ground (see II Chron. Xxxiii. 14), but in another (ib. xxxii. 30), it is said that Hezekiah stopped the "upper watercourse" of Gihon. This fountain is mentioned by Josephus as being outside the city ("Ant." Vii. 14, § 5). Robinson ("Researches," i. 513) came to the conclusion that "there existed anciently a fountain Gihon on the west of the city, which was 'stopped' or covered over by Hezekiah, and its waters brought down by subterranean channels into the city."[56]

The Jewish Virtual Library states that the waters King Hezekiah diverted was through a landmark that has been named "Hezekiah's Tunnel," stating:

> The project is mentioned in the Bible (II Kings 20:20): "...and how he made a pool, and a conduit, and brought water into the city..." and again in II Chronicles 32:30: "This same Hezekiah also stopped the upper watercourse of Gihon, and brought it straight down to the west side of the city of David."[57]

However, a tunnel is never mentioned in scripture, nor is a spring. Instead, relying solely on scripture, we would have to believe the Gihon mentioned in II Chronicles and I Kings to be the same Gihon spoken about in Genesis, a river that branches off out of the Garden of Eden that flows through the land of Kush, or at least a related waterway.

The Gihon, as we know it now, is the Nile River. Given the fact the Gihon was able to be redirected by Hezekiah, something that

---

[56] Emil G. Hirsch, M. Seligsohn, Gihon, Jewish Encyclopedia, https://www.jewishencyclopedia.com/articles/6668-gihon (*last visited* Aug 1, 2023).
[57] Jerusalem Archaeological Sites: Biblical Water Systems, Jewish Virtual Library, https://www.jewishvirtuallibrary.org/biblical-water-systems-in-jerusalem (*last visited* Jan. 10, 2024).

would be impossible with the actual Nile River, it's clear Yerusalem is not stationed on the Gihon itself, but a tributary to the Gihon that goes through Yerusalem. Thus, the question is whether there is a city surrounded by mountains with a tributary of the Nile that flows through it. There is only one city in the world that matches this description. That is the ancient city of Aksum.

Aksum (or Axum), which is near the base of the Adwa Mountains, is very visibly surrounded by mountains and has a small river that runs directly through the city, the Tekezē River. The Tekezē River is a major tributary of the Atbara River, which is a tributary of the Nile River. Aksum is in close proximity to this river, approximately 50 kilometers northeast, and a small non-perennial offshoot of the river diverts directly through the west side of the city of Aksum.[58](See Map 4) Thus, a direct tributary of the Gihon runs directly through Aksum, as described in scripture.

A shadow of its formal self, Aksum which is located in the Central Zone of the Tigray Region, was the capital of the marine trading power known as the Aksumite Empire. Aksum City has also been a hub for religion in Ethiopia. The city's Church of St. Mary of Zion is famous for being the home of the Ark of the Covenant.[59] One might also observe the recreations of the ruins of the Dungar Palace closely resemble recreations of the Temple of Solomon. Whether this is the actual site or whether this became the architectural style after the initial building of the temple is, of course, unknown.

What Does the New Testament Say?

Many will still be wedded to the idea of Palestine being Yahshar-el (Israel) as the testament of Yahusha (Jesus), his disciples and their

---

[58] Historical city travel guide: Aksum, 6th century AD, The British Museum, (July 17, 2020), https://www.britishmuseum.org/blog/historical-city-travel-guide-aksum-6th-century-ad.
[59] Aksum, Britannica, https://www.britannica.com/place/Aksum-Ethiopia (*last visited* Jan. 10, 2024)

apostles has been depicted throughout history in a way that is Romanized. However, erasing the depictions from our mind and focusing on what the scripture says, we learn that the geography described in the New Testament also does not comport to a Palestinian setting.

Yahusha's Travels

While geography is not as much of a focal point of the New Testament as it is in the Old Testament, where geography does come into play, there are some clear inconsistencies with what we read of Yahusha's travels while sharing the good news of His reign, and what we know of Palestine. This occurs in the Gospel of Mark, which is believed by many scholars to be the oldest gospel.[60] In Mark 5, we are told of a story where Yahusha travels to a foreign country by sea where he famously casts demons out of a man who then flees into a herd of pigs who then drown themselves in the sea. Mark 5:1-21 reads:

> **They came to the other side of the sea, into the region of the Gerasenes.** [2] When He got out of the boat, immediately a man from the tombs with an unclean spirit met Him. [3] He lived among the tombs; and no one was able to bind him anymore, not even with a chain, [4] because he had often been bound with shackles and chains, and the chains had been torn apart by him and the shackles broken in pieces; and no one was strong enough to subdue him. [5] Constantly, night and day, he was screaming among the tombs and in the mountains, and cutting himself with stones. [6] Seeing Jesus from a distance, he ran up and bowed down before Him; [7] and shouting with a loud voice, he said, "What business do You have with me, Jesus, Son of the Most High God? I implore You by God, do not torment me!" [8] For He had already been saying to him, "Come out of the man, you unclean spirit!" [9] And He was asking him, "What is your name?" And he said to Him, "My name is Legion, for we are many." [10] And he begged Him earnestly not to send them out of the region. [11] Now there was a large herd of pigs feeding nearby on the mountain. [12] And the demons begged Him, saying, "Send us into the

---

[60] Gospel According to Mark, Britannica, https://www.britannica.com/topic/Gospel-According-to-Mark (*last updated* Sept. 20, 2023).

pigs so that we may enter them." ¹³ Jesus gave them permission. **And coming out, the unclean spirits entered the pigs; and the herd rushed down the steep bank into the sea, about two thousand of them; and they were drowned in the sea....**
²¹ When Jesus had crossed over again in the boat to the other side, a large crowd gathered around Him; and He stayed by the seashore.

The Greek word here for "region" is *chóra*, which means a different country, and the Greek word used for the sea is "Thalassa," which is only translated as the sea and was personified by the Greeks as a sea goddess.[61] However, clearly, there is no sea bordering Palestine from which a simple journey to another region and back could have been executed.

To deal with this geographical issue, Biblical scholars, instead of applying the actual meaning of the word to the text, decided to attribute "the sea" to the Jordan River.[62] However, the scriptures use the Greek word *potamos* for rivers, including the Jordan River.[63] Thus, to apply a new meaning for the word Thalassa as the Jordan River is a clear misrepresentation of what the text says.

Applying what we know, that the Red Sea bordered Yahshar-el, this quick journey now makes sense. It was common in ancient times for travelers to voyage through the area known today as the Gulf of Aden, which encompasses modern-day Ethiopia and Djibouti on the western side, and the country of Yemen on the eastern side. According to historian Richard Pankhurst:

> The intervening strip of sea between South Arabia and the

---

[61] Thalassa, Behind the Name, https://www.behindthename.com/name/thalassa/ (*last visited* Aug. 24, 2023)

[62] Jewish Encyclopedia, Gadarenes https://www.jewishencyclopedia.com/articles/6458-gadarenes (*last visited*, Aug. 24, 2023); Gadarenes (Gergesenes), BibleStudy.org, https://www.biblestudy.org/meaning-names/gadarenes.html (*last visited* Aug 24, 2023).

[63] Potamos, Bible Hub, https://biblehub.com/greek/4215.htm (*last visited* Aug 24, 2023).

Ethiopian Horn of Africa is at its closest little more than fifty miles wide, and is believed ten thousand years ago to have been only eleven miles wide. This narrow stretch of water could be crossed, throughout the historic period, by the simplest of vessels, including rafts, within little more than a day.[64]

This points to Gerasene being located in modern-day Yemen. Ironically, Mark, who gives the most geographical details of Yahusha's travels, has been criticized by some Bible scholars for his ignorance of Palestinian geography. In the article "Mark: Failed Geography, but Great Bible Student," writer Neil Godfrey explains what he sees as a discrepancy in the geography of Yahusha's travels as detailed by Mark:

> Much has been said about Mark's poor knowledge of the geography of Palestine. A classic case is his bizarre itinerary for Jesus leaving Tyre to go north, then south-east, then back east again, to reach (h)is final destination. On the map here, locate Tyre, run your finger north to Sidon, then let it wander to the right and downwards till it reaches Decapolis, then zero up to the "lake" of Galilee.
>
> That is the route that the Gospel of Mark says Jesus took in order to get from Tyre to the "sea of Galilee."
>
> Jesus' travel agent must have been offering a super-bargain or Mark had little real knowledge of the geography of the area…[65]

This inconsistency does not exist within East Africa. From scripture, we can ascertain that both Tyre and Sidon were cities or regions that were seaports. Genesis 49:13 states, about Tyre, "Zebulun will reside at the seashore; and he shall be a harbor for ships, and his flank shall be toward Sidon."

Similarly, in Isaiah 23:1-8, we read of Tyre and Sidon's maritime access:

---

[64] Richard Pankhurst, Across the Red Sea and Gulf of Aden: Ethiopia's Historic Ties with Yemen, Africa: Rivista Trimestrale Di Studi e Documentazione Dell'Istituto Italiano per l'Africa e l'Oriente, vol. 57, no. 3, (2002), pp. 393–419.
[65] Neil Godfrey, Mark: failed geography, but great bible student, Vridar, (Aug. 8, 2006) https://vridar.org/2010/08/06/mark-failed-geography-but-great-bible-student/.

> The pronouncement concerning Tyre:
>
> Wail, you ships of Tarshish,
> For Tyre is destroyed, without house or harbor;
> It is reported to them from the land of Cyprus.
> ² Be silent, you inhabitants of the coastland,
> You merchants of Sidon;
> Your messengers crossed the sea
> ³ And were on many waters.
> The grain of the Nile, the harvest of the River was her revenue;
> And she was the market of nations.
> ⁴ Be ashamed, Sidon,
> For the sea speaks, the stronghold of the sea, saying,
> "I have neither been in labor nor given birth,
> I have neither brought up young men nor raised virgins."
> ⁵ When the report reaches Egypt,
> They will be in anguish over the report of Tyre.
> ⁶ Pass over to Tarshish;
> Wail, you inhabitants of the coastland.
> ⁷ Is this your jubilant city,
> Whose origin is from antiquity,
> Whose feet used to bring her to colonize distant places?
> ⁸ Who has planned this against Tyre, the bestower of crowns,
> Whose merchants were princes, whose traders were the honored of the earth?

Joshua 19:24-29 also described this region as it pertains to Yahshar-el:

> Now the fifth lot went to the tribe of the sons of Asher according to their families. ²⁵ Their territory was Helkath, Hali, Beten, and Achshaph,²⁶ Allammelech, Amad, and Mishal; and it reached to Carmel on the west and Shihor-libnath. ²⁷ **It turned toward the east to Beth-dagon and reached Zebulun, and to the Valley of Iphtahel [concealed] to Beth-emek and Neiel; then it proceeded on [concealed] to Cabul, ²⁸ Ebron, Rehob, Hammon, and Kanah, as far as Great Sidon. ²⁹ The border turned to Ramah and to the fortified city of Tyre; then the border turned to Hosah, and it ended at the sea by the region of Achzib.**

Sidon and Tyre were maritime cities that bordered the Tribe of Zebulun on the far end of Yahshar-el's territory. Zebulon's sea port would likely have been stationed in or around modern-day Djibouti. That would put Tyre and Sidon in modern-day Somaliland. We receive confirmation of this geographical reality in Ezekiel 27:3, where it states, "and say to Tyre, who sits at the **entrance** to the sea, merchant of the peoples to many coastlands..." Tyre sitting at the "entrance of the sea" makes no geographical sense if applied to Tyre in Lebanon, where there is no sea entrance. However, the location of Tyre on the horn of Africa, where the Arabian Sea enters before becoming the Red Sea, does match this description. (See Map 5)

Two possibilities for the locations of Tyre and Sidon are ancient Zeila or Berbera, both prominent historic maritime cities with a commanding presence in the region. During antiquity, Zeila and Berbera were involved in lucrative maritime trade with various commodities between empires such as Phoenicia, Ptolemaic Egypt, Greece, Saba, the Roman Empire and India.[66] f Tyre and Sidon were Berbera and Zeila, then suddenly, Mark's geography makes sense. Yahusha's travels were in a region south of Yahshar-el in modern-day Somaliland, before heading north to the southern end of the Red Sea, where he would have crossed the Gulf of Aden to spread the good news in Yemen.

The Apostle Paul

There is one more geographical anomaly worth mentioning from New Testament texts, that is the Apostle Paul's supposed reference to Arabia in the Book of Galatians. In Galatians 25:21-25 it reads:

> Tell me, you who want to be under law, do you not listen to the Law? [22] For it is written that Abraham had two sons, one by the slave woman and one by the free woman. [23] But the son by the slave woman was born according to the flesh, and the son by the free woman through the promise. [24] **This is speaking allegorically, for these women are two covenants: one coming from Mount Sinai giving birth to children who are to be slaves; she is**

---

[66] Mohamed Diriye Abdullahi, Culture and Customs of Somalia, Greenwood Press, (2001), 13–14.; John Donnelly Fage and Roland Anthony Oliver, Journal of African History, 50.

> Hagar. **²⁵ Now this Hagar is Mount Sinai in Arabia and corresponds to the present Jerusalem, for she is enslaved with her children. ²⁶ But the Jerusalem above is free; she is our mother.** ²⁷ For it is written:
>
> "Rejoice, infertile one, you who do not give birth;
> Break forth and shout, you who are not in labor;
> For the children of the desolate one aremore numerous
> Than those of the one who has a husband."

This is the second use of the word "Arabia" in the New Testament, the first being in Galatians 1:17: "nor did I go up to Jerusalem to those who were apostles before me; but I went away to Arabia, and returned once more to Damascus." The text would seem to support Mount Sinai, the mountain where Moses received the 10 Commandments shortly after the exodus from Egypt, as being in Arabia.[67]

Just reading the scripture itself, it reads in a confusing manner, as one would not think of Hagar, the mother of Ishmael, as having to do with the Law of Moses, as he was not born of Isaac and Jacob. As far as Biblical scripture is concerned, Ishmael has nothing to do with the covenant of the Torah. Thus, "Arabia" and even "Hagar" are likely mistranslated from what was written in Paul's original letter.

A similar conclusion was reached by Professor Stephen C. Carlson, who believes the mention of Hagar as Mount Sinai in Arabia was not originally in Paul's letter and may have been added as a marginal note:

> The note about Arabia sticks out like a sore thumb. It has no corresponding element on Sarah's side of the allegory. These considerations raise the possibility that at least some or all of the v. 25a parenthesis is a marginal note that was interpolated into the text

---

[67] Even locating Mount Sinai in Arabia causes geographical difficulties for those who believe Yahshar-el to be in Palestine, who usually put Mount Sinai in the Sinai Peninsula.

of Galatians, as some nineteenth-century textual critics have contended.[68]

Carlson also takes note of the seeming contradiction of this passage and Galatians 1:17, which notes Arabia as Gentile territory:

> Although some scholars have called attention to Paul's only other mention of Arabia in Gal 1:17, no one seems to have noticed that how Paul thinks of Arabia in Gal 1 conflicts with its use in Gal 4. In Gal 1:15–16, Paul told the Galatians in defense of his apostolic ministry that God was pleased to reveal his son in him so he would proclaim Christ among the Gentiles. As a result of this experience, Paul did not visit Jerusalem to confer with the apostles before him, but he immediately went to Arabia (v. 17). Thus, in Paul's mind, Arabia is coded as Gentile territory. Yet in the allegory of Sarah and Hagar, "Arabia" does not function as Gentile territory.[69]

Thus, similar to the Old Testament, New Testament geography establishes that something happened sometime between the original writing of the texts and the translating of the text into our modern Bibles.

---

[68] Stephen C Carlson, "For Sinai is a Mountain in Arabia," De Gruyter, 2014, 97.
[69] *Id.*, at 100.

Chapter 3: The Palestine Lie

"Thereby invalidating the word of God by your tradition which you have handed down, and you do many things such as that."

~Mark 7:13

Mainstream Christianity is wedded to the idea of Yahshar-el (Israel) in Palestine. There has been an entire genre of books, documentaries and articles, as well as a tourism industry of Holy Land tours that have been utilized to confirm the veracity of this location by engaging in the supposed identification of archeological sites. Not to mention the unholy alliance between Christianity and Zionism, and the devotion to the Israeli cause that, in the minds of many Christians, has justified genocidal acts of the State of Israel towards Palestinians. In this chapter, we will focus on the evidence that proves the world has invested in the wrong location of Yahshar-el.

Palestine Cannot be the Holy Land

Secular archeologists have long blasted the Biblical narrative of the powerful nation of Yahshar-el (Israel) as mere fiction and fantasy. From the enslavement in Egypt, to a major military conquest to expel the Canaanites, to the reign of a united monarchy under kings David and Solomon, all have been delegitimized by mainstream archeology. The reason is that despite the strong fervor towards these Biblical narratives, the archeological evidence is simply not there. Not only is the evidence not there, but the Palestinian geography is simply asinine to reconcile with the geography as outlined in the scriptures. However, because of the dubious field known as Biblical Archeology, Bible believers have been given a false sense of relief that the archeology does match up with that of Palestine. Not many experts, however, have asked the question as to whether the Bible is true, but the location is incorrect.

For Bible believers who will be confused by Palestine not being Yahshar-el, it is useful to understand how Biblical Archaeology has operated throughout the centuries. Like so many fields that operate out of bias, the field of Biblical Archaeology is a victim of its own partiality. In a world where *reason* has been used as justification in denying the validity of the Bible, Biblical archeologists, most of whom were devoted Christians or Jews, found themselves on the frontlines as having to prove the Bible to save it from the growing scrutiny from unbelievers. Nur Masalha, director of the Centre for Religion and History and the Holy Land Research Project at Mary's University College, details this approach to archeology in his book *The Bible & Zionism: Invented Traditions, Archology and Post Colonialism in Israel-Palestine*:

> The first biblically oriented topographical study of Palestine was carried out in 1828 by two American scholars, Dr. Edward Robinson and Eli Smith, who identified scores of 'biblical sites' on the basis of modern Arabic place names. At the end of the nineteenth century, archeologist Sir William Matthew Flinders Petrie began to explore a large number of mounds, or tells (tall in Arabic), as possible "biblical sites." From its beginning, the Western discipline was established 'to prove the veracity of scripture... William Foxwell Albright, "the son of a Christian priest," arrived in Palestine in December of 1919. "Albright began excavating in Palestine in the 1920s. His declared position was that biblical archeological was the scientific means to refute the critical claims against the historical veracity of biblical stories...For several decades Albright and his students would deploy linguistics and biblical archology to authenticate the historicity of the Hebrew Bible... During the Mandatory period, large-scale excavations were conducted by Albright and his students to create a reliable history of the Bible. These Western archeologists brushed aside the historical and contemporary social realities of Arab and Muslim Palestine in favor of the biblical paradigm; for them, the Palestinian uprisings raging in the late 1920s and 1930s meant little 'in comparison to the eternal verities' of the Bible. Adopting a virtually fundamentalist approach to archeology, Albright and his pupils based the site excavation on biblical names: Megiddo (the site of the biblical Armageddon), Lachish, Gezer, Shechem (Nablus), Jericho, Jerusalem, Ai, Gibeon, Beit Shean (Baysan), Beit Shemesh, Tanach and Hazor, the last site of the ancient Canaanites city-state mentioned in the book of

Joshua, the same city whose subsequent excavation later became a major landmark in the history of mobilized Israeli archeology.⁷⁰

This perception of a Holy Land was not based on clearly delineable evidence but was principally based on tradition. This tradition goes back to the famous journey of Helena, the mother of the Roman Emperor Constantine. After the emperor's conversion to Christianity, Helena journeyed to Palestine to identify the site of the crucifixion of Yahusha (Jesus) and his resurrection, marking a radical change in the perception of modern Jerusalem, now as a center of reverence and pilgrimage for Christianity.⁷¹

Jerusalem was also central to the religion of Islam since its beginning. According to the Muslim Prophet Mohammed's biographies, when he first began to preach at Mecca, Mohammed would have his converts prostate in prayer in the direction of Jerusalem in Palestine. It is also Muslims who first began the tradition of identifying the Temple Mount as Solomon's Temple after they conquered the city. As Masalha explains:

> ... with Muslim identification of the area as 'Solomon's temple,' an error was begun. European Christians, travelers, and later investigators all claimed that the walls of the al-Haram al-Sharif were remnants of the Jewish Temple Mount. For many Christians, Muslims, and Jews, the identification of the Moriah Mount as delineated by the walls of the Temple Mount has become a fundamental principle which needs no proof.⁷²

Arab invaders of Palestine in the 7ᵗʰ and 8ᵗʰ centuries CE also have much to do with the modern identification of Biblical geographic locations, having adopted some of the geographical names that were used in the Byzantine period. This led to the tradition of Palestine as

---

⁷⁰ Nur Masalha, The Bible & Zionism: Invented Traditions, Archology and Post Colonialism in Israel-Palestine, Zed Books, (2007) 102, 103, 104.
⁷¹ *Id.* at 111.
⁷² *Id.* at 122.

the Holy Land having been fully taken advantage of by the Zionist movement.[73]

According to Britannica, Zionism is a "Jewish nationalist movement that has had as its goal the creation and support of a Jewish national state in Palestine, the ancient homeland of the Jews."[74] This simple claim of the right to a homeland was not enough to propel the movement for the displaced Jewish population. Instead, using their status as "Jews," the supposed people of the Bible, and representing their movement as the return to the Holy Land of the dispersed children of Yahshar-el, Zionists appealed directly to the religious zeal of many in Christianity awaiting the return of the Messiah. [75]

Despite this religious connotation, the founding fathers of Zionism were almost completely atheist or religiously indifferent.[76] For example, in 1937, David Ben-Gurion, a Russian Jew who would later become the first prime minister and the chief architect for the State of Israel, told the British Royal Commission visiting Palestine, "The Bible is our Mandate." This is despite the fact Gurion was a non-believer and a deeply secular Zionist.[77]

It is, therefore, imperative to look at claims of a Yahshar-el in Palestine with an investigatory eye. Was the Christian church brought into this notion from reputable sources, or have they believed a convenient *truth* to usher in their own messianic ambitions? The evidence will prove the latter.

---

[73] *Id.*
[74] Zionism, Britannica (Oct. 19, 2023) https://www.britannica.com/topic/Zionism.
[75] *Supra* note 70 at 2.
[76] Bernard Leeman, Nubian Moses, Ethiopian Exodus, Arabian Solomon, Sheba University College, (Aug. 2, 2015) at 1.
[77] *Supra* note 70 at 16.

The Egyptian Captivity and the Exodus

Secular scholars have long scoffed at the idea of a historical Bible. As Zeev Herzog, Professor of Archeology at Tel Aviv University and the director of its Institute of Archeology explained, archeology based on an Exodus to Palestine shows that the Exodus, Joshua's conquest of Canaan and the united monarchy of David and Solomon could not have happened:

> This is what archeologists have learned from their excavations in the Land of Israel: the Israelites were never in Egypt, did not wander in the desert, did not conquer the land in a military campaign, and did not pass it on to the 12 tribes of Israel. Perhaps even harder to swallow is the fact that the united monarchy of David and Solomon, which is described by the Bible as a regional power, was, at most, a small tribal kingdom. And it will come as an unpleasant shock to many that the God of Israel, Jehovah, had a female consort and that the early Israelite religion adopted monotheism only in the waning period of the monarchy and not at Mount Sinai. Most of those who are engaged in scientific work in the interlocking spheres of the Bible, the field looking for proof to corroborate the Bible story – now agree that the historic events relating to the stages of the Jewish people's emergence are radically different from what the story tells.[78]

The major problem is that the Bible's archeology has been built around a narrative of Yahshar-el in the Levant. In the book of Genesis, we are told about a seven-year period of famine in Egypt that encompassed the entire region, including the land of the Biblical Patriarchs. However, if the Biblical Patriarchs originated in Arabia, a regional famine is highly unlikely, as the climatic systems responsible for weather in Arabia are independent of the systems causing the monsoon rains, which determine the annual water flow in the Nile.[79] Also, conceivably, the Hebrews who faced hardship securing food from their long-lost brother Joseph in Egypt could have also journeyed north towards modern Turkey or east towards modern Iraq, which are even further from this climatic system.

---

[78] *Id.* at 245- 246 (*citing* Herzog 1999: 6-8).
[79] Avner Ramu, Canaan? Opps Wrong Country, Isgav Publishing LLC, (2003) 18.

After settling in a community known as Goshen in Egypt, the Hebrews were forced into slavery until they received deliverance from Yahuah (God) through His servant Moses, who led them from Egypt to journey towards the land promised to Abraham, Isaac and Jacob. Because of distance, Biblical experts put the land of Goshen, as well as the exodus, in Northern Egypt (Lower Egypt). We are told the Hebrews left Egypt by crossing the "Sea of Reeds" (not the Red Sea as commonly mistranslated) and then exiting into the Sinai Peninsula. However, an additional problem occurs. Egypt controlled the Sinai Peninsula during the time of the Exodus. Undoubtedly, Egypt would have launched a new offensive against the Hebrews had they journeyed through the Sinai Peninsula after the captivity. As explained by Avner Ramu:

> From Egyptian sources, we know that at this period, the Egyptians controlled northern Sinai through a series of fortresses and garrisons built to protect the coastal road to their Canaanite province. A journey along this road of some 150 miles could have been completed in less than two weeks. Because of the Egyptian presence, the Hebrews could not have taken this eastern route, along the coast, to Canaan. However, a journey from Egypt toward the southern tip of the Sinai Peninsula is not plausible either, as the Egyptians secured the roads to the turquoise and copper mines and to the stone quarries in this region. If the Hebrews were indeed escaping from Egypt, choosing any of the eastward routes would not have been reasonable. In addition, William Ward indicated that between 1468 and 1150 BC, Canaan was dominated by Egypt politically and militarily, and the escaping Hebrews could not have found shelter from Egyptian subordination in this area.[80]

Joshua's Conquest and the United Monarchy

Joshua's conquests have long been a point of discontent for archeologists investigating the Biblical narrative. Probably the most controversial account is the fall of Jericho. As

---

[80] *Id.* at 60.

archeologists Israel Finkelstein and Neil Asher Silberman stated on Jericho:

> There is no sign of destruction. Thus, the famous scene of the Israelite forces marching around the walled town with the Ark of the Covenant, causing Jericho's mighty walls to collapse by blowing of their war trumpets was, to put simply, a romantic mirage.[81]

Daniel Gavron, a British Zionist journalist who heads English News at Radio Israel, wrote an article entitled "King David and Jerusalem: Myth and Reality," where he remarked on Joshua's conquest:

> The historical evidence to back up these events is sparse, and in some cases, contradictory. In particular, the account of Joshua's conquest of Canaan is inconsistent with archeological evidence. Cities supposedly conquered by Joshua in the 14th century BCE were destroyed long before he came on the scene. Some, such as Ai and Arad, had been ruins for 1000 years...The conclusion is somewhat startling to Bible readers who know the Canaanites portrayed in the Bible as immoral idolaters: most of the Israelites were in fact formerly Canaanites.[82]

As attested to by Daniel Gavron, modern archeology shows that the later inhabitants of contemporary Jerusalem were not genetically distinct from the previous inhabitants but were of the same ethnicity, meaning if Palestine were Yahshar-el, the Hebrews and the Canaanites were the same people.[83] There is also no proof of the "united monarchy" of David and Solomon, one of military conquests, achievements, riches and power. Instead, archeology only supports the presence of two modest communities in Palestine.[84] As Thomas L. Thompson, a minimalist scholar, has written:

> There is no evidence of a United Monarchy, a capital in Jerusalem, or any coherent, unified political force that dominated western Palestine, let alone an empire of the size the legends describe. We do not have evidence for the existence of kings named Saul, David, or Solomon,

---

[81] Israel Finkelstein and Neil Asher Silberman, The Bible Unearthed, The Free Press (2001) 82.
[82] *Supra*, note 70 at 248.
[83] *Id.* at 165-166.
[84] *Id.* at 247.

nor do we have evidence for any temple at Jerusalem in this early period. What we know of Israel and Judah of the tenth century does not allow us to interpret this lack of evidence as a gap in our knowledge and information about the past, a result merely of the accidental nature of archeology. There is neither room nor context, no artifact or archive that points to such historical realities in Palestine's tenth century. One cannot speak historically of a state without a population. Nor can one speak of a capital without a town. Stories are not enough.[85]

Palestine's Geography

When we read the Bible's descriptions of Yahshar-el's geography, we can also attest that the Yahshar-el in the Bible and Palestine do not match. After the Hebrews arrived in the Promised Land, a land flowing with "Milk and Honey," they also found a land of forests. Joshua 17:17-18 says:

> But Joshua spoke to the house of Joseph, to Ephraim and Manasseh, saying, "You are a numerous people and have great power; you shall not have one lot only, 18 but the hill country shall be yours. **For though it is a forest, you shall clear it**, and to its farthest borders it shall be yours; for you shall drive out the Canaanites, even though they have iron chariots and though they are strong."

Similarly, in 1 Samuel 14:25-26, we're told of Saul's military journeying though forests:

> **All the people of the land entered the forest**, and there was honey on the ground. 26 **When the people entered the forest**, behold, there was honey dripping; but no man put his hand to his mouth, because the people feared the oath.

Additionally, in 2 Samuel 18:6-8, we read of David's troops fighting his son Absalom's troops in the forest:

---

[85] Thomas L. Thompson, The Mythic Past: Biblical Archaeology And The Myth Of Israel, Basic Books (Apr. 6, 2000).

> Then the people went out to the field against Israel, and the battle took place in the forest of Ephraim. 7 The people of Israel were defeated there by the servants of David, and the slaughter there that day was great, twenty thousand men. 8 For the battle there was spread over the whole countryside, and **the forest devoured more people that day than the sword devoured**.

Despite the Biblical depiction of a forestry landscape, this landscape hardly exists in Palestine today or in the past.[86] As detailed by Ramu:

> As early as the Middle Ages, visitors and pilgrims who came to Palestine were struck by its barren landscapes. Europeans who were familiar with the Bible, were surprised that so few trees could be seen in the mountains of Samaria and Judea. After one hundred years of a reforestation effort by the Jewish National Fund, the British Mandatory government, and since 1949 AD by the State of Israel, only 3.7% of Israel's territory is covered by forests (mostly man-made)...[87]

In the 1960s, the Jewish National Fund (JNF) planted a human-made forest called Yatir, 30 miles from modern Jerusalem, where Aleppo pines were planted to match what was in the Bible. As detailed by National Geographic writer Josie Glausiusz:

> Though Aleppo pines are mentioned in the Bible, pollen surveys and archaeological studies suggest the species was rare in the region until the 20th century. First planted extensively in Palestine in the 1920s by the British Mandate Forestry Service, they constituted about 50 percent of the forests planted by the JNF by the 1980s. They grow rapidly and on any kind of soil. They can be seen now all over Israel, from the northern Galilee mountains to the northern Negev.[88]

In addition to forestry, there is also the issue of lions. Repeatedly, throughout the Bible, there are stories involving lions, from David

---

[86] *Supra* note 79 at 155.
[87] *Id.*
[88] Josie Glausiusz, They planted a forest at the edge of the desert. From there it got complicated, National Geographic, (Mar. 23, 2023) https://www.nationalgeographic.com/environment/article/carbon-sucking-forest-desert-israel-yatir.

killing a lion with his own hands, to Samson eating honey from a lion's carcass, to a lion killing a prophet in 1 Kings Chapter 13. However, there is no evidence that lions were ever dispersed throughout Palestine. As Ramu remarks, "Five species of wild big cats are found in Israel. Four of these species are too small to be considered a threat to humans – David likely lived in northern Ethiopia/Eritrea."[89] In Ethiopia, lions not only still exist despite their dwindling numbers, but are also a central feat of Ethiopian culture.[90]

An Alternative Account

The mainstream narrative of the Biblical Exodus has no historical, geographical, or archeological congruence with the truth. However, an alternative to this account, rooted in scripture, where the Exodus, the sojourn in the wilderness, and the establishment of the Kingdom of Yahshar-el (Israel) are given a completely different setting can make sense out of puzzlement. A willingness to shift our understanding of location will help us realize this is the story the Bible has told us all along. It was only conspirators against Yahuah's (God's) original chosen who ripped this story from its origin for their own political and spiritual objectives. [91]

    The revisionist account is that the Hebrews originally came into Egypt from the south of Egypt, likely Eritrea or Ethiopia. This region experiences the same climatic shifts as Egypt due to a similar dependency on the Nile, and thus a famine in Egypt would affect this entire region. Upon entering Egypt, Yahshar-el was given an abode in Goshen, located in Nubia where they were later forced into slavery. Goshen's location in Nubia is supported by the word *Goshen*, which resembles the word *Kushan*. The Egyptians used Kush to describe the

---

[89] *Supra* note 79 at 152-15.
[90] Fred Harter, 'Humans everywhere': lions cling on in Ethiopia's last patches of wilderness, The Guardian, (Aug. 17, 2023) https://www.theguardian.com/environment/2023/aug/17/ethiopias-lions-under-pressure-humans-farmers-aoe.
[91] Credit to the YouTube Channel, Revisionist – official channel, whose research was a helpful guide: https://www.youtube.com/@Revisionistsofficialchannel

regions south of Egypt.⁹² Even greater confirmation is the Soleb Inscription located in ancient Kush, and modern Sudan, which explicitly names the region "the Land of the Nomads of Yahuah." As stated by Jude Flurry from the Armstrong Institute of Biblical Archeology:

> ... one pillar at Soleb bears a cartouche (a term for an oval-shaped hieroglyphic inscription) of enormous biblical significance. It is badly damaged. Originally, the cartouche would have been accompanied by an image of a kneeling slave, matching the other pillars. However, only the cartouche and the prisoner's hands are still visible. Even the cartouche itself has been vandalized by locals within the past century. However, the inscription is still visible: It translates to "The land of the shasu of Yahweh."
>
> Almost all scholars believe the Egyptian word "shasu" should be translated as "cattle-herding nomads," or simply "nomads." More significant, though, is the other name in the inscription. "Yahweh" undoubtedly refers to the God of the Hebrews, mentioned over 6,800 times throughout the Hebrew Bible.⁹³

The term Flurry translated as "Yahweh" is "YHW," a portion of the tetragrammaton "YHWH." This inscription is located in Northern Sudan at the Soleb Temple built by Pharaoh Amenhotep III around 1400 BCE. There is also the Amarah West inscription, also in Northern Sudan, which was constructed by Rameses II in the 13th century BCE. This inscription also references, "The Shasu of YHWH's Land" which is believed to be referring to the Soleb Temple inscription.⁹⁴ This points a high probability that the Soleb Temple is located in the Biblical land of Goshen.

---

⁹² *Supra* note 79 at 35.
⁹³ Jude Flurry, Armstrong Institute of Biblical Archaeology, The Soleb Inscription: Earliest-Discovered Use of the Name 'Yahweh,' (Oct. 10, 2022) https://armstronginstitute.org/768-the-soleb-inscription-earliest-discovered-use-of-the-name-yahweh.
⁹⁴ Clyde E. Billington, The Name of Yahweh in Egyptian Hieroglyphic Texts, Associates for Biblical Research, https://biblearchaeology.org/research/exodus-from-egypt/3233-the-name-yahweh-in-egyptian-hieroglyphic-texts

There is little detail given in the Bible about what exact slave labor the Hebrews were subjected to other than making bricks and constructing cities.[95] However, with a Lower Egypt destination, mining gold was likely an aspect of their workload. (See Map 6) The gold mining business was lucrative for ancient Egypt, with most mines being state monopolies dominated by prisoners and slaves. According to ancient Greek historian Diodorus Siculus in his *Bibliotheca Historicam*, published around 60 BCE, these miners worked in shockingly difficult conditions, were given little food or water, and were often beaten if they didn't work hard enough.[96]

There is historical evidence of a Nubian religious group that worshipped the bull god Apis, a detail akin to what we know of the Hebrews, who, not long after leaving Egypt, created a golden calf they worshipped. As Professor Bernard Leeman of Queen of Sheba University remarked:

> The Egyptians certainly enslaved defeated Nubians on a huge scale for gold mining… If the Hebrew were indeed held captive in Nubia, it would explain their seeming rootlessness, their exposure to a bull deity (Apis) and a connection with gold (the Golden Calf). Arab sources and the Jewish historian Josephus both link Moses to Nubia.[97]

The Bible tells us Moses, after killing an Egyptian overseer, fled to a land called Midian. There, he married his wife Zipporah, a Kushite woman and the daughter of the Midian leader Jethro. There has been much speculation on whether Midian, which in Hebrew is *miḏ yān*[98] was, in fact, the territory of the Medjay of Nubia, given the semblance in names as well as their close proximity to Egypt. There is also scriptural confirmation of this association of the Medjay with Kush. Habakkuk 3:7 reads, "I saw the tents of Cushan under distress, the

---

[95] Exodus 1:14.
[96] Where Did the Ancient Egyptians Find All Their Gold?, Rare Gold Nuggets, (Aug. 24, 2017) https://raregoldnuggets.com/?p=5468.
[97] *Supra* note 76 at 10.
[98] 4080 miḏ·yān, Bible Hub, https://biblehub.com/hebrew/midyan_4080.htm (last visited Jan. 21, 2024).

tent curtains of the land of Midian were trembling." Egyptian sources depict the Medjay as a pastoral people who roamed the northeastern Nubian desert. Their land stretched between the Red Sea in the East and the Nile River. The Medjay people also served in the Egyptian military, initially as scouts and light infantry, but later as policemen.[99]

Seemingly, the only mention of Yahshar-el as a nation by the Egyptians is in Thebes in Upper Egypt on what is known as the Merneptah or Israel Stele of 1213-1203 BCE, discovered in 1896. The stele, dated to when many scholars believe the Exodus occurred, contains the hieroglyphs *I.si.ri.ar.* which has been thought to commemorate a defeat of the Hebrews, stating the message "Israel is no more." This understanding of "Israel is no more" is due to the assumption that Yahshar-el went into Palestine where Egyptian military raids were frequent. However, if Yahshar-el completed their departure in the south, "Israel is no more" may not refer to a military victory but have been a euphemism, meaning Israel escaped. This record of Israel being no more also comes from the same era where all the Medjay ceased to exist, gold production ceased and volcanic activity occurred in Nubia, which could run parallel to plagues, such as the Sun being darkened.[100]

The most dramatic turn of events during the Exodus occurs when Yahshar-el crosses the *Yam Suph*, which means the "Sea of Reeds." While tradition has held this body of water as the Red Sea, modern scholarship reveals this designation was an error of the translator based on their understanding of geography, as noted on BibleArcheology.org:

> Unfortunately, "Red Sea" was not a translation, and the LXX translators understood that. While we do not know their reasoning, they gave yam suph a historicized interpretation, based on their understanding of the region at the time. When the Bible indicated the Israelites crossed a significant body of water on Egypt's eastern border, the LXX translators connected it with the body of water they

---

[99] *Id.*
[100] *Id.* at 12 & 14; Exodus 10:21-23.

knew as the Red Sea. Instead of translating the Hebrew phrase literally, they offered this historical identification as their interpretation of the text... There is general agreement among scholars today, both liberal and conservative, that yam suph means "Reed Sea." **The Hebrew suph referred to a water plant, as indicated in Exodus 2:3–5 and Isaiah 19:6–7, where reeds in the Nile River are mentioned**. The Hebrew suph ("reed") is probably an Egyptian loan word—from the hieroglyph for water plants.[101]

Returning to the gold mining hypothesis, most archaeologists believe that most of the gold mined in Egypt was along the Nile River. Given the scriptural reference to "reeds" being used to refer to the Nile, as stated above by BibleArcheology.com, it is likely the actual Reed Sea crossing occurred through the Nile River.

---

[101] New Evidence from Egypt on the Location of the Exodus Sea Crossing, Associates for Biblical Research https://biblearchaeology.org/research/exodus-from-egypt/3191-new-evidence-from-egypt-on-the-location-of-the-exodus-sea-crossing-part-i?highlight=WyJuZXciLCJnbmV3IiwiJ25ldyciLCJ0ZXN0YW1lbnQiLCJ0ZXN0YW1lbnQiiwidGV4dCIsInRleHQncyIsInRleHQiiwibmV3IHRlc3RhbWVudCIsIm5ldyB0ZXN0YW1lbnQgdGV4dCIsInRlc3RhbWVudCB0ZXh0Il0= (*last visited* Nov. 7, 2023).

Chapter 4: Evidence From Hidden Scriptures

"For the wrath of God is revealed from heaven against all ungodliness and unrighteousness of people who suppress the truth in unrighteousness, because that which is known about God is evident within them; for God made it evident to them."

~ Romans 1:18-19

It has been demonstrated that the Hebrew translation of Bible scriptures reveals Biblical Yahshar-el (Israel) is in East Africa. We will now delve into confirmatory evidence from other ancient Hebrew scriptures.

The Hidden Books

In this section, we will explore two extrabiblical sources: 1) the Genesis Apocryphon and 2) the Book of Jubilees. The institutions of Rabbinical Judaism and Christianity have labeled both books as pseudepigrapha.

Apocrypha & Pseudepigrapha

Not all Christian believers know that many ancient Hebrew and New Testament writings are not included in their Christian Bibles, some for reasons they may agree with, others for reasons they may not agree with. Two labels are typically given to these books, the first being Apocrypha and the second being Pseudepigrapha. According to Christianity.com:

> the word "Apocrypha" comes from the Greek word meaning "hidden" or "secret." Initially, the term was reserved for books with content considered too sacred and grand to make accessible to the general public. Over time, "Apocrypha" took on a more negative connotation

due to the questionable origins and doubtful canonicity of these books."[102]

While apocrypha books are typically rejected as scripture by protestant denominations, they are deemed scriptural by the Catholic Church and included in Catholic Bibles. Books labeled Pseudepigrapha, however, receive almost universal banishment from all Christian churches, with a notable exception being the Ethiopian Orthodox Church, which has long held some Hebrew books labeled Pseudepigrapha as Holy scripture. According to the Christian Apologist website Got Questions, the reasons for the banishment of Pseudepigrapha are:

> The pseudepigrapha [are] the books that attempt to imitate Scripture, but that were written under false names. The term pseudepigrapha comes from the Greek pseudo, meaning "false," and epigraphein, meaning "to inscribe," thus, "to write falsely." The pseudepigraphal books were written anywhere from 200 BC to AD 300. They are spurious works written by unknown authors who attempted to gain a readership by tacking on the name of a famous biblical character.
>
> While the pseudepigrapha may be of interest to students of history and ancient religious thought, they are not inspired by God and therefore not part of the canon of Scripture. Reasons to reject the pseudepigrapha are 1) they were written under false names. Any pretense or falsehood in a book naturally negates its claim of truthfulness. 2) They contain anachronisms and historical errors.[103]

We are not told how church authorities know one or all of these books are written under false names. We are also not told the supposed "historical errors" of each book labeled Pseudepigrapha. Instead, these labels are applied to "they," all Pseudepigrapha, without qualification from the writer as to why and how.

---

[102] What Is the Apocrypha? Are Apocryphal Books Really Scripture?, Christianity.com, (Apr. 25, 2019) https://www.christianity.com/wiki/bible/what-is-the-apocrypha-are-apocryphal-books-really-scripture.html.
[103] What are the pseudepigrapha?, Got Questions, https://www.gotquestions.org/pseudepigrapha.html (*last visited* Oct. 5, 2023).

While we will later contend more with these objections to the "Pseudepigrapha" label, for purposes of this chapter, it should simply be noted 1) the Ethiopian Orthodox Church has long held the Book of Jubilees as canonical, 2) both the Genesis Apocryphon and the Book of Jubilees were found in the Dead Sea Scrolls, meaning ancient believers in Torah found these books of scriptural significance, and 3) these books are ancient books with much more closeness to the question of where Biblical Yahshar-el would be. Thus, even the Christian apologist, who almost always will concede the point that these books have historical value, or as noted above, "pseudepigrapha may be of interest to students of history and ancient religious thought," cannot simply write these books off as baseless, especially if they are corroborating what we have already established is present in Biblical texts.

The Dead Sea Scrolls

There is no doubt that Torah believers inhabited Palestine after 450 BCE.[104] One such community of Torah believers left us what is today the Bible's most significant physical and archeological confirmation: the Dead Sea Scrolls.

The Dead Sea Scrolls were mainly discovered during this last century in caves in Qumran, Palestine, and contain the earliest known copies of parts of almost every book of the Hebrew Bible (other than the Book of Esther and Nehemiah), written on parchment and papyrus and mainly in Hebrew. Dating to around the third century BCE to the first century CE, the Dead Sea Scrolls are widely considered the most significant archaeological find of the 20th century and remain the subject of heated academic debate worldwide.[105] The study of the scrolls has enabled Bible scholars to push back the date

---

[104] Bernard Leeman, Nubian Moses, Ethiopian Exodus, Arabian Solomon, Sheba University College, (Aug. 2, 2015) 7.
[105] Isabel Kershner, Israel Reveals Newly Discovered Fragments of Dead Sea Scrolls, New York Times, (Mar. 16. 2021)
https://www.nytimes.com/2021/03/16/world/middleeast/dead-sea-scrolls-israel.html.

of the Hebrew Bible to no later than 70 CE.[106] However, the evidence of the original Hebrew Bible, which includes Pseudepigrapha and Apocrypha texts, has been compartmentalized so as not to disrupt the Bible canon.

Before the Dead Sea Scrolls were discovered, the earliest known Hebrew Bible manuscript was dated to the 10th century CE. At that time, there was no "Bible," per se, but a loose collection of sacred writings belonging to different sects. The Dead Sea Scrolls, however, show that many of these books were a part of the Hebrew canon, despite some Jewish and Christian stances that they were not.[107] As Britannica details:

> A quarter of the texts are biblical manuscripts—to which can be added copies of works such as the books of Enoch, Jubilees, and Tobit, previously known and not thought to be sectarian. Thus, the scrolls shed light on more than merely the sect that possessed them. Indeed, it has been argued that the Qumran scrolls actually represent the contents of libraries in Jerusalem, hurriedly hidden shortly before the Roman siege of the city during the First Jewish Revolt (66–73 CE), and thus reflect quite varied Jewish [Hebrew] origins.[108]

It should be noted, however, that the Dead Sea Scrolls were not immediately made available to the public. Despite being discovered in the West Bank of Palestine, the scrolls were seized by the Israeli government, who kept the scrolls hidden only to be released under the direction of the Israeli government. As is detailed by Britannica:

> All the manuscripts were placed initially under the control of a small committee of scholars appointed by the Jordanian Department of Antiquities (a responsibility assumed after 1967 by what is now the Israel Antiquities Authority), who, some claim, monopolized access to

---

[106] The Scrolls in Context, Britannica, https://www.britannica.com/topic/Dead-Sea-Scrolls/The-scrolls-in-context (*last visited* Jan. 11, 2024).
[107] Jean-Pierre Isbouts, What do the Dead Sea Scrolls reveal about the origins of Christianity?, National Geographic, (Aug. 22, 2023) https://www.nationalgeographic.com/premium/article/dead-sea-scrolls-origins-christianity.
[108] *Supra* note 106.

the scrolls. Most of the longer, more complete scrolls were published soon after their discovery. The majority of the scrolls, however, consists of tiny, brittle fragments, which were published at a pace considered by many to be excessively slow. Even more unsettling for some was the fact that access to the unpublished documents was severely limited to the editorial committee.[109]

Any student of history should rightfully ask, why such secrecy in the discovery of the Dead Sea Scrolls, and why such a slow release? The author contends that the primary reason for the initial concealment of the Dead Sea Scrolls by the Israelis is they 100% prove that Palestine is not the ancient homeland of Hebrews, as widely published by Zionists, the Israeli authorities and their co-conspirators.

The Genesis Apocryphon

The Genesis Apocryphon found in the Dead Sea Scrolls is the only copy of the ancient text known to exist. This book is parallel to the Book of Jubilees' narrative and details. The Genesis Apocryphon, Column 16:8-19 gives an account of Abraham previewing the land promised to his descendants:

> Then God appeared to me in a vision in the night, and said to me, "Go up to Ramat-Hazor, which is to the north of 9. Bethel, the place where you are living. Lift up you eyes and look to the east, to the west, to the south, and to the north, and look at this entire 10. land that I am giving to you and to your descendants for all ages." So on the following day I went up to Ramat-Hazor and I saw the Land from 11. this high point: from the River of Egypt until Lebanon and Senir, and from the Great Sea to Hauran, and all the land of Gebal up to Kadesh, and the entire Great Desert 12. that is east of Hauran and Senir, up to the Euphrates. He said to me, "To your descendants I will give all of this land, and they will inherit it for all ages. 13. I will make your descendants as numerous as the dust of the earth, which no one is able to reckon. So too your descendants will be beyond reckoning. Get up, walk around, go 14. and see how great are its length and its width. For I shall give it to you and to you descendants after you unto all the ages. vacat 130 15. So I, Abram, went out to go around and look at the Land. I began to travel the circuit from the Gihon River,

---

[109] *Id.*

> and came alongside the Sea until 16. I reached Mount Taurus. I then traversed from alo[ng] this Great Sea of Salt and went alongside Mount Taurus to the east, through the breadth of the land, 17. until I reached the Euphrates River. I journeyed along the Euphrates until I reached the Erythrean Sea, to the East, and was traveling along 18. the Erythrean Sea until I reached the gulf of the Red Sea, which extends out from the Erythrean Sea. I went around to the south until I reached the Gihon 19. River, and I then returned, arriving at my house in safety.

What this passage reveals is astounding. Based on the text, the Erytheran Sea, another name for the Red Sea, is on the *east side* of Yahshar-el. In addition, the text points to a high point from which one can see the Gihon, or the Nile River, as far as the "Euphrates River," or the Perath River. This would be impossible if we accepted the translation of *Perath* as the Euphrates, as the Erythrean Sea is nowhere close to the Euphrates River. This geography is possible, however, based on our establishing the Perath as the Blue Nile, particularly if Abraham's journey had been through the Ethiopian Highlands, which reach both the Blue Nile and the Red Sea.

It is also profound that the Genesis Apocryphon corroborates our findings that the Salt Sea is Lake Abbe as Column 16 verse 17-18 iterates that: "... the gulf of 17. the Great Salt Sea. And this boundary goes as a spring from this gulf, wh[ich]... 18. to... up to the gulf of the sea that faces toward Eg[yp]t." This is also further confirmation that the Sea of Salt is not the Dead Sea but is Lake Abbe, with the gulf mentioned being the Gulf of Aden. Applying what has already been established in previous chapters, we will add the more correct geographical meanings:

> Then God appeared to me in a vision in the night, and said to me, "Go up to Ramat-Hazor, which is to the north of 9. Bethel, the place where you are living. Lift up you eyes and look to the east, to the west, to the south, and to the north, and look at this entire 10. land that I am giving to you and to your descendants for all ages." So on the following day I went up to Ramat-Hazor and I saw the Land from 11. this high point: from the *Nile River* of Egypt until Lebanon and Senir, and from the *Red Sea* to Hauran, and all the land of Gebal up to Kadesh, and the entire Great Desert 12. that is east of Hauran and Senir, up to the *Blue Nile River*. He said to me, "To your descendants I will give all of this land, and they will inherit it for all ages. 13. I will

make your descendants as numerous as the dust of the earth, which no one is able to reckon. So too your descendants will be beyond reckoning. Get up, walk around, go 14. and see how great are its length and its width. For I shall give it to you and to you descendants after you unto all the ages. vacat 130 15. So I, Abram, went out to go around and look at the Land. I began to travel the circuit from the *Nile River*, and came alongside the *Red Sea* until 16. I reached Mount Taurus. I then traversed from alo[ng] this *Lake Abbe* and went alongside Mount Taurus to the east, through the breadth of the land, 17. until I reached the *Blue Nile River*. I journeyed along the *Blue Nile* until I reached the *Red Sea*, to the East, and was traveling along 18. the *Red Sea* until I reached the gulf of the *Red Sea*, which extends out from the *Red Sea*. I went around to the south until I reached the *Nile* 19. *River*, and I then returned, arriving at my house in safety.

Amazingly, the Genesis Apocryphon unquestionably puts Yahshar-el in East Africa. One last point worth emphasizing is Abraham's origins. The Genesis Apocryphon states that after touring the promised land, Abraham returned south till he reached the Nile. This establishes that Abraham's origins were in Ethiopia. This is corroborated by the details of his travels in Genesis 12:9: "Abram journeyed on, continuing toward the Negev. Now there was a famine in the land; so Abram went down to Egypt to live there for a time, because the famine was severe in the land." We are told Abraham traveled through the desert, which we have established is the Nubian Desert. Thus, Abraham, who journeyed "down" to Egypt (north), was originally from Ethiopia.

The Book of Jubilees

The Book of Jubilees, as it is called today, is known by some as the "Lesser Genesis." Had it not been for the Ethiopian Orthodox Church, this book would have remained hidden until the release of the Dead Sea Scrolls.

There are numerous reasons why Jubilees could have been removed from the gaze of mainstream Judaism and Christianity. One apparent reason is that Jubilees calls our attention to the order of seasons, years, sabbaths and jubilees in a way that contradicts the Jewish lunar calendar. Another reason is Jubilees, like the Book of Enoch, provides details about the Watchers, fallen angels who once taught man many devices and mated with women to create the Nephilim, hybrid human-angel beings who oppressed humanity, a story not widely taught throughout mainstream Christianity. However, possibly the most significant reason why Jubilees was erased from the Biblical canon is that it plainly states that the Holy Land, which encompasses "the Holy of Holies," the Garden of Eden, Mount Sinai, and Mount Zion, are not in Palestine or even Arabia, but are in fact in East Africa.

Jubilees gives a detailed breakdown of the allotments of land given to Noah's three sons Shem, Ham and Japheth after the global flood. This allotment does not complement what is widely believed in mainstream Christianity and Judaism, where Arabia was given to Shem (hence the term Semitic being used today to describe Arabian ancestry), Africa to Ham and Europe to Japheth. (See Map 7). However, Jubilees gives a much more nuanced description of the allotments of the descendants of Noah.

The Book of Jubilees Chapter 8:9-17 details the division of the lands by Noah's sons:

> And they divided (it) secretly amongst themselves, and told it to Noah.
> 10. And it came to pass in the beginning of the thirty-third jubilee that they divided the earth into three parts, for Shem and Ham and Japheth, according to the inheritance of each, in the first year in the first week, when one of us who had been sent, was with them.
> 11. And he called his sons, and they drew nigh to him, they and their children, and he divided the earth into the lots, which his three sons were to take in possession, and they reached forth their hands, and took the writing out of the bosom of Noah, their father.
> 12. And there came forth on the writing as Shem's lot the middle of the earth which he should take as an inheritance for himself and for his sons for the generations of eternity, **from the middle of the mountain range of Rafa, from the mouth of the water from the river Tina, and his portion goes towards the west through the midst of this river, and it extends till it reaches the water of the abysses, out of which this river goes forth and pours its waters into the sea Me'at, and this river flows into the great sea.** And all that is towards the north is Japheth's, and all that is towards the south belongs to Shem.

> 13. And it extends till it reaches **Karaso**: this is in the bosom of the tongue which looks towards the south.
> 14. And his portion extends along the great sea, and it extends in a straight line till it reaches the west of the tongue which looks towards the south: for this sea is named the tongue of the Egyptian Sea.
> 15. And it turns from here towards the south towards the mouth of the great sea on the shore of (its) waters, and it extends to the west to 'Afra, and it extends till it reaches the waters of the river Gihon, and to the south of the waters of Gihon, to the banks of this river.
> 16. And it extends towards the east, till it reaches the Garden of Eden, to the south thereof, [to the south] and from the east of the whole land of Eden and of the whole east, it turns to the east and proceeds till it reaches the east of the mountain named Rafa, and it descends to the bank of the mouth of the river Tina.
> 17. This portion came forth by lot for Shem and his sons, that they should possess it for ever unto his generations for evermore.

Jubilees gives us three remarkable details here. 1) Jubilees identifies Shem's portion as extending west of the tongue of the Egyptian Sea that points south, called the "Karaso." This tongue of the Egyptian Sea is obviously the Sinai Peninsula. 2) Shem's portion extends west to 'Afra' till it reaches the Gihon, and 3) Shem's portion extends to the south where the Garden of Eden is located. This totally contradicts what Jewish and Christian theologians have depicted as the division of the world.

In Jubilees Chapter 8:18-21 we receive further details of Shem's portion, which encompasses the "Holy of Holies:"

> And Noah rejoiced that this portion came forth for Shem and for his sons, and he remembered all that he had spoken with his mouth in prophecy; for he had said: 'Blessed be the Lord God of Shem And may the Lord dwell in the dwelling of Shem.'
> 19. And he knew that the Garden of Eden is the holy of holies, and the dwelling of the Lord, and Mount Sinai the centre of the desert, and Mount Zion -the centre of the navel of the earth: these three were created as holy places facing each other.
> 20. And he blessed the God of gods, who had put the word of the Lord into his mouth, and the Lord for evermore.

21. And he knew that a blessed portion and a blessing had come to Shem and his sons unto the generations for ever - the whole land of Eden and the whole land of the Red Sea, and the whole land of the east and India, and on the Red Sea and the mountains thereof, and all the land of Bashan, and all the land of Lebanon and the islands of Kaftur, and all the mountains of Sanir and 'Amana, and the mountains of Asshur in the north, and all the land of Elam, Asshur, and Babel, and Susan and Ma'edai, and all the mountains of Ararat, and all the region beyond the sea, which is beyond the mountains of Asshur towards the north, a blessed and spacious land, and all that is in it is very good.

Thus, as for the total lot of Shem given to us by the Book of Jubilees, we can ascertain the following:

Jubilees 9 Geographical Identifications	
Rafa Mountains "from the middle of the mountain range of Rafa"	**Hijaz Mountains**
River Tina "from the mouth of the water from the river Tina, and his portion goes towards the west through the midst of this river, and it extends till it reaches the water of the abysses, out of which this river goes forth and pours its waters into the sea Me'at, and this river flows into the great sea."	**Kuwait River**
Mc'at Sea "and his portion goes towards the west through the midst of this river, and it extends till it reaches the water of the abysses, out of which this river goes forth and pours its waters into the sea Me'at."	**Persian Gulf**
Karaso "And it extends till it reaches Karaso: this is in the bosom of the tongue which looks towards the south."	**Sinai Peninsula**
Egyptian Sea/Great Sea "And his portion extends along the great sea, and it extends in a straight line till it reaches the	**Red Sea**

west of the tongue which looks towards the south: for this sea is named the tongue of the Egyptian Sea."	
Afra "and it extends to the west to 'Afra, and it extends till it reaches the waters of the river Gihon, and to the south of the waters of Gihon, to the banks of this river."	Africa

In Jubilees Chapter 9:1-5, Shem's portion is divided between his sons:

1. And Shem also divided amongst his sons, and the first portion came forth for Ham and his sons, to the east of the river Tigris till it approach the east, the whole land of India, and on the Red Sea on its coast, and the waters of Dedan, and all the mountains of Mebri and Ela, and all the land of Susan and all that is on the side of Pharnak to the Red Sea and the river Tina.
2. And for Asshur came forth the second Portion, all the land of Asshur and Nineveh and Shinar and to the border of India, and it ascends and skirts the river.
3. **And for Arpachshad came forth the third portion, all the land of the region of the Chaldees to the east of the Euphrates, bordering on the Red Sea, and all the waters of the desert close to the tongue of the sea which looks towards Egypt, all the land of Lebanon and Sanir and 'Amana to the border of the Euphrates.**
4. And for Aram there came forth the fourth portion, all the land of Mesopotamia between the Tigris and the Euphrates to the north of the Chaldees to the border of the mountains of Asshur and the land of 'Arara.
5. And there came forth for Lud the fifth portion, the mountains of Asshur and all appertaining to them till it reaches the Great Sea and till it reaches the east of Asshur, his brother.

We can ascertain numerous translation errors, notably "the region of the Chaldees," "the Euphrates," "Mesopotamia" and the "Tigris." We know they are errors because they are obvious contradictions. For example, the Chaldees are in Mesopotamia. However, verse 3 tells us Arpachshad, the ancestor of Yahshar-el, had territory boarding the Red Sea, close to the tongue pointing to the Egyptian Sea. It is no mistake all of these words have Greek origins, and thus comport to a

European understanding of the Holy Land. We, however, are concerned with the Hebrew original meanings.

The Hebrew word that has been translated as "Chaldees" by Bible translators is *Kasdi* or *Kasdimah*.[110] This is the region Abraham originated from, in modern day Ethiopia. The Tigris, or the *Hiddekel*, as stated previously, encompasses the Kuwait River and connects to the Nile River, and the Perath is the Blue Nile. In this case, the word "Mesopotamia" was mistranslated, and is the region from the Perath to the Hiddekel.

Jubilees Chapter 8:22-30 continues with a description of the allotments of Ham and Japheth:

> 22. And for Ham came forth the second portion, beyond the Gihon towards the south to the right of the Garden, and it extends towards the south and it extends to all the mountains of fire, and it extends towards the west to the sea of 'Atel and it extends towards the west till it reaches the sea of Ma'uk -that (sea) into which everything which is not destroyed descends.
> 23. And it goes forth towards the north to the limits of Gadir, and it goes forth to the coast of the waters of the sea to the waters of the great sea till it draws near to the river Gihon, and goes along the river Gihon till it reaches the right of the Garden of Eden.
> 24. And this is the land which came forth for Ham as the portion which he was to occupy for ever for himself and his sons unto their generations for ever.
> 25. And for Japheth came forth the third portion beyond the river Tina to the north of the outflow of its waters, and it extends north-easterly to the whole region of Gog, and to all the country east thereof.
> 26. And it extends northerly to the north, and it extends to the mountains of Qelt towards the north, and towards the sea of Ma'uk, and it goes forth to the east of Gadir as far as the region of the waters of the sea.
> 27. And it extends until it approaches the west of Fara and it returns towards 'Aferag, and it extends easterly to the waters of the sea of Me'at.

---

[110] 3778. Kasdi or Kasdimah, Bible Hub, https://biblehub.com/hebrew/3778.htm (*last visited* Jan. 11, 2024).

> 28. And it extends to the region of the river Tina in a north-easterly direction until it approaches the boundary of its waters towards the mountain Rafa, and it turns round towards the north.
> 29. This is the land which came forth for Japheth and his sons as the portion of his inheritance which he should possess for himself and his sons, for their generations for ever; five great islands, and a great land in the north.
> 30. But it is cold, and the land of Ham is hot, and the land of Shem is neither hot nor cold, but it is of blended cold and heat.

Again, this description is more complex than taught in Christianity and Judaism, where it is commonly believed that Africa is only Ham's territory, and Japheth's is Europe and East Asia. In reality, Shem shares the African continent with Ham, specifically, the land on the Eastern side of the Nile.(See Map 10) For Japheth, his descendants reached not just Europe and East Asia but also parts of the area that we call today the 'Middle East,' including Palestine. (See Map 8)Thus, Palestine and the State of Israel are not even "Semetic."

In Chapter 9 of Jubilees, we are also given a vital clue about where the infamous Canaanites, the people whom Yahshar-el would expel from the Holy Land, originated from. The story of the Canaanites begins with Shem, Ham and Japheth further dividing their lots by their children. In Jubilees, Chapter 9:1, Ham divided his between his four sons, Cush, Mizraim, Put and Canaan:

> 1.And Ham divided amongst his sons, and the first portion came forth for Cush towards the east, and to the west of him for Mizraim, and to the west of him for Put, and to the west of him and to the west thereof] on the sea for Canaan.

Essentially, the Canaanites were to inhabit a region west of Put. Put is the area known today as Libya. The Sahel countries of Algeria, Morocco, and Mauritania are to the west of Libya and bordering the ocean. This is the lot originally designated for Canaan.(See Map 9) However, Canaan did not accept this lot as his own and would go against his family by occupying Shem's lot. This is recorded in Jubilees 10:28-34:

> 28 And Ham and his sons went into the land which he was to occupy, which he acquired as his portion in the land of the south.

> 29 And Canaan saw the land of Lebanon to the river of Egypt, that it was very good, and he went not into the land of his inheritance to the west (that is to) the sea, and he dwelt in the land of Lebanon, eastward and westward from the border of Jordan and from the border of the sea.
> 30 And Ham, his father, and Cush and Mizraim his brothers said unto him: 'Thou hast settled in a land which is not thine, and which did not fall to us by lot: do not do so; for if thou dost do so, thou and thy sons will fall in the land and (be) accursed through sedition; for by sedition ye have settled, and by sedition will thy children fall, and thou shalt be rooted out for ever.
> 31 Dwell not in the dwelling of Shem; for to Shem and to his sons did it come by their lot.
> 32 Cursed art thou, and cursed shalt thou be beyond all the sons of Noah, by the curse by which we bound ourselves by an oath in the presence of the holy judge, and in the presence of Noah our father.'
> 33 But he did not harken unto them, and dwelt in the land of Lebanon from Hamath to the entering of Egypt, he and his sons until this day.
> 34 And for this reason that land is named Canaan.

This verse adds much-needed context to the "Curse of Ham" propagated in the Jewish Talmud, which teaches Ham engaged in sexual intercourse with Noah, for which he was cursed with Black skin:

> The Sages taught: Three violated that directive and engaged in intercourse while in the ark, and all of them were punished for doing so. They are: The dog, and the raven, and Ham, son of Noah. The dog was punished in that it is bound; the raven was punished in that it spits, and Ham was afflicted in that his skin turned black.[111]

However, as we read in both Jubilees 10 and Genesis 9, the "Curse of Ham" was a curse of Canaan and a prophecy by Noah. As is stated in Genesis 9:22-25:

> Ham, the father of Canaan, saw the nakedness of his father, and told his two brothers outside. [23] But Shem and Japheth took a garment and laid it on both their shoulders and walked backward and covered the nakedness of their father; and their faces were turned away, so that they did not see their father's nakedness. [24] When Noah awoke from

---

[111] Sanhedrin 108b:15.

his wine, he knew what his youngest son had done to him. [25] So he said,

> "Cursed be Canaan;
> A servant of servants
> He shall be to his brothers."

The Genesis Apocryphon also makes it clear Noah did not curse Ham, but Canaan specifically was cursed:

> On that day Noah went forth from the ark (viii, 18) at the end of a full year of three hundred and sixty-four days, on the first day of the week, on the seven[teenth] of the second month vacate on and six vacate Noah from the ark at the appointed time of a full year vacate And Noah awoke from his wine and knew what his youngest son had done to him. And he said, cursed be Canaan; a slave of slaves shall he be to [his] bro[thers] (ix, 24—5). **But he did not curse Ham but only his son, for God had blessed the sons of Noah.** And let him dwell in the tents of Shem (ix, 27). [112]

Before proceeding further, it is worth discussing Japheth's son's allotments. In Jubilees 9:7-13 we read:

> 7. And Japheth also divided the land of his inheritance among his sons.
> 8. **And the first portion came forth for Gomer to the east from the north side to the river Tina; and in the north, there came forth for Magog all the inner portions of the north until it reached the sea of Me'at.**
> 9. And for Madai came forth as his portion that he should posses from the west of his two brothers to the islands, and to the coasts of the islands.
> 10. And for Javan came forth the fourth portion every island and the islands which are towards the border of Lud.
> 11. And for Tubal there came forth the fifth portion in the midst of the tongue which approaches towards the border of the portion of Lud to the second tongue, to the region beyond the second tongue unto the third tongue.
> 12. And for Meshech came forth the sixth portion, all the region beyond the third tongue till it approaches the east of Gadir.

---

[112] Dead Sea Scrolls, 4Q252, fr. I (Gen. vi, 3—XV, 17).

> 13. And for Tiras there came forth the seventh portion, four great islands in the midst of the sea, which reach to the portion of Ham [and the islands of Kamaturi came out by lot for the sons of Arpachshad as his inheritance].[113]

Gomer's portion encompasses Arab territory north of the river Tina. To the north of the sea Me'at is the portion we know as Magog. Regarding Gog, Jubilees 9:25 reads: "And for Japheth came forth the third portion beyond the river Tina to the north of the outflow of its waters, and it extends north-easterly to the whole region of Gog, and to all the country east thereof." This territory extends from Western Europe, Eastern Europe to Asia. (See Map 11)

Our knowledge of the Kuwait River as the river Tina and the Me'at Sea as the Persian Gulf can give us rough estimates for the territory allotted to Gomer and Magog. Thus, we can conclude the following geographical descriptions from Jubilees 9:

1. Gomer is on the North side of the Rivet Tina (Kuwait River)
2. Magog is to the North of Gog
3. Magog reaches the Persian Gulf
4. Magog encompasses inner areas towards the north
5. The land of Gog encompasses territory Northeasterly from the outflow of the River Tina

The Truth is in the Scriptures

At this point, the case for Yahshar-el (Israel) in Africa has been made. A literal reading of scripture undoubtedly does not support the widely held belief that Palestine is Yahshar-el. Instead, it points to the Holy Land's location as East Africa, encompassing parts of Eritrea, Sudan, Ethiopia, and Djibouti. This location is unabashedly confirmed in ancient Holy books regarded by many as Pseudepigrapha.

---

[113] Without further geographical descriptors the writer will not hypothesize the location of the Islands of Kamaturi.

Additionally, Yerusalem (Jerusalem) is not the highly contested city in the modern state of Israel and Palestine, but is the city of ancient Aksum. Those still grappling with whether this is true or not based on what they have been told their entire lives have to grapple with whether they genuinely believe the Bible or their tradition.

In the next section of this book, we will endeavor to complete an almost impossible task. That is explain how the greatest deception known to man could have happened. Because the historical record is sparse, much of what can be uncovered are numerous seemingly unrelated historical occurrences pieced together. However, by the grace Most High, who has provided his word as a guide to us today, scripture gives us critical clues on how this geographical switch occurred and how the coverup transpired.

Part II: The Conspiracy

Chapter 5: How Could This Happen?

"For it is written

"I WILL DESTROY THE WISDOM OF THE WISE,
AND THE UNDERSTANDING OF THOSE WHO HAVE UNDERSTANDING, I WILL CONFOUND."
Where is the wise person? Where is the scribe? Where is the debater of this age? Has God not made foolish the wisdom of the world?"

~1 Corinthians 1:19-20

After receiving the truth, it is up to each individual to determine whether they believe it. For those who can now see, the next question they might have is how is this possible? How could the location of Yahshar-el (Israel), a setting central to the Abrahamic faiths, which make up two-thirds of the world's religion, be not only hidden for two millennia but be mistaken for a completely different location? I do not have all the answers to these questions, but I believe The Most High has left some central clues we have ignored. First and foremost, we have to contend with the fact the Bible has been corrupted.

The Bible Corrupted

Much of the distorted views of Bible believers on issues such as the location of Yahshar-el (Israel) stem from a distorted relationship Christians have with the Bible. Most who profess to follow The Way (the Christian faith) have thought very little about how the Bible arrived to them in the composition and format they have received it. To control the thought processes of believers, artificial doctrines have been created to ensure that Christians follow a standardized theology. They are then shamed and discouraged from exploring the merits of that system. However, to receive what Yahuah (God) has spoken to us through His Word, it is a necessity that we deconstruct what man has done to control this process.

What is the Bible?

To discern what man has taught from what Yahuah has spoken, we should understand the Bible and how it was created. The Bible is a compilation of books or letters collected into one book. It is estimated Biblical manuscripts were written over a period spanning 1,500 years and were written in Hebrew, koine or common Greek, and Aramaic. These books stem from two different eras of the faith, widely known as the "Old Testament" and the "New Testament," terms coined by the 2nd century church Bishop Melito of Sardis.[114]

The term "testament" means "covenant," signaling an old and new covenant Yahshar-el has with Yahuah. The old covenant was solely through the Torah or the Law of Moses. The new covenant is through the Law of the Spirit, through the death and resurrection of Yahusha Hamashiach (Jesus Christ).[115]

The "Old Testament"

The era and the circumstances wherein the Old Testament was composed were very different from that in which the New Testament was written. Foundationally, the words were written in Hebrew, a distinct dialect spoken only by Yah's chosen people, the Hebrews, keeping outside corruption of the original written scripture at bay even amid wars and captivities. Hebrew has long since passed out of common usage. Today, the vast majority of Jewish people who claim to "speak Hebrew" are not speaking the Hebrew of the Bible, but rather a language known as Yiddish, the Germanic language of Ashkenazism. However, some Hebrewisms are incorporated into that language.[116]

---

[114] Joshua Mark, Melito of Sardis and his Apology for Christianity, World Encyclopedia, (Nov. 3, 2022) https://www.worldhistory.org/article/2097/melito-of-sardis-and-his-apology-for-christianity/.
[115] Romans 8.
[116] The Editors of Encyclopaedia Britannica, Yiddish language, Britannica, (*last updated* Aug 18, 2023), https://www.britannica.com/topic/Yiddish-language.

During the era of the Old Testament, the Books of the Law were guarded by priests from the tribe of Levi of Yahshar-el, whom Yahuah specifically chose to keep, read and share The Word before the assembly. As is written in Deuteronomy 31:9-13:

> So, Moses wrote this Law and gave it to the priests, the sons of Levi who carried the ark of the covenant of the Lord, and to all the elders of Israel. Then Moses commanded them: "At the end of every seven years, in the year for canceling debts, during the Festival of Tabernacles, when all Israel comes to appear before the Lord your God at the place he will choose, you shall read this law before them in their hearing. Assemble the people—men, women, children, and the foreigners residing in your towns—so they can listen and learn to fear the Lord your God and follow carefully all the words of this law. Their children, who do not know this law, must hear it and learn to fear the Lord your God as long as you live in the land you are crossing the Jordan to possess."

While the people were instructed to write down the words of the law for their own remembrance and for teaching those around them, it was ultimately the Levites, the Priest of Yahuah, who were tasked with being keepers of the Law. However, this priesthood has long passed away. Following the Assur and Babylonian captivities of the kingdoms of Yahshar-el and Yahudah (Judah), newly self-appointed sects occupied the position that would have been ascribed to the holy priesthood. This cooptation of the priesthood is a trend that has continued until today.

The "New Testament" & Opportunity

The Old Testament and New Testament are not the same. The New Testament differs very much as far as content and style of writing. The Old Testament details the journey and travails of Abraham, Isaac, Jacob and their descendants through historical accounts, prophetic writings, and poetry. The New Testament, however, starts with four gospels, which have the names attached: Matthew, Mark, Luke and John. These names have been attributed to four apostles said to have been eyewitnesses or second-hand eyewitnesses of the ministry of Yahusha. The truth is this authorship is all tradition. Every one of the gospels was written anonymously.[117] What we know for sure about the authors is only what they wrote in their accounts.

The gospels are followed by the Books of Acts, which gives details of the activities of Yahusha's apostles following His resurrection. Then we read several letters written by the apostles giving spiritual instruction and insight to the assembly of Yahusha, and then a robust closure with the apocalyptic book of Revelations.

A key reason the New Testament differs from the Old Testament goes back to the original language Yahuah's people spoke, Hebrew. We know what language the Hebrews spoke; however, we genuinely do not know what language the original manuscripts of the New Testament were written in.[118] Knowledge of this issue has been controlled by religious institutions, who we are trusting to self-report on the New Testament's origins even if it conflicts with their power and influence. Not only this, but we are trusting the Catholic Church and its translators to have not changed the Greek words of the New Testament to reflect their own aspirations.

This is highly relevant because if the Greek translations of the New Testament contradicts the Hebrew written words of the Old Testament in geography, we would have to ascertain why. The most plausible reason would be that the Hebrew scriptures were written well before entities that controlled the discourse of the Bible could alter them in a language foreign to most. However, Greek translations of the Bible were ongoing at least until the 4th century Latin Vulgate, and thus more susceptible to hierarchical influence, particularly from Rome.

---

[117] Michael Horner, Are the Gospels Anonymous, The Life, https://thelife.com/are-the-gospels-anonymous (*last visited* Jan 12, 2024).

[118] Catholic Answers Staff, Was Matthew's Gospel First Written in Aramaic or Hebrew?, Catholic Answers, https://www.catholic.com/qa/was-matthews-gospel-first-written-in-aramaic-or-hebrew (*last visited* Jan. 12, 2024).

Canonization & Standardization

In addition to concerns about liberties taken in translating the Bible, there is also need to concern ourselves with the process by which certain books were chosen by church authorities to be in the Bible and others left out. For the Old Testament, the Levite Priesthood was supplanted by the Pharisees by the time of Yahusha. This sect was primarily opposed to the teachings of Yahusha and ultimately conspired to have him crucified for His message.

Yahuah, out of the new covenant, set Yahusha as the High Priest of Yahshar-el, and his followers as his royal priesthood.[119] This means that at all times, Yahusha was to be the ultimate keeper and Teacher of the Law, and not man. Romans 8:3 states, "For the law of the Spirit of life in Christ Jesus has set you free from the law of sin and of death." One would, therefore, need to not only know him but be guided by Him and the Ruach HaKodesh (Holy Spirit) in all teachings about His Word, not through mere debate or academic posturing, but through communion with the Son of Man and the Ruach HaKodesh.

Compare this spiritual relationship to the Son with what transpired in the creation of the Bible canon during the Catholic Church's ecumenical councils, as detailed by Got Questions:

> For the New Testament, the process of recognition and collection began in the first centuries of the Christian church. Very early on, some of the New Testament books were being recognized. Paul considered Luke's writings to be as authoritative as the Old Testament (1 Timothy 5:18; see also Deuteronomy 25:4 and Luke 10:7). Peter recognized Paul's writings as scripture (2 Peter 3:15-16). Some of the books of the New Testament were being circulated among the churches (Colossians 4:16; 1 Thessalonians 5:27). Clement of Rome mentioned at least eight New Testament books (A.D. 95). Polycarp, a disciple of John the apostle, acknowledged 15 books (A.D. 108). Ignatius of Antioch acknowledged about seven books (A.D.

---

[119] Hebrews 7.

115). Later, Irenaeus mentioned 21 books (A.D. 185). Hippolytus recognized 22 books (A.D. 170-235). The New Testament books receiving the most controversy were Hebrews, James, 2 Peter, 2 John, and 3 John.

The first "canon" was the <u>Muratorian Canon</u>, which was compiled in AD 170. The Muratorian Canon included all of the New Testament books except Hebrews, James, 1 and 2 Peter, and 3 John. In AD 363, the Council of Laodicea stated that only the Old Testament (along with one book of the Apocrypha) and 26 books of the New Testament (everything but Revelation) were canonical and to be read in the churches. The <u>Council of Hippo</u> (AD 393) and the Council of Carthage (AD 397) also affirmed the same 27 books as authoritative.

The councils followed something similar to the following principles to determine whether a New Testament book was truly inspired by the Holy Spirit: 1) Was the author an apostle or have a close connection with an apostle? 2) Is the book being accepted by the body of Christ at large? 3) Did the book contain consistency of doctrine and orthodox teaching? 4) Did the book bear evidence of high moral and spiritual values that would reflect a work of the Holy Spirit? Again, it is crucial to remember that the church did not determine the canon. No early church council decided on the canon. **It was God, and God alone, who determined which books belonged in the Bible. It was simply a matter of God's imparting to His followers what He had already decided. The human process of collecting the books of the Bible was flawed, but God, in His sovereignty, and despite our ignorance and stubbornness, brought the early church to the recognition of the books He had inspired.**[120]

Unfortunately, statements like the bold section are the norm in Christianity. They are made without spiritual qualification, and spiritual qualification is something every believer of Yahusha must require from those who claim to have Holy authority to make decisions about our understanding of His Word. The author recognizes all of the books in the New Testament as being scriptural. However, the logic and thinking conveyed throughout mainstream Christianity that assumes these men at various councils were being

---

[120] How and when was the canon of the Bible put together?, Got Questions, https://www.gotquestions.org/canon-Bible.html (*last visited* Jan. 12, 2024).

led by the Ruach, without any qualification proving so, is the dangerous mentality that has deceived the masses.

It is convenient to assume the ecumenical councils were spirit-filled retreats similar to the Pentecost instead of political dogmatic events. But it is not truthful, especially as the Roman Emperor called and oversaw the early councils.[121] However, this willful ignorance is encoded into church doctrine that has taught Christians to unthinkingly defer to church authority as being authorized by Yahuah. This tradition goes to the doctrine of church infallibility. As noted by Catholic Saint Thomas Aquinas:

> The doctrine of the *infallibility of ecumenical councils* states that solemn definitions of ecumenical councils, which concern faith or morals, and to which the whole church must adhere, are infallible. Such decrees are often labeled as 'Canons' and they often have an attached anathema, a penalty of excommunication, against those who refuse to believe the teaching. The doctrine does not claim that every aspect of every ecumenical council is dogmatic, but that every aspect of an ecumenical council is free of errors or impeccable.[122]

Again, remembering who our high priest is and who we are called to be, would Yahuah sanction this blind surrender? Something else often not spoken about here is the Bible canon accepted by the Western church is not universal. The Ethiopian Orthodox Church canon accepts numerous books as inspired by Yahuah that the Western church deems Apocrypha and Pseudepigrapha. How do we test, as Paul tells us to do[123] whether the Ethiopian church or the Western church has their canon correct?

---

[121] Ecumenical Council, Henry VIII, the Reign, https://www.henryviiithereign.co.uk/ecumenical-council.html (*last visited* Jan 12. 2024).
[122] Question 11. Heresy, New Advent, http://newadvent.org/summa/3011.htm#article2, (*last visited* Jan. 12, 2024).
[123] 1 Thessalonians 5:21.

Inerrancy Doctrine

According to 2 Timothy 3:16, "All Scripture is inspired by God and beneficial for teaching, for rebuke, for correction, for training in righteousness." The word "inspired" in the Greek is *theópneustos* which means "God-breathed."[124] It should go without saying that whatever words breathed by The Most High Yahuah are 100% without error. However, that which is written or translated by mankind is indeed subject to human error.

Because much of Christianity relies on culture and traditions, the church has walked itself into its own controversy. One of the traditions is the doctrine that teaches the Bible is the inherent word of Yahuah. Bible theologian E. J. Young gave a classical definition of this doctrine of Bible inerrancy:

> By this word (inerrancy), we mean that the Scriptures possess the quality of freedom from error. They are exempt from the liability to mistake, incapable of error. In all their teachings, they are in perfect accord with the truth.[125]

By this definition, Bible inerrancy means not a single word in the Bible is incorrect. Such a doctrine invites obvious ridicule towards Bible believers. There are hundreds of translations of just the English Bible. Which one is inerrant?

However, many Bible scholars have recognized this error in the doctrine of inerrancy and have modified the doctrine away from Young's ridged definition. According to Bible theologian J. Hampton Keathley, Bible inerrancy:

> does not demand rigidity of style and verbatim quotations from the Old Testament. 'The inerrancy of the Bible means simply that the Bible tells the truth. Truth can and does include approximations, free

---

[124] 2315. Theopneustos, Bible Hub, https://biblehub.com/greek/2315.htm (*last visited* Jan. 12, 2024).
[125] J. Hampton Keathley, The Bible: The Inerrant Word of God, (June 3, 2004) https://bible.org/seriespage/6-bible-inerrant-word-god.

quotations, language of appearances, and different accounts of the same event as long as those do not contradict.[126]

All credible Bible scholars acknowledge there are at least some errors in the Bible simply due to mistranslation. However, most in mainstream Christianity will claim these are all inconsequential errors, simple mistakes from copyists that do not change the overall meaning of the scriptures. This unqualified assumption is incorrect. Not only have Bible translators made mistakes in translating names and locations, but given the breadth of mistakes, we can only conclude that these errors were intentional.

Liberties have been taken in translating the scriptures in today's modern bible translation. Yet the institutions of the church and Christianity have made many believers feel it is morally wrong to question the originality of any words in the Bible. Thus, the doctrine of inerrancy is not helpful to the Bible believer, particularly if it reassures them that there is no need to look further into the meaning of scripture outside of what is written on the page. Having a greater willingness to critique what man has done for the 2000 years Holy scripture has been in his custody is reasonable and necessary if one is serious about uncovering the truth.

Understanding Translation vs. Transliteration

Before proceeding further, a quick note should be made about the difference between translation and transliteration. We will begin with transliteration. According to Truth Ministries Apostolic Faith Church:

> Transliteration is when a translator takes a word in one language (i.e., Greek word "apostlos"), adjusts it a little to make it look and sound more like another language (English word Apostle), and then places it within the rest of the text in that other language. So, in biblical translation, a translator would take, for example, a Greek word and

---

[126]*Id.*

adjust it to fit in our character set, usually changing the pronunciation a bit to make it sound more like English.[127]

Transliteration comes into play in the Bible when the translator seeks to bring Hebrew names, phrases or words into English pronunciation, perhaps most notably transliterating Yahushua (Jesus) into Iesous, as "I" carried the same sound as the "y" sound. The Hebrew sound "sh" was replaced with "s" to accommodate Greek pronunciation. [128]

While Transliteration at least attempts to reflect the original language as far as sound, translation instead looks for terms of "equivalence" in the language being used. As the Truth Ministries Apostolic Faith Church explains:

> A translation is when a translator takes the text of one language (i.e., Greek, Hebrew, and Aramaic), which is unreadable to the majority of Christians, and converts it to the equivalent text in English (*or the common language for another culture*).
>
> However, the problem with translation is that there is not always an equivalent text from one language to another. We don't just have different words; we have different sentence structures, different figures of speech, and some words which have no match in a different language or which carry different connotations and nuances.
>
> Sometimes translators will use a similar term and then expand the text to include a definition within it. But in many cases, when translators come across a word with no exact English equivalent, they will just skip translating that word entirely.[129]

While Biblical translators made some attempts to use transliteration of Biblical locations, much of what we know of as Biblical geography is

---

[127] The Oneness of God in Christ, Translation/Transliteration https://www.theonenessofgod.org/understanding-translation-transliteration/ (*last visited* Sept. 20, 2021).

[128] Pronunciation of the Messiah's Name (Yahushua), https://eliyah.com/pronunciation-messiahs-name/ (*last visited* Sept. 20, 2023).

[129] The Oneness of God in Christ, Translation/Transliteration https://www.theonenessofgod.org/understanding-translation-transliteration/ (*last visited* Sept. 20, 2021).

based on translation. Thus, rather than relying on Hebrew language and culture to identify specific locations, translators, specifically early translators, often used their own or common knowledge to identify locations. This fact, of course, would complicate matters if the translators are from a location where the geography is foreign to them. As detailed by Avner Ramu:

> While a literal translation of a Biblical verse from Hebrew to English could change its meaning because of inherent differences between the linguistic structure of these languages, the use of idiomatic translation may be influenced by the beliefs of the translator and his understanding of the spirit of the text. In addition, in both methods the accuracy of the translation depend on the understanding of the Hebrew Bible.[130]

The reader needs to understand how much power a translator has in determining the course of history. A failure or unwillingness to do proper research or translate work in truthfulness and sincerity can change the entire face of a faith and give cover to imposters from various factions.

Rule of Thumb: Trust the Geography First

While this work does not have all the answers regarding what has been mistranslated and what is accurately translated, a practical rule of thumb for Biblical geography is to lean on literal direction and descriptions over the usage of names, which, again, are the work of identification by translators. For example, this work subscribes to the commonly held understanding that the location of the kingdom identified by the Hebrews as *Mīṣrayīm* in the Bible is what we know of as Egypt today. But that is only because the description as far as direction points to Mīṣrayīm as being Egypt. However, in the case of the Euphrates River, this location as we know it today does not match the Bible's geographical descriptions. This can be difficult to parse. However, trusting and leaning on geography rather than the

---

[130] Avner Ramu, Canaan? Opps Wrong Country, Isgav Publishing LLC, (2003), 11.

translator's understanding of names is trusting the word for what it says rather than what man says.

Chapter 6: The Conspirators

"I praise You, Father, Lord of heaven and earth, that You have hidden these things from the wise and intelligent and have revealed them to infants. Yes, Father, for doing so was well-pleasing in Your sight."

~ Luke 10:21

We know a conspiracy happened. We know this because none of the three major Abrahamic religions acknowledge a foundational deception, that Yahshar-el (Israel) in the Bible is not the people or the location in Palestine. That level of deception only happens with the meeting of minds, intentional erasure of history and covering of tracks. In this chapter we will endeavor on the difficult task of detailing such a conspiracy.

The Players

While the nitty details are almost impossible to uncover at this juncture, we can start with some highly probable assumptions, starting with what is popularly considered the first Abrahamic religion, Judaism. Both Christianity and Islam have relied on Jewish expertise on issues of understanding the Hebrew people, as they claimed to be Yahuah's (God's) chosen people. Given that Judaism is the foundational religion of the Abrahamic faiths, knowledge of the true Yahshar-el (Isreal) must have been kept by the highest forces in the Sanhedrin, the governing council of Judaism. It is also not a coincidence that the Jewish sect of the Pharisees, with an adversarial positioning to Yahusha (Jesus), is the foundation of Rabbinical Judaism.[131]

One Pharisee, in particular, is a man widely beloved in many Jewish and Christian academic circles, so much so that many hold his words and his version of history as if they were *God breathed*

---

[131] Rebecca Denova, Pharisees, World History Encyclopedia (Feb. 2, 2022) https://www.worldhistory.org/Pharisees/.

scripture. That man is Flavius Josephus, a Jewish priest and historian who is mainly responsible for much of the beliefs held by theologians about Yahshar-el and the history of the Yahudi (Judeans).

Flavius Josephus

Most of what we know about Josephus is what he reported. Josephus was born around 37-38 CE and died in Rome in 100 CE. He was born into an aristocratic priestly family in "Jerusalem." By his own account, he was advanced as a youth and, by age 14, was consulted by high priests in matters of Jewish law. After a three-year sojourn in the wilderness with the hermit Bannus, a member of one of the popular Jewish sects in "Judaea," he returned to "Jerusalem" and joined the Pharisees.[132]

Josephus grew an affinity for Rome and Roman culture when, in 64 CE, he was sent as an emissary to Rome to secure the release of several Jewish priests. While there, he gained the favor of Poppaea Sabina, the wife of Emperor Nero, who helped make his mission a success. In 66 AD, Josephus was appointed by his fellow Jews to be a military commander during a Jewish revolt.[133]

Josephus records a story from his own life where his 40 forces were trapped in a cave in Jotapata in Galilee by Roman emperor Vespasian. Seeing little hope in surviving, his troops decided to commit mass suicide rather than surrender to the Romans. Josephus, who was against the suicide, convinced his troops to cast lots and have one man execute the other. Josephus contrived to draw the last lot so that it came down to him and a fellow soldier. Then, rather than carry through with the suicide, the two of them surrendered

---

[132] Gary William Poole, Flavius Josephus, Britannica, https://www.britannica.com/biography/Flavius-Josephus (*last updated* Jan. 1, 2024).
[133] *Id.*

themselves to the Romans.[134] This is the man so many Bible historians rely on.

From here, Josephus was led away in chains to Emperor Vespasian, where he assumed the position of "prophet" to him. Josephus then fully assumed a Roman identity, adopting Vespasian's family name of Flavius.[135] Although being regarded by many as a traitor, it is essential to note that for the rest of his life, Josephus acted as an apologist for Jewish people, telling the history of his people to a Roman audience that, at the time, was largely ignorant of their history.

Generally, Josephus has been trusted as a reliable source, and in many instances, primary source of Hebrew history by Christian, Jewish and secular scholars alike, despite numerous cases of his retelling of history being historically untrue. Perhaps the best example of this is the mass suicide at Masada. In *War of the Jews*, Josephus details a mass suicide at Masada told by Josephus alone, of 960 men, women and children who refused to surrender to Rome.[136] However, this version of events has been widely challenged by scholars today:

> Josephus gives a famous account of the last stand of the Jews atop Masada. Instead of surrendering, he says the Jews selected several men to slay the majority and then turn their swords upon themselves. Yet archaeologists have not found the bodies to verify his story.
>
> Also, like other historians of his day, Josephus sometimes invented heroic speeches and put them into the mouths of his subjects, such as the patriotic oratory of Eleazer, the leader of the Jews atop Masada. Since the men who heard Eleazer were slain in the siege, and since

---

[134] Daniel K. Judd, Suicide at Masada and in the World of the New Testament, BYE Studies, https://byustudies.byu.edu/article/suicide-at-masada-and-in-the-world-of-the-new-testament/ (*last visited* Jan. 13, 2024).
[135] *Supra* at note 132.
[136] Amanda Borschel-Dan, Maybe there was no mass suicide at Masada? Top archaeologist questions a legend, the Times of Israel, (Oct. 9, 2019) https://www.timesofisrael.com/maybe-there-was-no-mass-suicide-at-masada-top-archaeologist-questions-a-legend/.

Josephus wrote the account from Rome, he cannot possibly have had access to the full speech.[137]

Despite his inaccuracies, Josephus still enjoys unprecedented credence from theological circles. As Professor of Religion and Archeology of Duke University Eric Meyers stated:

> Josephus is our primary source for reconstructing history in the late second temple period and in the time of Jesus and the first century. Josephus is our Bible, he is our map. He is the guy we all turn to. And his complexity and his change of opinions on key ideas and key events of this time make him very difficult to take as a reliable source.[138]

Josephus, who lamented in *Antiquities* the difficulty of merely translating ancient Hebrew scriptures into Greek (despite the fact this was done later), essentially uses *Antiquities* to retell the entire Old Testament, but not with a measured and objective approach. As stated on the website Answers in Genesis:

> *Antiquities*, written later, attempts to show the superiority and antiquity of the Jewish culture. To achieve that end, it tends to exaggerate the good qualities and ignore the unflattering failures, such as Aaron's golden calf, in an effort to promote the Jewish cause.
>
> Historians now generally agree with Harold Attridge that Josephus's Antiquities were a "propagandistic history." His "paraphrasing [of] the narratives" of the Old Testament was a "creative adaptation" aimed at presenting Jewish history as "relevant, comprehensible and attractive in a new environment."[139]

Not only was Josephus telling history as pro-Jewish, but also one that was pro-Palestine for the location of Yahshar-el. On Yahshar-el's geography, Josephus states:

---

[137] Brenton H. Cook, Is Josephus Reliable?, Answers in Genesis, (Jan. 1, 2013) https://answersingenesis.org/bible-history/is-josephus-reliable/.
[138] Josephus, Our Primary Source, Frontline, https://www.pbs.org/wgbh/pages/frontline/shows/religion/portrait/josephus.html (*last visited*, Jan. 13, 2024)
[139] *Supra* note 137.

To Joshua took both Eleazar and the senate, and with them the heads of the tribes, and distributed the land to the nine tribes, and to the half-tribe of Manasseh, appointing the dimensions to be according to the largeness of each tribe. So when he had cast lots, Judah had assigned him by lot the upper part of Judea, reaching as far as Jerusalem, and its breadth extended to the Lake of Sodom. Now in the lot of this tribe there were the cities of Askelon and Gaza. **The lot of Simeon, which was the second, included that part of Idumea which bordered upon Egypt and Arabia.** As to the Benjamites, their lot fell so, that its length reached from the river Jordan to the sea, but in breadth it was bounded by Jerusalem and Bethel; and this lot was the narrowest of all, by reason of the goodness of the land, for it included Jericho and the city of Jerusalem. The tribe of Ephraim had by lot the land that extended in length from the river Jordan to Gezer; but in breadth as far as from Bethel, till it ended at the Great Plain. The half-tribe of Manasseh had the land from Jordan to the city of Dora, but its breadth was at Bethsham, which is now called Scythopolis. And after these was Issachar, which had its limits in length, Mount Carmel and the river, but its limit in breadth was Mount Tabor. The tribe of Zebulon's lot included the land which lay as far as the Lake of Genesareth, and that which belonged to Carmel and the sea. The tribe of Aser had that part which was called the Valley, for such it was, and all that part which lay over against Sidon. The city Arce belonged to their share, which is also named Actipus. The Naphtalites received the eastern parts, as far as the city of Damascus and the Upper Galilee, unto Mount Libanus, and the Fountains of Jordan, which rise out of that mountain; that is, out of that part of it whose limits belong to the neighboring city of Arce. The Danites' lot included all that part of the valley which respects the sun- setting, and were bounded by Azotus and Dora; as also they had all Jamnia and Gath, from Ekron to that mountain where the tribe of Judah begins. [140]

This account promotes the Palestine lie, specifically where Josephus describes the lot of Simeon, which "included that part of Idumea which bordered upon Egypt and Arabia." Palestine is the only region in the world bordering Egypt and Arabia. We also see the renaming of cities attributed to scriptural locations, most explicitly where he writes of the Hebrew city Beth Shan, "the half-tribe of Manasseh had

---

[140] Flavius Josephus, Antiquities of the Jews, Book 5, (93-94 CE).

the land from Jordan to the city of Dora; but its breadth was at Bethsham, which is now called Scythopolis." Scythopolis is a city in Roman Palestine.[141]

However, Josephus's description of geography was not thoroughly thought out, as his description of the four rivers of Eden still resembles one where Eden would be based in East Africa. According to Josephus, on the geography of the Garden of Eden:

> Now the garden was watered by one river, which ran round about the whole earth and was parted into four parts. And Phison, which denotes a multitude, running into India, makes its exit into the sea, and is by the Greeks called Ganges. **Euphrates also, as well as Tigris, goes down into the Red Sea.** Now the name Euphrates, or Phrath, denotes either a dispersion, or a flower: by Tiris, or Diglath, is signified what is swift, with narrowness; **and Geon runs through Egypt, and denotes what arises from the east, which the Greeks call Nile.**[142]

Here, Josephus mysteriously connects the Euphrates and the Tigris to the Red Sea. As stated previously, the Hiddekel, as the "Tigris," would connect to the other three rivers of Eden through the Red Sea. We also see Josephus agrees with the Septuagint that the Gihon was, in fact, the Nile River. However, as explained previously, if the Gihon is the Nile, then Yahshar-el, which had an offshoot of the Gihon running through Yerusalem (Jerusalem), could not be in Palestine.

It seems unlikely that Josephus alone contrived to change the location of Yahshar-el from East Africa to Palestine. We can assume that as the Jewish community in Palestine did not come out against his telling of a Palestinian Yahshar-el, that most had already adopted this narrative of history at the time his accounts were published. He was, however, the most prominent voice to make this claim, making it

---

[141] Scythopolis (Bet She'an), Rome in the Footsteps of an XVIIIth Century Traveller, https://www.romeartlover.it/Schytopolis.html (*last visited* Jan. 13, 2024).
[142] *Supra* note 140, at Book 1.

highly probable that Josephus was commissioned by his Pharisee affiliates to write books that would overshadow and even replace the Biblical narrative, as did happen.

This is not to say the entire history told by Josephus was a fabrication. A significant presence of converts and possibly some Hebrews resided in Palestine. Thus, if true, this history told by Josephus, including of the Hasmoneans, the Maccabees and the different Jewish sects, is not the history of Yahshar-el but, at best, the history of the Palestinian-based Jewish religion.

The Romans

Josephus may have been the first progenitor of status in Rome to propagate a Palestinian Holy Land, but what evidence is there of compliance within Christianity? Given the fact Judaism and Christianity have, since the beginning of Christianity, had an antagonistic relationship with one another, wouldn't the agreeance of Palestine as the Holy Land in itself be evidence of the truth of the matter?

The first thing that needs to be questioned is whether the Romans would benefit from recognizing the Holy Land in Palestine versus East Africa. The answer is yes. At the time Christianity became the religion of Rome, Palestine was firmly under Roman control. Aksum, however, the East African kingdom that existed in the land of Yahshar-el at that time, was fully flourishing on its own, and while a Roman presence existed in the region, Aksum was in no way a province of Rome. For the Romans to knowingly yield to another territory as being the Holy Land would have been politically asinine. The convenient lie that the Holy Land was Roman Palestine would have undoubtedly been preferred.

The second thing that should be understood is the Roman world's general ignorance of Biblical Yahshar-el and authentic Hebrew practices, history and culture. In the early apostolic age (before the Catholic takeover of the faith), believers of the Way (the Christian faith) were almost immediately persecuted by Rome, as detailed by the Church of God:

> In the early days of the Apostolic Age, Christianity was persecuted by the Jews who did not recognize Jesus as the Christ. Later, as Christianity spread not only to Jerusalem but also to Asia Minor and Rome, it was oppressed by the Roman Empire. At that time, the Roman Empire implemented a moderate tolerance in the empire. However, Christianity was an exception. It was because they considered that Christians would damage the stability of the empire.
>
> Christians worshiped only their own God, and did not participate in social ritual or religious ceremonies of those days. They did not even mingle with the pagans in the temple or in the theater. This was considered to harm the stability and unity of the empire. In particular, the Christians' refusal to worship the Roman gods was regarded as a threat to the peace and prosperity that gods brought to the empire.
>
> In addition, the Christians refused to worship the emperor because they could not worship anyone other than God. For the Romans, emperor worship was the most powerful means to unify the empire and the standard of loyalty to the empire. The Roman government regarded the attitude of Christians as disloyal and rebellious against the emperor and the empire, and so Christianity was persecuted as an illegal religion.[143]

This undoubtedly led to quashing the original voices that arose from Yahshar-el. Compare this to the treatment of Judaism in the Roman Empire, which was recognized as the religion of its adherents. While the original followers of the Way were facing immense persecution, Josephus had liberty to give what would become the accepted narrative of Yahshar-el and the Hebrew people to a gentile audience who were oblivious to the matters of worship of Yahuah (God). This cooptation of the Way would play a pivotal role in a pseudo version of the Way emerging under Roman Catholicism.

Even with the antagonistic relationship that did exist between the Roman Catholic Church and Judaism, there was immense influence of

---

[143] Roman Persecution of Christians: The Cause, Reason, and Details of 10 Great Persecutions, Christ Ahnsahnghong, https://ahnsahnghong.com/en/church-of-god/persecution-in-the-roman-empire/ (*last visited* Nov. 12, 2023).

Judaism and its understanding of the Bible which was taught to Roman Christians. By the time of the Catholic Church, Palestine as the Holy Land had been cemented in the minds of the Catholic faith. Similarly, a Pro-Palestine Holy Land worldview was held firmly by the Catholic Church fathers who made Palestine the center of their study about the Hebrew faith and traditions, the most famous of whom was Catholic Saint Jerome.

"Saint" Jerome

The Catholic Saint Jerome, also known as Eusebius Sophronius Hieronymus, was born in 347 CE in what is today's terms, probably near Ljubljana, Slovenia, but died in 420 CE in Bethlehem, Palestine, where he established a monastery. Jerome became a priest and secretary to Pope Damascus I, who commissioned him to translate a Latin version of the Bible. In undergoing this task, Jerome deemed the Septuagint non-satisfactory and instead decided to use "the Hebrew Bible." [144]

Because of his choice to use this version, his translation faced scrutiny.[145] The so-called "Hebrew Bible" or the Tanakh Jerome used was not as old or well regarded as the Septuagint. This "Hebrew Bible" resembles what we know today as the Masoretic text, a translation of Hebrew scriptures written by a Jewish group of scribes based primarily in Palestine.[146] The Jewish scribes also separated scriptures they designated Apocrypha or Pseudepigrapha from books they considered canonical.[147] While there was much backlash against the usage of the "Hebrew Bible" as opposed to the Septuagint, in 1546, the Council of Trent still decreed the Vulgate was the exclusive

---

[144] Melissa Snell, A Concise Biography of Saint Jerome, ThoughtCo. https://www.thoughtco.com/saint-jerome-profile-1789037 (*last updated* Feb. 8, 2019).
[145] Vulgate, Britannica, https://www.britannica.com/topic/The-History-of-Susanna (*last visited* Oct. 13, 2023).
[146] Edmund F. Sutcliffe, Notes on St. Jerome's Hebrew Text, The Catholic Biblical Quarterly, Catholic Biblical Association, 139-143.
[147] What is the Masoretic Text?, Got Questions, https://www.gotquestions.org/Masoretic-Text.html (*last visited* Nov. 12, 2023).

Latin authority of the Bible. In 1592, a Clementine version of the Vulgate was issued by Pope Clement VIII and became the authoritative text of the Roman Catholic Church.[148]

As stated, Jerome had an orientation towards the Bible and the Hebrew people that was centered around Palestine. In 374, Jerome decided to go to Jerusalem in Palestine, where he stayed for three years. While there, Jerome met an "apostate Jew" who is said to have taught him Hebrew. Jerome continued his studies in Bethlehem, Palestine, where several Jewish teachers taught him.[149]

In addition to his pro-Palestine orientation, Jerome was influenced by early church fathers who similarly had a pro-Palestine orientation. In Thomas Scheck's translation of *Jerome's Commentary on Matthew, The Fathers of the Church*, Scheck states:

> Jerome dictated his Commentary on Matthew over the course of two weeks. The work shows signs of hasty composition, such as, at times, extreme brevity and numerous inaccurate citations from the Bible and Josephus. Jerome's commentary is not very extensive. ... In his explanation of Matthew's text, Jerome occasionally relies on Josephus, Origen, or Eusebius for information about geographical or historical details, but he also shows evidence of a personal knowledge of the biblical sources, of the topography of Palestine, and of current traditions, both Jewish and Christian. In an influential article, G. Bardy argued that Jerome took from Origen all of what he claimed to know firsthand from the Jews.[150]

All three influences, Josephus, Origen and Eusebius, espoused a stout Palestine-Holy Land orient. We have already detailed Josephus's reconstructing the Bible into a Palestinian narrative. Origen, a Christian Biblical critic, also spent immense time in Roman Palestine and taught in Caesarea Maritima. As stated by the Jewish Virtual

---

[148] *Supra* note 145.
[149] Jerome, Jewish Virtual Library, https://www.jewishvirtuallibrary.org/jerome-x00b0 (*last visited* Oct. 13, 2023).
[150] Thomas Scheck', The Fathers of the Church: St Jerome Commentary on Mathew, The Catholic University of America Press, (2008), 16-17.

Library on Origen, "Having encountered personally the Jewish teachers of his time, Jewish customs, and Jewish relations with non-Jews, he interspersed his works with knowledge about Judaism, including non-rabbinic Judaism."[151] Origen also relied on Jewish scholars to understand the text of the Bible, as written by Rabbi N. R. M. de Lang during the World Congress of Jewish Studies' proceedings.

> Origen's contacts with Jews took two forms: discussions of the text and interpretation of the Bible and debates about the rival claims of Judaism and Christianity. His activities as a controversialist did not apparently impair his good relations with Jewish scholars, and it has even been suggested that he had Jewish copyists working in his scriptorium[152]

Similarly, Eusebius of Caesarea became prominent in Palestine in the 4th century. While his relationship with the Jewish people was less favorable, he espoused a pro-Palestine Holy Land orientation and relied heavily on Josephus in his landmark work, *Ecclesiastical History*.[153] Thus, Jerome's academic foundation was set as Palestinian-Yahshar-el.

    While it would be nearly impossible, absent gaining access to the highly secretive Vatican archives, to ascertain if Jerome's reliance on the "Hebrew Bible" and Jewish teachers was a collaboration to cover up the true Yahshar-el, we should take note of the willingness of the Roman Catholic Church to break tradition in deferring to Judaism in determining scripture, despite their less than favorable views of the Jewish religion. This is the same Catholic Church who was so antagonistic to Judaism that they released the following cannon from the 4th Century Council of Laodicea:

---

[151] Origen, Jewish Virtual Library, https://www.jewishvirtuallibrary.org/origen-x00b0 (*last visited* Nov. 11, 2023).

[152] De Lange, N. R. M., ORIGEN AS A SOURCE FOR JEWISH HIStORY." Proceedings of the World Congress of Jewish, (1973), 1–7.

[153] Eusebius of Caesarea, Britannica, https://www.britannica.com/biography/Eusebius-of-Caesarea, (*last updated* Sep. 23, 2022).

Christians must not judaize by resting on the Sabbath, but must work on that day, rather honouring the Lord's Day; and, if they can, resting then as Christians. But if any shall be found to be judaizers, let them be anathema from Christ.[154]

The Conspiracy to Hide Jubilees

Yahuah never gave us a list of scripture. While we are given the description of scripture by the Apostle Paul as "inspired by God" or *God breathed*,[155] In the hands of institutional Christianity, this definition has been used haphazardly to negate the veracity of some books with little thought. When books such as Jubilees, with content highly inflammatory to the doctrines of both Judaism and Catholicism alike, are easily brushed aside without much critical thought, it would be rash to not consider whether decisions were made in an effort to conceal inconvenient truths.

Again, as the Apostle Paul has written, we should test everything. While not all books which claim to be scripture are scripture, the author would suggest some means by which one can test these books:

- ⇒ How old is the book based on available evidence?
- ⇒ Does the book have a history of being revered by ancient Hebrews?
- ⇒ Does the book have a history of being revered as scripture by the ancient ekklesia (assembly or church)?
- ⇒ Does the book corroborate books already long held to be scripture?
- ⇒ Is the book mentioned or referenced in books we already consider scripture?
- ⇒ Does the book contain prophesy predicted accurately?
- ⇒ Does the book contain spiritual revelations about books already held as scripture?

---

[154] Synod of Laodicea (4th Century) https://www.newadvent.org/fathers/3806.htm (*last visited* Jan. 13, 2024).
[155] 2 Timothy 3:16.

The Hebrew Bible?

Today, most Bible believers have felt comfortable relying on institutional findings on what we should regard as scripture or not, without proof of spiritual revelation from The Most High in the reaching of such conclusions. Essentially, the way the church has operated is *if it's not broken, don't fix it*. Because the books found in the canon have been sufficient for the average believer to develop a personal relationship with Yahusha (Jesus), there is little to no reason to investigate whether scriptures omitted from that canon were done so haphazardly or even with hidden agendas.

The first step in understanding Apocrypha and Pseudepigrapha is understanding the standard "Hebrew Bible." When one seeks a definition of the "Hebrew Bible," they will likely be pointed to the Tanakh, which includes the Torah, or Books of the Law, the "Nevi'im" or Books of the Prophets, and "Ketuvim Writings" meaning miscellaneous sacred writings. There is no consensus on when this canon of books was established, some arguing that the Hasmonean dynasty fixed it, while others argue it was only fixed in the second century CE or even later.[156] In whatever case scenario, it is essential to question the idea that the "Hebrew Bible" is the Hebrew Bible. Essentially, did the ancient Hebrews really not keep any of the books called Apocrypha and Pseudepigrapha as scripture?

The designation of Apocrypha and Pseudepigrapha as not scripture occurred in hierarchal circles where the average believer was not allowed to test these books for themselves. The status of these books, determined by Jewish scribes long after the last books of the Bible had been written, were done under the judgment of fallible humans. This includes the Catholic Saint Jerome, who merely accepted Jewish expertise on the subject that the Apocrypha and

---

[156]Philip Davies, The Jewish Scriptural Canon in Cultural Perspective, McDonald, Lee Martin; Sanders, James A., The Canon Debate. Baker Academic (2001) "With many other scholars, I conclude that the fixing of a canonical list was almost certainly the achievement of the Hasmonean dynasty."

Pseudepigrapha books were not *God-Breathed*. As stated by BlueLetterBible.org, on the Apocrypha:

> Jerome explicitly denied that they should have the status as scripture. Jerome said they were not books of the canon but books of the church. He believed they could be helpful to people, but he clearly stated his belief that they were not divinely authoritative."[157]

The Book of Jubilees is Scripture

The most evident proof of a conspiracy to hide the location of Biblical Yahshar-el is the displacement, concealment and debasement of the Book of Jubilees, as well as the mysterious disappearance of the Genesis Apocryphon from Judaism and Christianity. While almost all of the church holds that these book are not scripture, the reasoning is faulty. Hope Bolinger from Christianity.com wrote on the Book of Jubilees, giving the following critique:

> This book undoubtedly failed the canonicity test and does not belong in the Bible. Although it played an important role in the culture of those in the Qumran region, Essenes who wrote the Dead Sea Scrolls, the Book of Jubilees does not come directly from God and does not belong in the Old Testament canon.[158]
>
> First, we have a problem with authorship. In other words, **we don't know who wrote the book.** Because of its emphasis on the laws and practices of Jewish culture, we can assume it was someone of a Pharisaic or Essenic background. But aside from that, we don't know who the author is. Furthermore, and more problematic, this book claims to be a revelation to Moses, but if Moses didn't write the book, we can consider much of the information suspect.

---

[157] Christianity.com, What Is the Apocrypha? Are Apocryphal Books Really Scripture?, (Apr. 25, 2019) https://www.christianity.com/wiki/bible/what-is-the-apocrypha-are-apocryphal-books-really-scripture.html; Don Stewart, WHAT IS THE HISTORY OF THE OLD TESTAMENT APOCRYPHA?, Blue Letter Bible, https://www.blueletterbible.org/Comm/stewart_don/faq/books-missing-from-old-testament/question3-history-old-testament-apocrypha.cfm (last visited Jan. 13, 2024).
[158] Hope Bolinger, What Is the Book of Jubilees?, Christianity.com, (Feb. 18, 2020) https://www.christianity.com/wiki/bible/what-is-the-book-of-jubilees.html.

This places the Book of Jubilees firmly in the Pseudepigrapha, a group of books written under a pen name. The author, assuming the authorship of Moses, was not actually Moses. Even though more than a dozen copies of this book were found amongst the Dead Sea Scrolls and given scriptural authority by the Ethiopic Church, most Christians and Jewish scholars have not placed this book in the Old Testament canon.[159]

Second, we have a problem with the date it was written. Because it was written about 100 years before the time of Christ, the author wrote the events thousands of years after they had transpired, allowing for possible errors and exaggerations to seep into the text.

We will deal with the question of the Essenes in the next chapter. However, Bolinger's chief objection, that we don't know who wrote Jubilees, is very odd. Many Christians believe that Moses wrote Genesis, Exodus, Leviticus, Numbers and Deuteronomy. However, the Bible does not say Moses wrote these books and not someone who may have acted as a scribe.

While the scriptures are clear that Moses wrote the Torah, Genesis records the history before the Torah was given. Deuteronomy gives details on Moses's death and Joshua's ascension to leadership, meaning Moses could not have written the entire book. Thus, while some may assume Moses wrote the first five books of the Bible himself, there is no definitive proof. Further, this fact is inconsequential. There are numerous books in the Bible where the author is not mentioned, yet, they are considered scripture and not Apocrypha or Pseudepigrapha. They include Joshua, Judges, I-II Samuel, I-II Kings, I-II Chronicles, Job, Jonah, the four Gospels and the Book of Hebrews, none of which name their author.

As far as the perceived issues with the dating of Jubilees, while it is believed by some that Jubilees dates to the first century BCE, there is no definitive proof of this claim. The late dating of Jubilees is based

---

[159] *Id.*

strictly on the hypothesis that Jubilees may have been written in 135 BCE by a Pharisee when Hyrcanus of the Hasmoneans is purported to have become a high priest due to his break with the Pharisees some years before he died in 105 BCE.[160] Of course, if the book originated in East Africa and not Palestine, then none of this history matters. In addition, given the fact this book was carried to Ethiopia by first temple-era Jewish believers known today as Beta Israel, Jubilees would at least have to have been written before 586 BCE.

Thus, authorities in Christianity and Judaism have no foundational basis to deny Jubilees as scripture. Doing so would put many other books held as scripture up for being negated based on the same arguments. Here is the uncontested truth on Jubilees. Jubilees is an ancient Hebrew book hidden from the Christian and Jewish Canon. We know this as it was maintained by the Falasha (Beta Israel) early on and is found in the Dead Sea Scrolls, the only library of ancient Hebrew scriptures known to exist from that era. Jubilees was also well known to Early Christian writers in the East and the West. However, it was later so thoroughly suppressed that no complete Greek or Latin version has survived.[161] The fact Pharisaic/Rabbinical sources do not recognize Jubilees despite other groups with closer relationships to the Biblical Hebrews regarding the book as scripture only tells of a later agenda to erase the book from the record.[162]

---

[160] Jubilees, Book of, New World Encyclopedia, https://www.newworldencyclopedia.org/entry/Jubilees,_Book_of (*last visited* Jan. 13, 2024).
[161] Book of Jubilees, New World Encyclopedia, https://www.newworldencyclopedia.org/entry/Jubilees,_Book_of (*last visited* Nov. 12, 2023).
[162] *Id.*

Chapter 7: The Edomite Religion

"For Esau is the end of the world, and Jacob is the beginning of it that followeth."

~2 Esdras 6:9

Yahshar-el (Israel) had many enemies, some from before even becoming a nation. Many Bible believers make the false assumption that all of Yahshar-el's enemies carry the same significance, them being enemy nations that were to be destroyed. This scriptural reading robs the reader of a proper understanding of Yahshar-el's history and present reality. As we will detail in this chapter, Yahshar-el's first enemy was its most significant enemy, and this enemy still exists in antipathy to Yahshar-el.

Jacob and Esau: The Full Story

The story of Yahshar-el (Israel) begins with its patriarch, Jacob. The Bible tells us the story of twins Jacob and Esau, the descendants of Abraham and his son Isaac. Abraham was chosen by Yahuah (God) out of all men on earth to have a covenant with him to make his descendants into a mighty nation. Abraham passed this covenant on to his son Isaac, and only one of Isaac's two sons would inherit the covenant of Abraham. Genesis 25:22-34 details the early struggle of Jacob and Esau in their mother Rebecca's womb:

> But the children struggled together within her; and she said, "If it is so, why am I in this condition?" So, she went to inquire of the Lord. [23] And the Lord said to her,
> **"Two nations are in your womb;**
> **And two peoples will be separated from your body;**
> **And one people will be stronger than the other;**
> **And the older will serve the younger."**
> [24] When her days leading to the delivery were at an end, behold, there were twins in her womb. [25] Now the first came out red, all over like a hairy garment; and they named him Esau. [26] Afterward his brother came out with his hand holding on to Esau's heel, so he was named Jacob; and Isaac was sixty years old when she gave birth to them.

27 When the boys grew up, Esau became a skilful hunter, a man of the field; but Jacob was a civilized man, living in tents. 28 Now Isaac loved Esau because he had a taste for game; but Rebekah loved Jacob. 29 When Jacob had cooked a stew one day, Esau came in from the field and he was exhausted; 30 and Esau said to Jacob, "Please let me have a mouthful of that red stuff there, for I am exhausted." **Therefore, he was called Edom by name.** 31 But Jacob said, "First sell me your birthright." 32 Esau said, "Look, I am about to die; so of what use then is the birthright to me?" 33 And Jacob said, "First swear to me"; so he swore an oath to him, and sold his birthright to Jacob. 34 Then Jacob gave Esau bread and lentil stew; and he ate and drank, and got up and went on his way. So, Esau despised his birthright.

The sibling rivalry between Jacob and Esau grew tense after Esau sold Jacob his birthright. The rivalry culminated in Jacob tricking his father Isaac into giving him Esau's blessing as the inheritor of the Promise of Abraham. Genesis 27:1-29 details Jacob's deceit and the blessing given to Jacob:

Now it came about, when Isaac was old and his eyes were too dim to see, that he called his older son Esau and said to him, "My son." And he said to him, "Here I am." 2 Then Isaac said, "Behold now, I am old and I do not know the day of my death. 3 Now then, please take your gear, your quiver and your bow, and go out to the field and hunt game for me; 4 and prepare a delicious meal for me such as I love, and bring it to me that I may eat, so that my soul may bless you before I die."

5 Now Rebekah was listening while Isaac spoke to his son Esau. So when Esau went to the field to hunt for game to bring home, 6 Rebekah said to her son Jacob, "Behold, I heard your father speak to your brother Esau, saying, 7 'Bring me some game and prepare a delicious meal for me, so that I may eat, and bless you in the presence of the Lord before my death.' 8 So now, my son, listen to me as I command you. 9 Go now to the flock and bring me two choice young goats from there, so that I may prepare them as a delicious meal for your father, such as he loves. 10 Then you shall bring it to your father, that he may eat, so that he may bless you before his death." 11 But Jacob said to his mother Rebekah, "Behold, my brother Esau is a hairy man and I am a smooth man. 12 Perhaps my father will touch me, then I will be like a deceiver in his sight, and I will bring upon myself a curse and not a blessing." 13 But his mother said to him, "Your curse be on me, my son; only obey my voice, and go, get the goats for me." 14 So he went and got them, and

brought them to his mother; and his mother made a delicious meal such as his father loved. [15] Then Rebekah took the best garments of her elder son Esau, which were with her in the house, and put them on her younger son Jacob. [16] And she put the skins of the young goats on his hands and on the smooth part of his neck. [17] She also gave the delicious meal and the bread which she had made to her son Jacob.

[18] Then he came to his father and said, "My father." And he said, "Here I am. Who are you, my son?" [19] Jacob said to his father, "I am Esau your firstborn; I have done as you told me. Come now, sit and eat of my game, so that you may bless me." [20] Isaac said to his son, "How is it that you have it so quickly, my son?" And he said, "Because the Lord your God made it come to me." [21] Then Isaac said to Jacob, "Please come close, so that I may feel you, my son, whether you are really my son Esau or not." [22] So Jacob came close to his father Isaac, and he touched him and said, "The voice is the voice of Jacob, but the hands are the hands of Esau." [23] And he did not recognize him, because his hands were hairy like his brother Esau's hands; so he blessed him. [24] And he said, "Are you really my son Esau?" And he said, "I am." [25] So he said, "Bring it to me, and I will eat of my son's game, that I may bless you." And he brought it to him, and he ate; he also brought him wine and he drank. [26] Then his father Isaac said to him, "Please come close and kiss me, my son." [27] So he came close and kissed him; and when he smelled the smell of his garments, he blessed him and said,

"See, the smell of my son
Is like the smell of a field which the Lord has blessed;
[28] Now may God give you of the dew of heaven,
And of the fatness of the earth,
And an abundance of grain and new wine;
[29] May peoples serve you,
And nations bow down to you;
Be master of your brothers,
And may your mother's sons bow down to you.
Cursed be those who curse you,
And blessed be those who bless you."

As Jacob takes the blessing, Esau is left with a promise of barbary and restlessness, as detailed in Genesis 27:30-46:

Now it came about, as soon as Isaac had finished blessing Jacob, and Jacob had hardly gone out from the presence of his father Isaac, that his brother Esau came in from his hunting. [31] Then he also made a delicious meal, and brought it to his father; and he said to his father, "Let my father arise and eat of his son's game, that you may bless me." ³² His father Isaac said to him, "Who are you?" And he said, "I am your son, your firstborn, Esau." ³³ Then Isaac trembled violently, and said, "Who then was he who hunted game and brought it to me, so that I ate from all of it before you came, and blessed him? Yes, and he shall be blessed." ³⁴ When Esau heard the words of his father, he cried out with an exceedingly great and bitter cry, and said to his father, "Bless me, me as well, my father!" ³⁵ And he said, "Your brother came deceitfully and has taken away your blessing." ³⁶ Then Esau said, "Is he not rightly named Jacob, for he has betrayed me these two times? He took away my birthright, and behold, now he has taken away my blessing." And he said, "Have you not reserved a blessing for me?" ³⁷ But Isaac replied to Esau, **"Behold, I have made him your master, and I have given to him all his relatives as servants; and with grain and new wine I have sustained him.** What then can I do for you, my son?" ³⁸ Esau said to his father, "Do you have only one blessing, my father? Bless me, me as well, my father." So, Esau raised his voice and wept.

³⁹ Then his father Isaac answered and said to him,

**"Behold, away from the fertility of the earth shall be your dwelling,
And away from the dew of heaven from above.
⁴⁰ And by your sword you shall live,
And you shall serve your brother;
But it shall come about when you become restless,
That you will break his yoke from your neck."**

⁴¹ So Esau held a grudge against Jacob because of the blessing with which his father had blessed him; and Esau said to himself, "The days of mourning for my father are near; then I will kill my brother Jacob." ⁴² Now when the words of her elder son Esau were reported to Rebekah, she sent word and called her younger son Jacob, and said to him, "Behold your brother Esau is consoling himself concerning you by planning to kill you. ⁴³ Now then, my son, obey my voice, and arise, flee to Haran, to my brother Laban! ⁴⁴ Stay with him a few days, until your brother's fury subsides, ⁴⁵ until your brother's anger against you subsides and he forgets what you did to him. Then I will send word and get you from there. Why should I lose you both in one day?"

⁴⁶ And Rebekah said to Isaac, "I am tired of living because of the daughters of Heth; if Jacob takes a wife from the daughters of Heth like these from the daughters of the land, what good will my life be to me?"

While many church congregations talk extensively about Jacob's promise, mainly, "Cursed be those who curse you, and blessed be those who bless you," the promise of Esau is wholly overlooked. It must be remembered that Esau's promise runs contrary to Jacobs. Therefore, like Jacob's descendants, Esau's descendants would carry his promise to the end.

The first portion of Esau's promise is again: "Behold, away from the fertility of the earth shall be your dwelling, and away from the dew of heaven from above." This description indicates that Esau's descendants would be driven to arid or otherwise unfruitful regions, leaving the possibility of desert and cold climates open. It goes on to say: "And by your sword you shall live, and you shall serve your brother; but it shall come about when you become restless, that you will break his yoke from your neck." This verse indicates that Esau's descendants would be warlike, and while they would serve Jacob at first, eventually, they would break this yoke off their necks. We will demonstrate that after Esau's descendants broke the yoke of Jacob from their necks, they went to war against Jacob.

The next saga in the Jacob and Esau story is an amicable reunion. In Genesis 33:1-17 it reads:

> Then Jacob raised his eyes and looked, and behold, Esau was coming, and four hundred men with him. So, he divided the children among Leah and Rachel, and the two slave women. ² He put the slave women and their children in front, and Leah and her children next, and Rachel and Joseph last. ³ But he himself passed on ahead of them and bowed down to the ground seven times, until he came near to his brother.
>
> ⁴ Then Esau ran to meet him and embraced him, and fell on his neck and kissed him, and they wept. ⁵ He raised his eyes and saw the women and the children, and said, "Who are these with you?" So he said, "The children whom God has graciously given your servant." ⁶ Then the slave women came forward with their children, and they bowed down. ⁷ And Leah likewise came forward with her children, and they bowed down; and afterward Joseph came forward with Rachel, and they bowed down. ⁸ And he said, "What do you mean by all this company which I have met?" And he said, "To find favor in the sight of my lord." ⁹ But Esau said, "I have plenty, my brother; let what you have be your own." ¹⁰ Jacob said, "No, please, if now I have found favor in your sight, then accept my gift from my

hand, for I see your face as one sees the face of God, and you have received me favorably. ¹¹ Please accept my gift which has been brought to you, because God has dealt graciously with me and because I have plenty." So he urged him, and he accepted it.

¹² Then Esau said, "Let's journey on and go, and I will go ahead of you." ¹³ But he said to him, "My lord knows that the children are frail and that the flocks and herds that are nursing are a matter of concern to me. And if they are driven hard just one day, all the flocks will die. ¹⁴ Please let my lord pass on ahead of his servant, and I will proceed at my leisure, at the pace of the cattle that are ahead of me and at the pace of the children, until I come to my lord at Seir."

¹⁵ Then Esau said, "Please let me leave with you some of the people who are with me." But he said, "What need is there? Let me find favor in the sight of my lord." ¹⁶ So Esau returned that day on his way to Seir. ¹⁷ But Jacob journeyed to Succoth, and built for himself a house and made booths for his livestock; therefore the place is named Succoth.

In Genisis 36:6-8, we are given further details on the dwelling of Esau:

> ⁶ Then Esau took his wives, his sons, his daughters, and all his household, and his livestock and all his cattle, and all his property which he had acquired in the land of Canaan, and went to another land away from his brother Jacob. ⁷ For their possessions had become too great for them to live together, and the land where they resided could not support them because of their livestock. ⁸ **So Esau lived in the hill country of Seir; Esau is Edom.**

In most church pulpits, this is where the story ends. There is forgiveness on the part of Esau and reconciliation. Esau accepts his brother as the promise's rightful heir, and they separate. However, the struggle between Jacob and Esau did not end when Esau retreated to the hill country of Seir. Esau was not a momentary struggle for Jacob that he would overcome when returning to his mother and father's home. The struggle between Jacob and Esau would continue until the end of this world.

One would only get the full story of Jacob and Esau from reading the Book of Jubilees. Jubilees 35 gives us more details on what happened after the siblings supposedly made peace. We learn that before Rebecca and Isaac's deaths, Rebecca convened a meeting with

Esau, asking him to maintain peace with Jacob after they pass away. As the Book of Jubilees 35:18-28 explains:

> 18. And Rebecca sent and called Esau and he came to her, and she said unto him: 'I have a petition, my son, to make unto thee, and do thou promise to do it, my son.'
> 19. And he said: 'I will do everything that thou sayest unto me, and I will not refuse thy petition.'
> 21. And she said unto him: 'I ask you that the day I die, thou wilt take me in and bury me near Sarah, thy father's mother, and that thou and Jacob will love each other and that neither will desire evil against the other, but mutual love only, and (so) ye will prosper, my sons, and be honoured in the midst of the land, and no enemy will rejoice over you, and ye will be a blessing and a mercy in the eyes of all those that love you.'
> 22. And he said: 'I will do all that thou hast told me, and I shall bury thee on the day thou diest near Sarah, my father's mother, as thou hast desired that her bones may be near thy bones.
> 23. And Jacob, my brother, also, I shall love above all flesh; for I have not a brother in all the earth but him only: and this is no great merit for me if I love him; for he is my brother, and we were sown together in thy body, and together came we forth from thy womb, and if I do not love my brother, whom shall I love?
> 24. And I, myself, beg thee to exhort Jacob concerning me and concerning my sons, for I know that he will assuredly be king over me and my sons, for on the day my father blessed him he made him the higher and me the lower.
> 25. And I swear unto thee that I shall love him, and not desire evil against him all the days of my life but good only.'
> 26. And he sware unto her regarding all this matter. And she called Jacob before the eyes of Esau, and gave him commandment according to the words which she had spoken to Esau.
> 27. And he said: 'I shall do thy pleasure; believe me that no evil will proceed from me or from my sons against Esau, and I shall be first in naught save in love only.'
> 28. And they eat and drank, she and her sons that night, and she died, three jubilees and one week and one year old, on that night, and her two sons, Esau and Jacob, buried her in the double cave near Sarah, their father's mother.

However, we learn that the peace would not last. After the death of Isaac, Esau goes back on his promise and, at the insistence of his sons, pursues Jacob. As Jubilees 37:1-25 details:

1. And on the day that Isaac the father of Jacob and Esau died, the sons of Esau heard that Isaac had given the portion of the elder to his younger son Jacob and they were very angry.
2. And they strove with their father, saying 'Why has thy father given Jacob the portion of the elder and passed over thee, although thou art the elder and Jacob the younger?'
3. And he said unto them 'Because I sold my birthright to Jacob for a small mess of lentils, and on the day my father sent me to hunt and catch and bring him something that he should eat and bless me, he came with guile and brought my father food and drink, and my father blessed him and put me under his hand.
4. And now our father has caused us to swear, me and him, that we shall not mutually devise evil, either against his brother, and that we shall continue in love and in peace each with his brother and not make our ways corrupt.'
5. And they said unto him, 'We shall not hearken unto thee to make peace with him; for our strength is greater than his strength, and we are more powerful than he; we shall go against him and slay him, and destroy him and his sons. And if thou wilt not go with us, we shall do hurt to thee also.
6. And now hearken unto us: Let us send to Aram and Philistia and Moab and Ammon, and let us choose for ourselves chosen men who are ardent for battle, and let us go against him and do battle with him, and let us exterminate him from the earth before he grows strong.'
7. And their father said unto them, 'Do not go and do not make war with him lest ye fall before him.'
8. And they said unto him, 'This too, is exactly thy mode of action from thy youth until this day, and thou art putting thy neck under his yoke.
9. We shall not hearken to these words.' And they sent to Aram, and to 'Aduram to the friend of their father, and they hired along with them one thousand fighting men, chosen men of war.
10. And there came to them from Moab and from the children of Ammon, those who were hired, one thousand chosen men, and from Philistia, one thousand chosen men of war, and from Edom and from the Horites one thousand chosen fighting men, and from the Kittim mighty men of war.
11. And they said unto their father: Go forth with them and lead them, else we shall slay thee.'
12. And he was filled with wrath and indignation on seeing that his sons were forcing him to go before (them) to lead them against Jacob his brother.
13. But afterward he remembered all the evil which lay hidden in his heart against Jacob his brother; and he remembered not the oath which he had sworn to his father and to his mother that he would devise no evil all his days against Jacob his brother.

14. And notwithstanding all this, Jacob knew not that they were coming against him to battle, and he was mourning for Leah, his wife, until they approached very near to the tower with four thousand warriors and chosen men of war.
15. And the men of Hebron sent to him saying, 'Behold thy brother has come against thee, to fight thee, with four thousand girt with the sword, and they carry shields and weapons'; for they loved Jacob more than Esau. So they told him; for Jacob was a more liberal and merciful man than Esau.
16. But Jacob would not believe until they came very near to the tower.
17. And he closed the gates of the tower; and he stood on the battlements and spake to his brother Esau and said, 'Noble is the comfort wherewith thou hast come to comfort me for my wife who has died. Is this the oath that thou didst swear to thy father and again to thy mother before they died? Thou hast broken the oath, and on the moment that thou didst swear to thy father wast thou condemned.'
18. **And then Esau answered and said unto him, 'Neither the children of men nor the beasts of the earth have any oath of righteousness which in swearing they have sworn (an oath valid) for ever; but every day they devise evil one against another, and how each may slay his adversary and foe.**
19. **And thou dost hate me and my children for ever. And there is no observing the tie of brotherhood with thee.**
20. **Hear these words which I declare unto thee, If the boar can change its skin and make its bristles as soft as wool,**
Or if it can cause horns to sprout forth on its head like the horns of a stag or of a sheep,
Then will I observe the tie of brotherhood with thee
And if the breasts separated themselves from their mother, for thou hast not been a brother to me.
21. And if the wolves make peace with the lambs so as not to devour or do them violence,
And if their hearts are towards them for good,
Then there shall be peace in my heart towards thee
22. And if the lion becomes the friend of the ox and makes peace with him
And if he is bound under one yoke with him and ploughs with him,
Then will I make peace with thee.
23. And when the raven becomes white as the raza,
Then know that I have loved thee
And shall make peace with thee
Thou shalt be rooted out,
And thy sons shall be rooted out,
And there shall be no peace for thee'

24. And when Jacob saw that he was (so) evilly disposed towards him with his heart, and with all his soul as to slay him, and that he had come springing like the wild boar which comes upon the spear that pierces and kills it, and recoils not from it;
25. then he spake to his own and to his servants that they should attack him and all his companions.

A battle ensues between the twin brothers wherein Jacob, at the direction of his son Yahudah (Judah), bends his bow, killing his twin brother, as detailed in Jubilees 38:1-14:

1. And after that Judah spake to Jacob, his father, and said unto him: 'Bend thy bow, father, and send forth thy arrows and cast down the adversary and slay the enemy; and mayst thou have the power, for we shall not slay thy brother, for he is such as thou, and he is like thee let us give him (this) honour.'
2. Then Jacob bent his bow and sent forth the arrow and struck Esau, his brother (on his right breast) and slew him.
3. And again he sent forth an arrow and struck 'Adoran the Aramaean, on the left breast, and drove him backward and slew him.
4. And then went forth the sons of Jacob, they and their servants, dividing themselves into companies on the four sides of the tower.
5. And Judah went forth in front, and Naphtali and Gad with him and fifty servants with him on the south side of the tower, and they slew all they found before them, and not one individual of them escaped.
6. And Levi and Dan and Asher went forth on the east side of the tower, and fifty (men) with them, and they slew the fighting men of Moab and Ammon.
7. And Reuben and Issachar and Zebulon went forth on the north side of the tower, and fifty men with them, and they slew the fighting men of the Philistines.
8. And Simeon and Benjamin and Enoch, Reuben's son, went forth on the west side of the tower, and fifty (men) with them, and they slew of Edom and of the Horites four hundred men, stout warriors; and six hundred fled, and four of the sons of Esau fled with them, and left their father lying slain, as he had fallen on the hill which is in 'Aduram.
9. And the sons of Jacob pursued after them to the mountains of Seir. And Jacob buried his brother on the hill which is in 'Aduram, and he returned to his house.
10. And the sons of Jacob pressed hard upon the sons of Esau in the mountains of Seir, and bowed their necks so that they became servants of the sons of Jacob.
11. And they sent to their father (to inquire) whether they should make peace with them or slay them.

12. And Jacob sent word to his sons that they should make peace, and they made peace with them, and placed the yoke of servitude upon them, so that they paid tribute to Jacob and to his sons always.
13. And they continued to pay tribute to Jacob until the day that he went down into Egypt.
14. And the sons of Edom have not got quit of the yoke of servitude which the twelve sons of Jacob had imposed on them until this day.

Yahshar-el reigned over Edom until the great famine drove the clan to Egypt where they later became enslaved by the Egyptians. This account is drastically different from what we have been authorized to know about Jacob and Esau by the institutions of mainstream Christianity and Judaism. Jacob and Esau did not live on in peace, Jacob killed Esau.

Esau's Dispersion

Genesis 36 gives us the first location of settlement for Esau and his descendants, a mountainous region known as Seir. We know Seir ran parallel to Yahshar-el (Israel) as Numbers 34:3 states: "Your desert region shall extend from the wilderness of Zin along the side of Edom, and your desert border shall extend from the end of the Salt Sea eastward." As we have already established, the Wilderness of Zin would have been in the Nubian Desert connecting Egypt/Kush and Yahshar-el on its northern border. With "from the wilderness of Zin along the side of Edom" we can determine that Edom would have also bordered the Wilderness of Zin alongside Yahshar-el. That would put Edom on the western side of Yahshar-el, in modern-day Sudan.

The Yoke of Jacob

As we know, Edom was based primarily in a hill country. This location would likely put Edom in the modern-day province of Kurdufan, Dufan, with the hill country of Seir being the Nuba Mountains or Nuba Hills of South Kurdufan. From their domain in Seir, Edom held onto their grudge against Yahshar-el for their enslavement. Numbers 20:14-21 tells us that as Yahshar-el began their journey through the wilderness after leaving Egypt,

Yahshar-el sought permission to pass through Edom's land, but Edom refused:

> From Kadesh Moses then sent messengers to the king of Edom to say, "This is what your brother Israel has said: 'You know all the hardship that has overtaken us; [15] that our fathers went down to Egypt, and we stayed in Egypt a long time, and the Egyptians treated us and our fathers badly. [16] But when we cried out to the LORD, He heard our voice and sent an angel, and brought us out from Egypt; now behold, we are at Kadesh, a town on the edge of your territory. [17] Please let us pass through your land. We will not pass through field or vineyard; we will not even drink water from a well. We will go along the king's road, not turning to the right or left, until we pass through your territory.'"
>
> [18] Edom, however, said to him, "You shall not pass through us, or I will come out with the sword against you." [19] Again, the sons of Israel said to him, "We will go up by the road, and if I and my livestock do drink any of your water, then I will pay its price. Let me only pass through on my feet, nothing more." [20] But he said, "You shall not pass through." And Edom came out against him with a heavy force and a strong hand. [21] So Edom refused to allow Israel to pass through his territory; then Israel turned away from him.

After Yahshar-el entered the Promised Land, the Edomites lived independently until the reign of King David. As Isaac prophesied, Esau fell into captivity to Yahshar-el. I Chronicles 18:12-13 states, "… Abishai the son of Zeruiah defeated eighteen thousand Edomites in the Valley of Salt. [13] Then he put garrisons in Edom, and all the Edomites became servants to David. And the LORD helped David wherever he went." Thus, Edom was made Yahshar-el's tributary.[163] The yoke of Jacob was around Esau's neck.

Out for Revenge

Edom did not submit to Yahshar-el's rule and, as occurred in Rebecca's womb, wrestled against Yahshar-el continually. While there would be several revolts of Edom against Yahshar-el, the most

---

[163] 1 Kings 22:47 Now there was no king in Edom; a deputy was king.

notable one was a confederacy with several other enemies. Psalm 83:5-8 states:

> For they have conspired together with one mind;
> They make a covenant against You:
> ⁶ The tents of Edom and the Ishmaelites,
> Moab and the Hagrites;
> ⁷ Gebal, Ammon, and Amalek,
> Philistia with the inhabitants of Tyre;
> ⁸ Assyria also has joined them;
> They have become a help to the children of Lot.

We read further details of this confederacy against Yahshar-el in Amos 1:6-12:

> This is what the Lord says:
>
> "For three offenses of Gaza, and for four,
> I will not revoke its punishment,
> Because they led into exile an entire population
> To turn them over to Edom.
> ⁷ So I will send fire on the wall of Gaza
> And it will consume her citadels.
> ⁸ I will also eliminate every inhabitant from Ashdod,
> As well as him who holds the scepter, from Ashkelon;
> And I will direct My power against Ekron,
> And the remnant of the Philistines will perish,"
> Says the Lord God.
>
> ⁹ This is what the Lord says:
>
> "For three offenses of Tyre, and for four,
> I will not revoke its punishment,
> Because they turned an entire population over to Edom
> And did not remember the covenant of brotherhood.
> ¹⁰ So I will send fire on the wall of Tyre,
> And it will consume her citadels."
>
> ¹¹ This is what the Lord says:
>
> "For three offenses of Edom, and for four,
> I will not revoke its punishment,
> Because he pursued his brother with the sword
> And stifled his compassion;
> His anger also tore continually,

And he maintained his fury forever.
**¹² So I will send fire upon Teman
And it will consume the citadels of Bozrah."**

The confederacy against Yahshar-el is unsuccessful, and instead, Edom and its allies are marked for destruction. Throughout the scriptures, we read of Yahuah's judgment against those aggressors, with Malachi 1:1-5 speaking directly to Edom:

> The pronouncement of the word of the LORD to Israel through Malachi:
>
> ² "I have loved you," says the LORD. But you say, "How have You loved us?" "Was Esau not Jacob's brother?" declares the LORD. **"Yet I have loved Jacob; ³ but I have hated Esau, and I have made his mountains a desolation and given his inheritance to the jackals of the wilderness."** ⁴ Though Edom says, **"We have been beaten down, but we will return and build up the ruins"; this is what the LORD of armies says: "They may build, but I will tear down; and people will call them the territory of wickedness, and the people with whom the LORD is indignant forever."** ⁵ And your eyes will see this, and you will say, "The LORD be exalted beyond the border of Israel!"

The Bible is clear. The Edomites did not become the territory known as Idumea, as told by Josephus and the Maccabees[164]. The nation of Edom was destroyed, and they could never rebuild. The question we are thus presented with is where did Yahshar-el's arch nemesis go? Did they disappear from history as commonly believed?

Where Edom Went

Nowhere in Isaac's prophecy is it foreseen that Edom would disappear from history. We must, therefore, assume this people continued to exist, even after the destruction of their nation. In fact, Jeremiah 49:7-22 gives explicit details about Edom's relocation:

---

[164] Flavius Josephus, Antiquities of the Jews, Book 1, (93-94 CE); 1 Maccabees 5:3–5:5.

Concerning Edom.
This is what the LORD of armies says:

"Is there no longer any wisdom in Teman?
Has good advice been lost by the prudent?
Has their wisdom decayed?
8 Flee away, turn back, dwell in the depths,
**You inhabitants of Dedan,
For I will bring the disaster of Esau upon him
At the time I punish him.**
9 If grape pickers came to you,
Would they not leave gleanings?
If thieves came by night,
They would destroy only what was sufficient for them.
**10 But I have stripped Esau bare,
I have uncovered his hiding places
So that he will not be able to conceal himself;
His offspring have been destroyed along with his brothers
And his neighbors, and he no longer exists.**
11 Leave your orphans behind, I will keep them alive;
And let your widows trust in Me."
12 This is what the LORD says: "If those who do not deserve to drink the cup must drink it, why should you go unpunished? You will not go unpunished, but must drink it.
13 I swear by myself," declares the LORD, "that Bozrah will become a ruin and a curse, an object of horror and reproach; and all its towns will be in ruins forever."
14 I have heard a message from the LORD;
an envoy was sent to the nations to say,
"Assemble yourselves to attack it!
Rise up for battle!"
15 "Now I will make you small among the nations,
     despised by mankind.
**16 The terror you inspire
    and the pride of your heart have deceived you,
you who live in the clefts of the rocks,
    who occupy the heights of the hill.
Though you build your nest as high as the eagle's,
    from there I will bring you down,"
declares the LORD.
17 "Edom will become an object of horror;
    all who pass by will be appalled and will scoff
    because of all its wounds.**
18 As Sodom and Gomorrah were overthrown,
    along with their neighboring towns,"
says the LORD,

> "so no one will live there;
>   no people will dwell in it.
> 19 **"Like a lion coming up from Jordan's thickets
>   to a rich pastureland,
> I will chase Edom from its land in an instant.**
>   Who is the chosen one I will appoint for this?
>   Who is like me and who can challenge me?
>   And what shepherd can stand against me?"
> **20 Therefore, hear what the LORD has planned against Edom,
>   what he has purposed against those who live in Teman:
> The young of the flock will be dragged away;**
>   their pasture will be appalled at their fate.
> **21 At the sound of their fall the earth will tremble;
>   their cry will resound to the Red Sea.
> 22 Look! An eagle will soar and swoop down,
>   spreading its wings over Bozrah.
> In that day the hearts of Edom's warriors
>   will be like the heart of a woman in labor.**

Verse 10 of Jeremiah 49 says explicitly: "I have uncovered his hiding places so that he will not be able to conceal himself." This scripture tells us that Esau goes into hiding places and conceals himself. However, the prophet Jeremiah does not stop there. The scripture explicitly calls out three names associated with Edom: Teman, Dedan and Bozrah. Teman is a chief son of Esau's oldest son Eliphaz. Bozrah was a city in Edom.[165] Dedan was an ancient kingdom that may have been a part of the kingdom Lihyan, an ancient Arabian kingdom that ruled over Yathrib to the Levant in the north.[166] The fact Yahuah is bringing the disaster of Edom on the nation of Dedan tells us that Dedan became one of Edom's hiding places. As is shown here, their association with Edom particularly comes into play when judgment is pronounced against Edom. Thus, Dedan becomes another Edom.

This is also significant because according to Genesis 25:1, Dedan, Shaba and Asshurim descend from Abraham and his third wife

---

[165] Genesis 36:11,15,33.
[166] Alsuhaibani, Abdulrahman, Dadan and Lihyan, a Kingdom or Two Kingdoms: A Critical Study through Archaeological Evidence, Jordan Journal for History and Archaeology, (2023).

Keturah. This blood relation might be a part of the motivation behind Edom's intermixing with Dedan. Jeremiah 25:21-24 also speaks to this other Edom:

> To Edom, Moab, and the sons of Ammon; 22 and to all the kings of Tyre, all the kings of Sidon, and the kings of the coastlands which are beyond the sea; 23 **and to Dedan, Tema, Buz, and all who trim the corners of their hair; 24 and to all the kings of Arabia and all the kings of the foreign people who live in the desert;**

Tema is an abbreviation for Teman while Buz is one of Bozrah. The fact that this scripture references Edom, Moab, Sidon, and Tyre as "beyond the Sea" is confirmation that this is not about when those nations bordered Yahshar-el. Instead, Teman and Bozrah found refuge in Arabia. This is confirmed again in Isaiah 21:13:

> A prophecy against Arabia:
>
> **You caravans of Dedanites,
> who camp in the thickets of Arabia,
> 14. bring water for the thirsty;
> you who live in Tema,**
> bring food for the fugitives.
> 15. They flee from the sword,
> from the drawn sword,
> from the bent bow
> and from the heat of battle.

We see Dedan again mentioned in a lament over Tyre in Ezekiel 27:12-23

> "Tarshish was your customer because of the abundance of all kinds of wealth; with silver, iron, tin, and lead they paid for your merchandise. 13 **Javan, Tubal, and Meshech**, they were your traders; with human lives and vessels of bronze they paid for your merchandise. 14 Those from Beth-togarmah gave horses, war horses, and mules for your merchandise. 15 **The sons of Dedan were your traders. Many coastlands were your market; they brought ivory tusks and ebony as your payment.** 16 Aram was your customer because of the abundance of your goods; they paid for your merchandise with emeralds, purple, colorfully woven cloth, fine linen, coral, and rubies. 17 Judah and the land of Israel, they were your traders; with the

wheat of Minnith, cakes, honey, oil, and balsam they paid for your merchandise. 18 Damascus was your customer because of the abundance of your goods, because of the abundance of all kinds of wealth, because of the wine of Helbon and white wool. 19 Vedan and Javan paid for your merchandise from Uzal; wrought iron, cassia, and spice reed were among your merchandise. **20 Dedan traded with you in saddlecloths for riding. 21 Arabia and all the princes of Kedar, they were your customers for lambs, rams, and goats; for these they were your customers. 22 The traders of Sheba and Raamah, they traded with you; they paid for your merchandise with the best of all balsam oil, and with all kinds of precious stones, and gold. 23 Haran, Canneh, Eden, the traders of Sheba, Asshur, and Chilmad traded with you.**

As is attested to here, Dedan became traders of both humans and goods in a network that extended to Sheba, Assur and even Haran. As for Assur, going back to the Jubilees description, Assur was described as being in this area of southern Arabia, and not the location of Assyria we typically associate with this name. Given the account given in the book of 2 Kings 23:29 where Egyptian Pharaoh Necho went south to the Perath River to attack Assur, but was met by King Josiah who he killed, this confirms that *Assur* mentioned in scripture is not the Assyrian Empire, but the modern-day province of Asir in Arabia. For this reason, the author takes the position that the "Assyrian captivity" may have been a captivity in Arabia.

There is more significant evidence the Edomites fled to Arabia. Omar is another chief son of Edom's firstborn Eliphaz.[167] Teman and Omar carry great semblance to two modern countries which border one another, Yemen and Oman. In fact, "Yemen" is a literal transliteration of the Hebrew name *Teman*.[168] The word "Bozrah" is actually *Botsrah* in Hebrew and closely matches the name of the city Basrah in Yemen.[169] Timna, an ancient city that was the capital of the

---

[167] Genesis 36:11,15.
[168] Teman, Christian Answers, https://christiananswers.net/dictionary/teman.html (*last visited* Jan. 14, 2024).
[169] 1224. Botsrah, Bible Hub, https://biblehub.com/hebrew/1224.htm (*last visited* Jan. 14, 2024).

Qataban kingdom in Yemen, also resembles the name Teman.[170] There is also a destination between Medina and Dumah carrying the Hebrew name Tema in Saudi Arabia.[171] Thus, the Edomite trifecta mentioned in Jeremiah 49 of Teman, Dedan and Bozrah are all found in Arabia. We will see Edom settled in Arabia from the south and gradually began a move upwards.

Into Palestine

If the true nation of Yahshar-el (Israel) was in East Africa, then how did Judaism and the Hebrew people become associated with Palestine? It is reasonable to conclude that many Edomites practiced Torah, especially out of reverence to Abraham and Isaac, from whom both Edom and Yahshar-el descended. It just so happens that the Edomite presence did not remain in Arabia but crept into the Levant, and eventually into Palestine through the Minaeans.

The Minaeans and the Move Into Palestine

The Minaeans, a people from the South Arabian kingdom of Ma'in that was eventually eclipsed by Saba, left southern Arabia and gradually made their way into modern-day Jordan. Minaeans are mentioned in the Bible as the "Meunites," as translated by the Septuagint.[172] In I Chronicles 4:41-42, we read of the Meunites association with Mount Seir, and thus with Edom:

> These people, recorded by name, came in the days of Hezekiah king of Judah, and they attacked their tents and the Meunites who were found there, and utterly destroyed them to this day; and they lived in their place, because there was pasture there for their flocks. 42 From them, from the sons of Simeon, five hundred men went to Mount

---

[170] Stone picked up in Timnah, Yemen, A History of the World, BBC, https://www.bbc.co.uk/ahistoryoftheworld/objects/4kSbm2gzRC2NOBupHZELAw (*last visited* Nov. 23, 2023).
[171] Tayma, Nabataea.Net, https://nabataea.net/explore/cities_and_sites/tayma/ (*last visited* Dec. 13, 2023).
[172] Who were the Meunites?, Got Questions, https://www.gotquestions.org/Meunites.html (*last visited* Jan. 16, 2024).

Seir, with Pelatiah, Neariah, Rephaiah, and Uzziel, the sons of Ishi, as their leaders.

In Jordan, Minaeans founded a city known as *Ma'an*. The semblance between the words *Ma'an* and *Teman* has led to many identifying Ma'an as the likely location of a town called *Teman*, known to be in Arabia Petrea as attested to by ancient historian Eusebius of Caesarea and the Catholic Saint Jerome.[173] Like other Arabian and Yemenite kingdoms of the same period, the Minaeans were heavily involved in the lucrative spice trade, especially frankincense and myrrh.[174]

Traces of Minaeans are found throughout Palestine. This presence was recorded by 'Ptolemy son of Ptolemy' and dated to around 263 BCE when the trade of incense between Gerrhaeans and Minaeans was in Syria-Palestine.[175] The Minaean presence in Palestine would later take on religious overtones, as eventually, Minaeans became synonymous with a later Jewish Christian sect known as the Nazarenes. Jerome spoke of the Nazarenes, stating:

> Until now a heresy is to be found in all of the synagogues of the East among the Jews; it is called 'of the Minaeans' and is cursed by the Pharisees until now. Usually they are called Nazarenes… until today they blaspheme the Christian people in their synagogues under the name of Nazarenes…They curse him [Christ] three times a day in their synagogues under the name of Nazarenes.[176]

Sabianism, Zoroastrianism, Mandeanism, & Rise the of Judaism

---

[173] Amos 1:12, Bible Hub, https://biblehub.com/commentaries/amos/1-12.htm (*last visited* Jan. 16, 2024).; Duke Tabor, Where is Teman in the Bible?, Viral Believer, (Aug. 17, 2023) https://viralbeliever.com/where-is-teman-in-the-bible/.
[174] Minaeans, Academic Dictionaries and Encyclopedias, https://en-academic.com/dic.nsf/enwiki/2280674 (*last visited* Jan. 16, 2024).
[175] Languages of Southern Arabia, Elmaz O. & Watson J.C.E. (eds), (2014) https://www.academia.edu/8279492/The_Minaeans_beyond_Ma_%C4%ABn, Footnote 18.
[176] Ray Pritz, Nazarene Jewish Christianity, Magnes Press, (1992).

The Minaeans becoming known as the Nazarenes, a sect recognized as Jewish, gives credence to the presupposition that Edomites carried the knowledge of Yahuah (God) and the Torah into the realm of Palestine. We now move specifically to the issue of the founding of Judaism, a religious system that should be differentiated from the practice of Torah, as many aspects of this religion go beyond the mosaic law and the Old Testament.

Before coming to the origins of Judaism, one must understand the religious doctrines rampant in the region. One significant and mysterious group is the Sabians of Harran. There is no scholarly agreeance on the origins of this group. However, they have been distinguished from the Sabeans of Sheba, as the name *Sabians* in this instance is believed to not derive from Saba but was Syriac. Interestingly enough, the Sabians of Harran later became associated with Torah beliefs, as they are documented to have identified themselves as "People of the Book."[177]

The Sabians are spoken about in the Quran, where they are said to have had cultic practices, and being of ancient heathen sects of several nationalities, namely Greeks, Persians and Indians.[178] The principal deity they worshipped was in the form of a pillar or holy stone, and under him was Shamash the sun god, Sin the moon god, Saturn, Jupiter, Mars, Venus, and Mercury. Like the days of the week in modern Western culture, every day was dedicated to one of these deities.[179] There are also Torah-based practices engrained into some of their beliefs, suggesting that practitioners of Torah intermixed with the Sabians. Some even reported that the Sabians originated from

---

[177] J. B. Segal, The Sabian Mysteries, The Planet Cult of Harran, Vanished Civilizations, (1963), 202-220.
[178] Muhammad Azizan Sabjan, The Al-s~biã'n (The Sabians): An Overview from the Quranic Commentators, Theologians and Jurists, Universiti Sains Malaysia (2011), 163.
[179] Michel Gybels, Harran, Turkish Archeological News, https://turkisharchaeonews.net/site/harran, (*last updated* May 31, 2020).

groups that identified as exiled Hebrews, who became exposed to Zoroastrianism.[180]

Zoroastrianism is a religion established by the Persian prophet Zoroaster between 1500 and 1000 BCE. The religion is both monotheistic and dualistic with beliefs in astrology and magic. It holds that there is one supreme deity, Ahura Mazda, the "Lord of Wisdom" and creator of all things. Because of the semblance in beliefs, it is widely believed that Zoroastrianism influenced the development of Judaism and thereby Christianity.[181] As detailed by Bahá'í scholar Christopher Buck:

> The remnants of the captive Jews in Babylonia, whom Nebuchadnezzar had transferred from Jerusalem to that country after having freely moved
> about in Babylonia, and having acclimatized themselves to the country, they found it inconvenient to return to Syria. Therefore, they preferred to
> stay in Babylonia. Their religion wanted a specific solid foundation, a consequence of which they listened to the doctrines of the Magians and
> inclined towards some of them. So their religion became a mixture of Magian and Jewish elements like that of the so-called Samaritans who were
> transferred from Babylonia to Syria.[182]

Many Jewish concepts are influenced by Zoroastrian beliefs, notably beliefs in an afterlife immediately after death where one enters heaven or hell. This belief differs from the scriptural understanding of descending to Sheol, followed by a resurrection of all the dead before

---

[180] *Supra* note 178 at 163-164.
[181] Joshua J. Mark, Zoroastrianism, World History Encyclopedia, (Dec. 12, 2019) https://www.worldhistory.org/zoroastrianism/; Jacques Duchesne-Guillemin, Zoroastrianism, Britannica, (*last updated* Jan. 4, 2024) https://www.britannica.com/topic/Zoroastrianism.
[182] Christopher Buck, The Identity of the Ṣābi'ūn: An Historical Quest", the Muslim World, (1984).

Judgement Day.[183] Judaism also encompasses several Zoroastrian beliefs in the realm of astrology and cosmology. As stated on the Jewish Hasidic website Chabad.org:

> It is fascinating to note that the rabbis of the Talmud gave considerable credence to astrology. The Talmud states that "upon entry into the month of Adar one should become increasingly joyous. Rav Papa said: 'Therefore a Jew should avoid litigation with gentiles in the month of Av, because his *mazal* is bad; and he should move the court case to the month of Adar, when his *mazal* is good.'"¹ The Hebrew word which Talmud uses here, *mazal*, is usually translated "luck" but literally means "constellations."'
>
> Astrology is not only a factor to be taken into account when planning future events—it also influences human nature. According to the Talmud, one born under the constellation of the sun will achieve eminence, and one born under Venus will become wealthy and immoral. One born under Mercury will be wise and have a retentive memory. One born under the Moon will suffer evil. One born under Saturn will suffer frustration, one born under Jupiter will be righteous, and one born under Mars will become either a surgeon or a slaughterer.²A birthday is therefore viewed by the rabbis as a day on which personal astrological fortune is at its most potent.[184]

Chabad gives further details on the role astrology plays in Judaism:

> In Judaism, Astrology is not regarded as "idol worship," even though the generic name for "idol worship" is "Avodat Kochavim U'Mazalot," Worship of the Stars and the Signs of the Zodiac."
>
> From the Jewish perspective, the stars are not unrelated to events on earth. It is not irrelevant whether one was born on Pesach, or Yom Kippur, or Lag Ba'Omer or on any particular day. Each day is special and has a unique imprint.

---

[183] Hannah M.G.Shapero, Zoroastrianism, Judaism, and Christianity, George Mason University, (Aug. 6, 1997) https://olli.gmu.edu/docstore/600docs/1403-651-3-Zoroastrianism,%20Judaism,%20and%20Christianity.pdf.
[184] Levi Brackman, Is Astrology Kosher?, Chabad, https://www.chabad.org/library/article_cdo/aid/269721/jewish/Is-Astrology-Kosher.htm(*last visited* Jan. 17, 2024).

On the other hand, if an individual was born under the "sign" of Mars, the Talmud says that he will have a tendency to spill blood. This tendency can be realized in a number of very different ways, however, which are subject to an individual's choice. In this case, options might be a soldier, a surgeon, a murderer, a "shochet," a ritual slaughterer of animals, or a "mohel," one who performs ritual circumcisions. These options correspond to a potential hero, a healer, one who violates the "image of G-d," to those who do "holy work" of different types.[185]

This reliance on astrology does not even take into account the widely popular Jewish mystical system of Kabbalah, which relies heavily on astrology and magic.[186] Such embracing of astrology and mysticism could not have come from the Torah, as astrology is consistently condemned in Biblical scripture. As Isaiah 47:13-14 states:

> You are wearied with your many counsels;
> Let now the astrologers,
> Those who prophesy by the stars,
> Those who predict by the new moons,
> Stand up and save you from what will come upon you.

Mandaeans

The Mandaeans, a group closely associated with the Sabians of Haran, who also regarded themselves as the chosen people, established a strong presence in Palestine where they were later absorbed into Judaism and Jewish Christianity.[187] Like the Sabians of Haran, the Mandaeans saw Haran as their celestial homeland.[188] Mandaean

---

[185] Significance of Astrology in Judaism, Orthodox Union, (Feb. 12, 2014) https://www.ou.org/judaism-101/resources/significance-astrology-judaism/
[186] DovBer Pinson, What is Kabbalah, Chabad, https://www.chabad.org/library/article_cdo/aid/170308/jewish/What-is-Kabbalah.htm (*last visited* Jan. 17, 2024); Astrology, The Kabbalah Centre, https://www.kabbalah.com/en/topics/astrology/ (*last visited* Jan. 17, 2024).
[187] Richard Thomas, The Israelite Origins of the Mandaean People, Studia Antiqua 5, no. 2 (2007). https://scholarsarchive.byu.edu/studiaantiqua/vol5/iss2/4.
[188] *Id.* at 11.

religion believes that there is a supreme god (not Yahuah), and carries dualism beliefs from Zoroastrianism, with a strong reverence for John the Baptist.[189] The Mandaean Associations Union summarizes their dualistic beliefs as the following:

> The Mandaean worldview is stamped by gnostic dualism. A World of Light (nhura) and a World of Darkness (hshuka) exist in mutual hostility. The World of Light is a world of light and brilliance, of goodness and truth, and eternity without death. Heading the World of Light is a sublime being, The King of Light "Life" (Haii). Countless number of light beings "angels" (uthra) surrounds this God. The World of Darkness is a similar construction to the World of Light, but it stems originally from the chaos or 'dark waters'. The World of Darkness is full of evil and falsehood. Hostile relations between light and darkness, life and death, good and evil have always existed. These relations led to the creation of the earthly world (Tibil). Earth was created as a result of joint actions from darkness and light. Basically, it was an evil act with the interference by the World of Light to tilt the balance in its favor.[190]

Certain followers of the Mandaean religion are called the Nasoraeans/Nasaraeans, the guardians or possessors of secret rites and knowledge. The name is, of course, almost exactly the name that would be applied to the Minaean Jewish Christian sect, the Nazarenes. The Mandaean Nasoraeans may come from the root n-ṣ-r, which means "to keep," meaning keepers of Gnosis. Just as the Minaean Nazarenes, Epiphanius, the Bishop of Salamis attributed the Nasoraeans to being Jews, and even mentions their origins as Jordan, the same as the Minaeans who established Ma'an:

> **The Nasaraeans - they were Jews by nationality - originally from Gileaditis, Bashanitis and the Transjordan ...** They acknowledged Moses and believed that he had received laws - not this law, however, but some other. And so, they were Jews who kept all

---

[189] Mandaean Religion, Encyclopedia.com, https://www.encyclopedia.com/environment/encyclopedias-almanacs-transcripts-and-maps/mandaean-religion (*last visited* Jan. 17, 2024).

[190] Mandaean Association Union, The Mandaeans: Their History, Religion and Mythology, (Mar. 27, 2013), https://www.mandaeanunion.com/history-english/item/170-brief-history-on-the-mandaeans.

the Jewish observances, but they would not offer sacrifice or eat meat. They considered it unlawful to eat meat or make sacrifices with it. They claim that these Books are fictions, and that none of these customs were instituted by the fathers. This was the difference between the Nasaraeans and the others.[191]

Careful reading of Mandaean texts reveals Mandaeans originally worshipped the god of Judaism before engaging in Sun worship. Mandaeans themselves claim that they were initially the same people as the Jewish people, but Judaism became corrupted and began to practice evil rituals, such as circumcision.[192] It was not until the time of Yahusha (Jesus) that the Mandaeans claimed to have lost their faith in the Jewish god.[193] Also, according to Jewish tradition, Jewish ancestors persecuted the Mandaean's ancestors, resulting in a strong anti-Jewish sentiment among Mandaeans. [194]

Based on the Mandaean account, the religion we know today as Judaism is the religious group from which the Mandaeans branched off. This is corroborated by the fact the religion of Mandaeism has many feats that greatly resemble what we know today as Judaism, despite what seems to be a later adoption of Gnosticism. Professor Richard Thomas also argued in his study, *The Israelite Origins of the Mandaean People*, that the Gnostic group found their origins in Judaism:

> They claim to have a secret knowledge which makes it possible for their souls, after death, to return to the "Worlds of Light" from whence they came. Their gnosis is manifest in a complex series of sayings, ordinances, and rituals which are absolutely necessary for salvation. They have multiple books of scripture which gave them protection as "People of the Book" under Arab rule. Primary among these books is the Ginza, which includes creation myths, underworld journeys, the story of Noah, words of wisdom from John the Baptist, doctrinal poetry, and Old Testament history with a Mandaean twist. The similarities to these Near Eastern religions are far less significant

---

[191] Epiphanius, The Panarion of Epiphanius of Salamis, Book I, Section 18.
[192] *Supra*, 187 at 9.
[193] *Id.*
[194] *Id.*

and numerous than similarities with Judean groups. ...Similar concepts are to be found in Valentinian Gnosticism and in Jewish mystical circles. The Jewish mystical system of Kabbalah, for example, also claims an ancient Judean origin and is very heavily reliant on astrology and magic...Though it is diametrically opposed to Judaism, Mandaeism shares many traits with it. In addition to revering many biblical figures, including Adam, Abel, Seth, Enoch, Eve, Noah, and Shem, it has traditions regarding Abraham, Moses, David, Solomon, Satan, Gabriel, Michael, and Raphael. Most of these names appear in the very early Mandaean literature. In addition to these figures, it refers to biblical events, including the crossing of the Red Sea and the Great Flood. Mandaeans also embrace much of the same legal terminology and ethics as their Jewish counterparts. One of the most important similarities between the two is their ritual practices. Parallels exist between the ordination ritual of the Mandaean and the Jewish priests, and in their foot washing, enthronement, laying on of hands, and ritual kissing. [195]

The True Origins of the Dead Sea Scrolls

Most scholars have presumed the original keepers of the Dead Sea Scrolls to have been Essenes, a religious group within Judaism known to be reclusive and Baptist.[196] This belief, which was almost universal until the 1990s, was primarily based on the fact the Qumran communities' communal living arrangement and ritual bathing rules resemble what is known of the Essenes.[197] However, this evidence is circumstantial. Not one word of the Dead Sea Scrolls names the Essenes as the writers.[198] In addition, the scrolls do not name other divisions of Judaism, such as the Pharisees and the Sadducees, who are known to have been the Essenes' rivals. Instead, scholars

---

[195] *Id.* at 4,7,9.
[196] *Id.* at 12.
[197] Alex P. Jassen, The Dead Sea Scrolls Community, https://www.bibleodyssey.org/articles/the-dead-sea-scrolls-community/ (*last visited* Dec. 13, 2023).
[198] Essenes, Encylopedia.com, https://www.encyclopedia.com/philosophy-and-religion/judaism/judaism/essenes (*last visited* Jan 17, 2024).

interpreted the terms "Seekers after Smooth Thing" or "Ephraim" as speaking to the Pharisees metaphorically.[199]

While the Essenes have much in common with the writers of the scrolls, the Mandaeans do as well. The Mandaeans believed they were the true "Sons of Light," a term used by the Qumran community in the scrolls. Also notable are the phrases "the Great building of Truth" and "house of Perfection" in Mandaean texts such as the Qolasta, Ginza Rabba, and the Mandaean Book of John, which carry semblance to "House of Perfection and Truth in Israel" in the Dead Sea Scrolls.[200]

One very remarkable account given in the Dead Sea Scrolls is the Damascus Covenant. The Damascus Covenant attests to a teacher called *moreh ha-yahid*, "the unique teacher," "the teacher of the One," or "the teacher of the community." This person played the role of organizing the community and pushing them into the covenant made at Damascus. There is also "the man of mockery" or "preacher of falsehood," who arose and misled the adherents to the covenant, causing many members to leave the community. It has been inferred that the people of mockery were the Pharisees who are said to have engaged in fornication for marrying more than one wife, but again, this in itself is not a clear identification of the Pharisees.[201]

The Dead Sea Scrolls also tell a story of piety and mass conversion. We can glean from the scrolls that whoever wrote and kept them saw themselves as a sect of the original community that began in Damascus. This feature replicates the original Torah-practicing Mandaeans, who believed themselves to be the original holders of knowledge. The founders of Judaism, in their view, broke

---

[199] John Merrill, In Quest of the Historical Pharisees, (Nov. 4, 2011) https://www.biblicalarchaeology.org/reviews/in-quest-of-the-historical-pharisees/.
[200] David Hamidovic, About the links between Dead Sea Scrolls and Mandaean Liturgy, ARAM Periodical, (Dec. 2010).
[201] Jewish Virtual Library, The Dead Sea Scrolls: The Book of Covenant of Damascus, https://www.jewishvirtuallibrary.org/the-book-of-covenant-of-damascus (*last visited* Jan. 17, 2024).

from their way of life. In addition, something repeatedly overlooked by scholars is the writers of the scrolls not explicitly identifying themselves as Hebrew. The Exhortation Scroll tells the story of the true Hebrews and their rebellion against Yahuah (God):

> For when they were unfaithful and forsook Him, He hid His face from Israel and His Sanctuary and delivered them up to the sword. But remembering the Covenant of the forefathers, He left a remnant to Israel and did not deliver it up to be destroyed. And in the age of wrath, three hundred and ninety years after He had given them into the hand of King Nebuchadnezzar of Babylon, He visited them, and He caused a plant root to spring from Israel and Aaron to inherit His Land and to prosper on the good things of His earth. And they perceived their iniquity and recognized that they were guilty men, yet for twenty years they were like blind men groping for the way.
>
> Hear now, all you who enter the Covenant, and I will unstop your ears concerning the ways of the wicked. God loves knowledge. Wisdom and understanding He has set before Him, and prudence and knowledge serve Him. Patience and much forgiveness are with Him towards those who turn from transgression; but power, might, and great flaming wrath by the hand of all the Angels of Destruction towards those who depart from the way and abhor the Precept. **They shall have no remnant or survivor. For from the beginning God chose them not; He knew their deeds before ever they were created and He hated their generations, and He hid His face from the Land until they were consumed.** For He knew the years of their coming and the length and exact duration of their times for all ages to come and throughout eternity. He knew the happenings of their times throughout all the everlasting years. **And in all of them He raised for Himself men called by name that a remnant might be left to the Land, and that the face of the earth might be filled with their seed**. And He made known His Holy Spirit to them by the hand of His anointed ones, and He proclaimed the truth (to them). But those whom He hated He led astray. [202]

Here, we see the community at Qumran distinguishes between a remnant of Hebrews and the entirety of Yahshar-el (Israel). To them,

---

[202] Geza Vermes, The Exhortation, The Complete Dead Sea Scrolls in English, Penguin Books, (1962), Sections I-II.

from the beginning, Yahuah did not choose the whole lot of Yahshar-el, as he had foreknown their future iniquity. Only a remnant would be redeemed. What is most surprising is that rather than identifying themselves as people of Yahshar-el, the keepers of the scrolls identify themselves as converts to the Torah. The scrolls go on to say:

> But with the remnant which held fast to the commandments of God He made His Covenant with Israel for ever, revealing to them the hidden things in which all Israel had gone astray. He unfolded before them His holy Sabbaths and his glorious feasts, the testimonies of His righteousness and the ways of His truth, and the desires of His will which a man must do in order to live. And they dug a well rich in water; and he who despises it shall not live. Yet they wallowed in the sin of man and in ways of uncleanness, and they said, 'This is our (way).' But God, in His wonderful mysteries, forgave them their sin and pardoned their wickedness; and He built them a sure house in Israel whose like has never existed from former times till now. Those who hold fast to it are destined to live for ever and all the glory of Adam shall be theirs. As God ordained for them by the hand of the Prophet Ezekiel, saying, **The Priests, the Levites, and the sons IV of Zadok who kept the charge of my sanctuary when the children of Israel strayed from me, they shall offer me fat and blood.**
>
> **The Priests are <u>the converts of Israel</u> who departed from the land of Judah, and (the Levites are) those who joined them.** The sons of Zadok are the elect of Israel, the men called by name who shall stand at the end of days. Behold the exact list of their names according to their generations, and the time when they lived, and the number of their trials, and the years of their sojourn, and the exact list of their deeds... **The Well is the Law, and those who dug it were <u>the converts of Israel</u> who went out of the land of Judah to sojourn in the land of Damascus. God called them allprinces because they sought Him, and their renown was disputed by no man.** The Stave is the Interpreter of the Law of whom Isaiah said, He makes a tool for His work; and the nobles of the people are those who come to dig the Well with the staves with which the Stave ordained that they should walk in all the age of wickedness - and without them they shall find nothing - until he comes who shall teach righteousness at the end of days.
>
> I ... ... [that they may bring near] each according to [his] spirit [and deeds] ... they shall depart by the decision of the Guardian (cf. 1QS VI, 16-17) ... **[And these are the precepts] in which all <u>the converts of Israel</u> [shall wa]lk ... the sons of Zadok, the**

> **Priests (cf. CD IV, 2-3), behold the[y are the converts of Israel**... [the interpretation of the] last Law. And these are the precepts for the Mas[ter] in which [he shall walk (1QS IX, 12)] in regard to all Israel, for [God] shall not save any of those who are not established] in His ways to walk perfec[tly] ...[203]

We are, also, given some details of the intentions of the adherents to the Damascus Covenant:

> At the time of the former Visitation they were saved, whereas the apostates VIII were given up to the sword; and so shall it be for all the members of His Covenant who do not hold steadfastly to these (MS. B: to the curse of the precepts).[204]

> None of the men who enter the New Covenant in the land of Damascus, (B I) and who again betray it and depart from the fountain of living waters, shall be reckoned with the Council of the people or inscribed in its Book from the day of the gathering in (B II) of the Teacher of the Community until the coming of the Messiah out of Aaron and Israel.

> ... And thus, shall it be for all among the first and the last who reject (the precepts), who set idols upon their hearts and walk in the stubbornness of their hearts; they shall have no share in the house of the Law. They shall be judged in the same manner as their companions were judged who deserted to the Scoffer. For they have spoken wrongly against the precepts of righteousness, and have despised the Covenant and the Pact - the New Covenant - which they made in the land of Damascus. Neither they nor their kin shall have any part in the house of the Law.[205]

We can see here that the Qumran community were also awaiting the Hebrew Messiah. Interestingly, there is talk of a messiah of Aaron, or out of the priesthood, which goes contrary to the messiah coming out of Yahudah. We are also given details of a future battle that

---

[203] *Id.*
[204] *Id.*
[205] *Id.*

would happen between Kittim, who are the Romans,[206] and Yahshar-el. This prophecy is recorded in the War Scroll, which states:

> The sons of Levi, Judah, and Benjamin, the exiles in the desert, shall battle against them in … all their bands when the exiled sons of light return from the Desert of the Peoples to camp in the Desert of Jerusalem; and after the battle they shall go up from there (to Jerusalem).
>
> [The king] of the Kittim [shall enter] into Egypt, and in his time he shall set out in great wrath to wage war against the kings of the north, that his fury may destroy and cut the horn of [Israel]. This shall be a time of salvation for the people of God, an age of dominion for all the members of His company, and of everlasting destruction for all the company of Belial. The confusion of the sons of Japheth shall be [great] and Assyria shall fall unsuccoured. The dominion of the Kittim shall come to an end and iniquity shall be vanquished, leaving no remnant; [for the sons] of darkness there shall be no escape. **[The sons of righteous]ness shall shine over all the ends of the earth; they shall go on shining until all the seasons of darkness are consumed and, at the season appointed by God, His exalted greatness shall shine eternally to the peace, blessing, glory, joy, and long life of all the sons of light.**[207]

This gives us an alternative account of the possible origins of Jewish zealots combating Yahusha and his assent to the throne. These converts viewed the children of Yahshar-el as having not been chosen by Yahuah. However, due to Yah's mercy, he left a remnant in the land. This remnant needed guidance about the law from those who regarded themselves as the "Sons of Light." These "Sons of Light" foresaw a future battle with Rome against the tribes of Levi, Yahudah and Benjamin, the remnant of the "exiles in the desert." For this reason, the "Sons of Light" would return to the Hebrews in East

---

[206] "Kition was the name for an ancient city in the southeastern part of the island of Cyprus (modern Larnaca).¹ In its original, limited sense, the Biblical Hebrew term Kittim means the island of Cyprus (Isa 23,1.12). In the expanded sense of »the isles of the Kittim« it can mean Cyprus and neighboring islands of the Eastern Mediterranean (Jer 2,10, Ez 27,6). In post–Biblical literature such as the Dead Sea Scrolls and the Targums, Kittim can be a code name for Rome." Benjamin Scolnic,Thomas Davis, How
Kittim Became Rome, De Gruyter, (2015).
[207] *Supra* 202 at the War Scroll, (IQM, 1Q33, 4Q491-7, 4Q471).

Africa to lead them to Yahuah, establishing the dominion of the new Yahshar-el.

In this version of events, the writers of the scrolls were Mandeans who had some branch off from their original group who later founded Judaism. This gives us an understanding of what the Pharisee priesthood was doing in Yahshar-el. This priesthood of converts saw it their duty to return the remnant of Yahshar-el to Yahuah by teaching them the ways of the law, as revealed to them at Damascus.

Khazar Conversion & Gog and Magog

It is necessary to mention the Khazar conversion in this conversation about converts. Most people who speak of Judaism and converts to the faith are speaking specifically about Ashkenazi Jews. Arthur Koestler details this story in the infamous book *The Thirteenth Tribe*. Koestler, a Jewish man himself, gives a highly compelling historical account that the Ashkenazi Jews did not come from Palestine but from the Caucasus Mountains and are genetically more related to the Turkish Hun, Uigur, and Magyar tribes than Hebrew people. [208] As Koestler writes:

> At the beginning of the eighth century, the world was polarized between the two super-powers representing Christianity and Islam. Their ideological doctrines were welded to power-politics pursued by the classical methods of propaganda, subversion and military conquest. The Khazar Empire represented a Third Force, which had proved equal to either of them, both as an adversary and an ally.[209]

The Khazar Empire's history has been almost totally erased from modern discourse, despite the former power and prominence of the kingdom. This erasure of a significant world power from history had to be intentional. Also interesting, several historical figures identified the Khazars as the Biblical Gog and Magog. Koestler cites a Georgian chronicle describing the Khazars as Gog and Magog with "wild men

---

[208] Arthur Koestler, The Thirteenth Tribe, 1976, Last Century Media, 18.
[209] *Id.* at 71.

with hideous faces and the manners of wild beasts, eaters of blood." The Gog and Magog connection is also chronicled by Ibn Fedlan, who states, "The Khazars and their Kings are all Jews. The Bulgars and all their neighbors are subject to him. They treat him with worshipful obedience. Some are of the opinion that Gog and Magog are the Khazars."[210]

Returning to the Book of Jubilees' account of Gog & Magog, this is a territory that encompasses Eastern Europe and Western Asia. The Khazar territory is located in this area, between the Black Sea and the Caspian Sea. The relevance of Gog and Magog should not be taken for granted. Ezekiel 38 speaks directly to a principality over the region of Magog known as "Gog," where it states:

> Now the word of the Lord came to me, saying,[2] "Son of man, set your face toward Gog of the land of Magog, the chief prince of Meshech and Tubal, and prophesy against him, [3] and say, 'This is what the Lord God says: "Behold, I am against you, Gog, chief prince of Meshech and Tubal. [4] So I will turn you around and put hooks into your jaws, and I will bring you out, and all your army, horses and horsemen, all of them magnificently dressed, a great contingent *with* shield and buckler, all of them wielding swords; [5] Persia, Cush, and Put with them, all of them *with* buckler and helmet; [6] Gomer with all its troops; Beth-togarmah *from* the remote parts of the north with all its troops—many peoples with you.
>
> [7] "Be ready, and be prepared, you and all your contingents that are assembled around you, and be a guard for them. [8] After many days you will be summoned; in the latter years you will come into the land that is restored from the sword, *whose inhabitants* have been gathered from many nations to the mountains of Israel which had been a continual place of ruins; but its people were brought out from the nations, and they are living securely, all of them. [9] And you will go up, you will come like a storm; you will be like a cloud covering the land, you and all your troops, and many peoples with you."
>
> [10] 'This is what the Lord God says: "It will come about on that day, that thoughts will come into your mind and you will devise an evil plan, [11] and you will say, 'I will go up against the land of unwalled

---

[210] *Id.* at 55.

villages. I will go against those who are at rest, who live securely, all of them living without walls and having no bars or gates, ¹² to capture spoils and to seize plunder, to turn your hand against the ruins that are *now* inhabited, and against the people who are gathered from the nations, who have acquired livestock and goods, who live at the center of the world.' ¹³ **Sheba and Dedan and the merchants of Tarshish with all its villages will say to you, 'Have you come to capture spoils? Have you assembled your contingent to seize plunder, to carry away silver and gold, to take away livestock and goods, to capture great spoils?'"**

¹⁴ "Therefore prophesy, son of man, and say to Gog, 'This is what the Lord God says: "On that day when My people Israel are living securely, will you not know *it*? ¹⁵ You will come from your place out of the remote parts of the north, you and many peoples with you, all of them riding horses, a large assembly and a mighty army; ¹⁶ and you will come up against My people Israel like a cloud to cover the land. It shall come about in the last days that I will bring you against My land, so that the nations may know Me when I show Myself holy through you before their eyes, Gog."

¹⁷ 'This is what the Lord God says: "Are you the one of whom I spoke in former days through My servants the prophets of Israel, who prophesied in those days for *many* years that I would bring you against them? ¹⁸ It will come about on that day, when Gog comes against the land of Israel," declares the Lord God, "that My fury will mount up in My anger. ¹⁹ In My zeal and in My blazing wrath I declare *that* on that day there will certainly be a great earthquake in the land of Israel. ²⁰ The fish of the sea, the birds of the sky, the animals of the field, all the crawling things that crawl on the earth, and all mankind who are on the face of the earth will shake at My presence; and the mountains will be thrown down, the steep pathways will collapse, and every wall will fall to the ground. ²¹ And I will call for a sword against him on all My mountains," declares the Lord God. "Every man's sword will be against his brother. ²² With plague and with blood I will enter into judgment with him; and I will rain on him and on his troops, and on the many peoples who are with him, a torrential rain, hailstones, fire, and brimstone. ²³ So I will prove Myself great, show Myself holy, and make Myself known in the sight of many nations; and they will know that I am the Lord.'"

Ezekiel 39:1-16 goes on to describe the doom of Gog and Magog:

> "And you, son of man, prophesy against Gog and say, 'This is what the Lord God says: "Behold, I am against you, Gog, chief prince of Meshech and Tubal; ² and I will turn you around, lead you on a rope,

take you up from the remotest parts of the north, and bring you against the mountains of Israel.³ Then I will strike your bow from your left hand and make your arrows fall from your right hand. ⁴ You will fall on the mountains of Israel, you and all your troops, and the peoples who are with you; I will give you as food to every kind of predatory bird and animal of the field. ⁵ You will fall on the open field; for it is I who have spoken," declares the Lord God.⁶ "And I will send fire upon Magog and those who inhabit the coastlands in safety; and they will know that I am the Lord.

⁷ "And I will make My holy name known in the midst of My people Israel; and I will not allow My holy name to be profaned anymore. But the nations will know that I am the Lord, the Holy One in Israel.⁸ Behold, it is coming and it shall be done," declares the Lord God. "That is the day of which I have spoken.

⁹ "Then those who inhabit the cities of Israel will go out and make fires with the weapons and burn *them*, both bucklers and shields, bows and arrows, war clubs and spears, and for seven years they will make fires of them. ¹⁰ They will not take wood from the field or gather firewood from the forests, because they will make fires with the weapons; and they will take the spoils of those who plundered them and seize the plunder of those who plundered them," declares the Lord God.

¹¹ "On that day I will give Gog a burial place there in Israel, the valley of those who pass by east of the sea, and it will block the way of those who would pass by. So they will bury Gog there with all his horde, and they will call *it* the Valley of Hamon-gog. ¹² For seven months the house of Israel will be burying them in order to cleanse the land. ¹³ And all the people of the land will bury *them*; and it will be to their renown *on* the day that I appear in My glory," declares the Lord God. ¹⁴ "They will also select men who will constantly pass through the land, burying those who were passing through, those left on the surface of the ground, in order to cleanse it. At the end of seven months they will conduct a search. ¹⁵ As those who pass through the land pass through and anyone sees a human bone, then he will set up a marker by it until the burial detail has buried it in the Valley of Hamon-gog.¹⁶ And even *the* name of *the* city will be Hamonah. So they will cleanse the land.'"

In addition, in Revelations 2:12-13, we are told that Pergamum, Turkey, is where the Seat of Satan is. This country is also within the realm of Gog and Magog:

"And to the angel of the church in Pergamum write:

> The One who has the sharp two-edged sword says this:
>
> 13 'I know where you dwell, where **Satan's throne is**; and you hold firmly to My name, and did not deny My faith even in the days of Antipas, My witness, My faithful one, who was killed among you, where Satan dwells.

In this same chapter in Revelations 2:9, we read of a people falsely claiming to be "Jews," where it states "'I know your tribulation and your poverty (but you are rich), and the **slander by those who say they are Jews, and are not, but are a synagogue of Satan.**" In Revelations 3:9, we similarly read: "Behold, **I will make those of the synagogue of Satan, who say that they are Jews and are not, but lie**—I will make them come and bow down before your feet, and *make them* know that I have loved you."

No scripture is inconsequential. These scriptures point us to one reality: out of this region comes the principality of Gog of Magog. Given the context of the final battle with this entity, it is clear that from out of these regions comes "the end of the world." We cannot, thus, ignore the religious system that comes diametrically opposed to the truth of scripture and the people of scripture, one which switched the location of the Promised Land and changed the identity of the Chosen Ones. We also cannot ignore Esau's presence in this religious system, and the unholy alliance Esau has with Gog and Magog.

Edom in the End Times

Edom's links to the Mineans, Mandaeans and, ultimately, Judaism carries great end-time significance. 2nd Esdras is another book considered pseudepigrapha, although it is recognized as scripture by the Ethiopian Orthodox Church, and has fragments maintained in the Dead Sea Scrolls.[211]

---

[211] Timothy Jay Schwab, Anna Zamoranos, The Book of 2nd Esdras, The Levite Bible, Independently Published (2021).

2nd Esdras pronounces a prophecy about Edom that is attention-grabbing. As stated in 2nd Esdras 6:9, "For Esau is the end of the world, and Jacob is the beginning of it that followeth." This scripture tells us outrightly that Esau's significance did not end in the Old Testament but that Esau would be the end of the world, while Jacob would be the beginning that follows. We know that the Messiah, Yahusha, is of Jacob and that he will be Jacob's beginning that follows with the reign of Elohim. Until then, we live in a world Esau-ran and controlled.

As with all scripture, there is Biblical confirmation of this prophecy in Obadiah 1:1-10 reads:

> 1 The vision of Obadiah.
>
> This is what the Lord God says concerning Edom—
> We have heard a report from the Lord,
> And a messenger has been sent among the nations saying,
> "Arise, and let's go up against her for battle"—
> 2 "Behold, I will make you small among the nations;
> You are greatly despised.
> 3 The arrogance of your heart has deceived you,
> **The one who lives in the clefts of the rock,**
> **On the height of his dwelling place,**
> **Who says in his heart,**
> **'Who will bring me down to earth?'**
> 4 **Though you make your home high like the eagle,**
> **Though you set your nest among the stars,**
> **From there I will bring you down," declares the Lord.**
> 10 "Because of violence to your brother Jacob,
> Shame will cover you, And you will be eliminated forever
> 11 On the day that you stood aloof,
> On the day that strangers carried off his wealth,
> And foreigners entered his gate
> And cast lots for Jerusalem—
> You too were as one of them.
> 12 Do not gloat over your brother's day,
> The day of his misfortune.
> And do not rejoice over the sons of Judah
> On the day of their destruction;
> Yes, do not boast
> On the day of *their* distress.
> 13 Do not enter the gate of My people

On the day of their disaster.
You indeed, do not gloat over their catastrophe
On the day of their disaster.
And do not lay *a hand* on their wealth
On the day of their disaster.
¹⁴ Do not stand at the crossroads
To eliminate their survivors;
And do not hand over their refugees
On the day of their distress.
¹⁵ "For the day of the Lord is near for all the nations.
Just as you have done, it will be done to you.
Your dealings will return on your own head.
¹⁶ For just as you drank on My holy mountain,
All the nations will drink continually.
They will drink to the last drop,
And become as if they had never existed.
¹⁷ But on Mount Zion there will be those who escape,
And it will be holy.
And the house of Jacob will possess their property.
¹⁸ Then the house of Jacob will be a fire,
And the house of Joseph a flame;
But the house of Esau *will be* like stubble.
And they will set them on fire and consume them,
So that there will be no survivor of the house of Esau,"
For the Lord has spoken.
¹⁹ Then *those of* the Negev will possess the mountain of Esau,
And *those of* the Shephelah the Philistine *plain*;
Also, they will possess the territory of Ephraim and the territory of Samaria,
And Benjamin *the territory of* Gilead.
²⁰ And the exiles of this army of the sons of Israel,
Who are *among* the Canaanites as far as Zarephath,
And the exiles of Jerusalem who are in Sepharad,
Will possess the cities of the Negev.
²¹ **The deliverers will ascend Mount Zion**
To judge the mountain of Esau,
And the kingdom will be the Lord's.

This prophecy tells us that Esau would make his home high like the eagle and set his nest in the stars. It is evident this was not the Edom that was a tributary, who was a servant to Yahshar-el. This prophecy would have to pertain to Edom's future and present reality.

Chapter 8: The Real Yahshar-el

"Listen to the word of the Lord, you sons of Israel, Because the Lord has a case against the inhabitants of the land, For there is no faithfulness, nor loyalty, Nor knowledge of God in the land... My people are destroyed for lack of knowledge. Since you have rejected knowledge, I also will reject you from being My priest. Since you have forgotten the Law of your God, I also will forget your children."

~ Hosea 4:1, 6

We will now discuss the location of the true Yahshar-el (Israel). As has been stated, the landmass of Yahshar-el encompassed parts of the modern-day countries of Ethiopia, Eritrea, Sudan, and Djibouti. Much of what we know about the history of this region is shrouded in mystery; however, we do know that three powerful kingdoms controlled this region during Biblical times. Despite well-documented relationships with some of the most prominent empires, including the Egyptians, the Greeks and the Romans, all three kingdoms have largely disappeared from the history books. We will begin with the first kingdom, the mysterious "Land of Punt."

The Land of Punt

The ancient Egyptian civilization remains unrivaled. From architecture to technology and military might, the ancient Egyptians stand out as an empire that awes historians today, with a culture still copied and displayed throughout the world. Thus, to imagine another civilization so impressive that even the ancient Egyptians marveled at this land's beauty and resources, yet is largely forgotten today, is unfathomable. Such a kingdom did exist, and is known as the Land of Punt.

Egyptians first explored the Land of Punt when, Pharaoh Sesostris took a fleet of ships to the land on the shores of the Red Sea. This tradition of state visits to Punt would be kept by numerous other Pharaohs. During the reign of Pharaoh Pepi II Neferkare at about 2200 BCE, an expedition was made to the land of Punt. Queen Hatshepsut, who reigned 1472–1458 BCE, also traveled to

Punt and detailed her journey on the temple walls at Dayr al-Bahrī. The last recorded expedition to Punt occurred under Rameses III in the 12th century BCE. [212]

The Land of Punt was remarked as a "Divine Land" and called "the Land of the gods."[213] It was described by the Egyptians as rich in incense, ebony, gold and carried many exotic animals. However, despite this land's distinct features, no Egyptian Pharaoh detailed the exact location of Punt. Still, several possible locations have been put forth by academics over the years, most notably in Arabia and East Africa. While some Egyptian sources detail crossing the Red Sea to arrive at Punt, others imply that Punt could be reached by traveling south along the Nile through Nubia. The two routes to Punt were likely due to the southern passage being avoided when hostile kingdoms were blocking the closest route. The passage through the Red Sea has led many experts to conclude the Land of Punt must have been in Arabia. However, because the Egyptians also recorded taking the southern route to arrive at Punt, Arabia is incompatible. Therefore, Punt could not have been in Arabia but south of Egypt, in East Africa.[214] (See Map 12)

In the 1960s, Rolf Herzog conducted a detailed study of the flora and fauna mentioned in Queen Hatshepsut's records, wherein he located Punt as being along the Upper Nile River, south of Egypt, specifically between the Atbara River and the confluence of the White and Blue Niles. Scholar Kenneth Kitchen pointed out in 1971 that the fish that Hatshepsut's carvings depicted beneath Punt's ships, in addition to other marine creatures such as spiny lobster and squid, are recognizable as fish species that are to this day in the Red Sea. The most widely held consensus has been that the territory must

---

[212] Joshua J. Mark, Punt, World History Encyclopedia, (Aug. 11, 2011) https://www.worldhistory.org/punt/.
[213] Britannica, Punt, https://www.britannica.com/place/Punt-historical-region-Africa (*last visited* Aug. Jan. 22, 2024).
[214] *Supra* note 212.

have been from Sudan to Ethiopia.[215] Herzog's and Kitchens's conclusions put Punt right in the territory we have uncovered as Biblical Yahshar-el (Israel), which stretches from the Blue Nile to the Red Sea.

Based on what we know of Punt, the kingdom Punt began to appear somewhere between 2613 and 2498 BCE.[216] Rameses III's rule is the last to mention this mighty nation in the 12th century BCE.[217] From here, Punt vanishes from history, never to be seen or heard of again. Later, Punt was replaced by a new empire known today as D'mt, which became a significant kingdom by the 10th century BCE before disappearing from history around 300 BCE.[218] D'mt then is eventually eclipsed by a kingdom more known to the modern world yet still shrouded in mystery, known as Aksum. This kingdom declined in influence and splintered by the 10th century CE.[219]

This timeline of the region is nothing short of remarkable. The Bible tells us of the Land of Canaan, which first occupied the Promised Land before being destroyed. Then, Yahshar-el took control of the land and ruled before being taken into the Babylonian and Assur captivities. Later, the exiled tribe of Yahudah (Judah) returns to the land. Comparing the timelines of these kingdoms, we can ascertain that the Land of Punt, which disappeared from history, is what we know today as the Land of Canaan.[220] D'mt, the kingdom that is formed in place of Punt is Yahshar-el. This kingdom weakened under the Assur and Babylonian captivities, wherein only a remnant of Yahshar-el remained or returned. Aksum, the kingdom formed in

---

[215] Peter Tyson, Where Is Punt?, PBS, (Dec. 1, 2009) https://www.pbs.org/wgbh/nova/article/egypt-punt/.
[216] Punt Timeline, World History Encyclopedia, https://www.worldhistory.org/timeline/punt/ (*last visited* Oct. 13, 2023).
[217] *Supra* note 212.
[218] Ethiopia, Britannica, https://www.britannica.com/place/Ethiopia/Sports-and-recreation#ref419476 (*last visited* Oct. 14, 2023).
[219] Aksum, Britannica, (Aug 22, 2023), https://britannica.com/place/Aksum-ancient-kingdom-Africa.
[220] Canaan Timeline, World History Encyclopedia (*last visited* Oct. 13, 2023), https://www.worldhistory.org/timeline/canaan/.

place of D'mt, is what we know as "Judea," the Yahudi (Judean) resettlement. However, unlike the history Josephus records, the real Yahudah was not destroyed in 70AD.

	TIMELINE		
	Canaan	**Yahshar-el**	**Yahudah or "Judea"**
Estimates According to Bible "Experts"	Destroyed 1250 BCE - 1150 BCE	Assyrian Captivity 722 BCE Babylonian Captivity 586 BCE	Return from Captivity 516 BCE
	Punt	**Dm't**	**Aksum**
According to History	Disappears from History after 1493 BCE	Disappears from History by 300 BCE	Appears by 300 BCE

Dm't: Yahshar-el & Yahudah

History has preserved very little information on the Land of Punt. This is even more the case with D'mt. Despite this empire forming later, as few inscriptions have survived and few archeological excavations have taken place, information on D'mt is minimal. Essentially, what is known about D'mt is the following.

    D'mt (Di'amat or Damont) is known to have existed in the Northern Ethiopia region of Tigray and Eritrea, becoming a regional power by roughly 950 BCE. One of the kingdom's capitals, is believed to have been Yeha, as a temple to the god Ilmuqah was built there around 800 BCE.[221] This area's climate experienced rainfall patterns, making the soil fertile and suitable for herding livestock and

---

[221] A summary of Ethiopian History- 5,000 years in 3,000 words, Ethiopian Adventure Tours, https://www.ethiopianadventuretours.com/about-ethiopia/ethiopian-history (*last visited* Oct 16, 2023); The Kingdom of Aksum, National Geographic,

agriculture, and thus, a pastoral population occupied this region. [222] There is evidence this was a complex agricultural kingdom that built irrigation schemes, used plows, grew cereal grains such as millet, and made iron tools and weapons. The kingdom obtained prominence trading ivory, tortoiseshell, rhinoceros horn, gold, silver and enslaved people with South Arabian merchants. [223] We also know to some degree this culture was influenced by a Sabean culture of Yemen, although to what degree is debated.

Even with our sparse information on this kingdom, some key details support the location of D'mt as Yahshar-el. According to Enclylopedia.com:

> The D'mt kingdom was a powerful and prosperous African kingdom that ruled for over 200 years. Located in what is today Ethiopia, the kingdom of D'mt was one of the most influential political entities that emerged during Africa's "era of kingdoms" from the 14th to 19th centuries. The ruling dynasty was believed to have been founded by two brothers and traced its lineage through ten ruling families. The people who resided within the boundaries of this great realm were known as Oromo or Wolamo as they referred to themselves, and their language was called Afaan Oromo.[224]

This narrative of ten ruling families founding D'mt is eerily similar to the Bible's 12 Tribes of Yahshar-el. Archeologist Rodolfo Fattovich also believed there to be a division in D'mt between the northern and southern regions.[225] From the biblical account, we know that this split occurred when Yahshar-el, the southern kingdom, split off from Yahudah (Judah), the northern kingdom. It is also very telling that the port city of Adulis, according to legend, was founded by escaped

---

https://education.nationalgeographic.org/resource/kingdom-aksum/10th-grade/ (*last visited* Jan. 18, 2024).
[223] Britannica, Ethiopia, https://www.britannica.com/place/Ethiopia/Sports-and-recreation#ref419476 (*last visited* Oct. 14, 2023).
[224] EthiopCylopedia, Damot Kingdom, http://ethiocyclopedia.com/damot.html (*last visited* Aug. 23, 2023).
[225] Dʻmt or Damot Kingdom Ethiopia, OrignalPeople.Org (Nov. 15, 2021) https://originalpeople.org/d%CA%BFmt-or-damot-kingdom-ethiopia/#cite_note-4.

Egyptian slaves.[226] Also, two Sabaean inscriptions have been uncovered at separate temples in the Adi Kaweh settlement, specifically describing Black Hebrews.[227]

Scholars do not know why or how, but D'mt declined in prominence around 500 BCE before completely deteriorating into smaller kingdoms sometime after 300 BCE.[228] This timeline conforms to what is known of the timeframe of Yahshar-el and Yahudah, who became a powerhouse under King Solomon around 950 BCE before the southern Kingdom was conquered by Assur around 700 BCE. The northern kingdom of Yahudah, however, continued in power until around 500 BCE.[229]

Aksum: The Return from Captivity

The Bible does not mention what happened after the Babylonian and Assur captivities. We know there was a return from captivity for Yahudah and a rebuilding of Solomon's temple that was destroyed by Nebuchadnezzar. However, the Bible does not tell us what government was instituted after the return from exile. Instead, Bible scholars have accepted the history that is recorded in the Book of Maccabees (not included in the Dead Sea Scrolls) and from Josephus.

Sometime after the fall of D'mt, Aksum arose as the empire that would dominate the region. Like D'mt, Aksum is known to have been principally located in Ethiopia's Tigray region and Eritrea, exercising

---

[226] Ed Whelan, Slave Trade and Exotic Animals Made the Ancient Port of Adulis Rich, Ancient Origins, (Sept 28, 2019) https://www.ancient-origins.net/ancient-places-africa/adulis-0012642.

[227] Bernard Leeman, Nubian Moses, Ethiopian Exodus, Arabian Solomon: Reconstructing the Old Testament Narrative, Queen of Sheba University, (Aug. 2, 2015), 11.

[228] *Supra* note 221; David Baker, Ancient Agrarian Societies: Aksum, World History Project.

[229] Kingdom of Israel Timeline, World History Encyclopedia, https://www.worldhistory.org/timeline/Kingdom_of_Israel/ (*last visited* Jan. 18, 2024)

administrative and economic control that extended to modern-day Djibouti and Somalia.[230] (See Map 13.1-13.2) Many experts believe that Aksum, from the outset, was ruled by the Sabeans of Saba. [231]

A Persian writer described Aksum as one of the four greatest powers in the world at the time. It was a wealthy civilization that thrived for centuries and controlled access to vast trade routes linked to the Roman Empire, Arabia and India. Gold and ivory were their most valuable exports as well as, tortoise shells, rhinoceros' horns, frankincense, myrrh, emeralds, salt, live animals and enslaved people.[232]

The Aksumites developed Africa's only surviving indigenous written script used today, Ge'ez.[233] However, while written scripts existed, no histories or thorough descriptions of this civilization have survived. Aksum was also the first African country to mint its gold, silver, and bronze coins, all of which were the standard weights used in the Roman Empire. [234] Aksum also stands out as becoming the first Christian kingdom in the 4th Century.[235] However, according to legend, the kingdom would collapse in 960 CE after a Jewish Queen sacked the empire burning its literature and churches. [236]

---

[230] *Supra* note 221, The Kingdom of Aksum.
[231] *Id.*
[232] *Id.*
[233] The British Museum, The Kingdom of Aksum, https://smarthistory.org/the-kingdom-of-aksum/ (*last visited* Jan 18, 2024).
[234] *Supra* note 230.
[235] Mario Alexis Portella, Ethiopia – The First Christian Nation?, Latin Mass, (2015)
[236] Gudit, Dictionary of African Christian Biography, https://dacb.org/stories/ethiopia/gudit/ (*last visited* Oct. 16, 2023).

Chapter 9: The First Jewish State

"Jerusalem will be trampled underfoot by the Gentiles until the times of the Gentiles are fulfilled."

~Luke 21:24

We have demonstrated that the roots of Judaism are found with Mandaeans in Palestine. According to the New Testament, Jewish groups such as the Pharisees and the Sadducees imposed their religion on the people of Yahudah (Judah). They were believed to have been given a protectorate status by the Roman Empire. The biggest hole in this story is the issue of the Roman presence, as there is no clear history of Rome's empire extending to a territory in East Africa or south of Egypt. However, while the record is scarce, there is sufficient evidence of Rome's push to occupy this territory during this period.

A Roman Protectorate?

There is clear evidence that the Romans ruled over Palestine. However, there is no evidence of a Roman protectorate colony in East Africa or south of Egypt. To deal with this issue, we should first consider what the Bible does and does not tell us about the Roman presence in and around Yahudah (Judah). For this discussion, the reader must separate tradition from reality. Most Bible believers have been enshrouded with the image of Yahudah being in a Roman setting with Roman garrisons stationed throughout the region to the point where many see Yahudah as Roman. However, this is not substantiated by scripture.

Rome in Scripture

The four gospels of the New Testament do attest to a Roman presence and authority in the region; however, they do not go into detail about what this relationship entailed. One supposed reference is in the book of Mark 12:12-17:

> Then they *sent some of the Pharisees and Herodians to Him in order to trap Him in a statement. ¹⁴ They came and *said to Him, "Teacher, we know that You are truthful and do not care what anyone thinks; for You are not partial to anyone, but You teach the way of God in truth. Is it permissible to pay a poll-tax to Caesar, or not? ¹⁵ Are we to pay, or not pay?" But He, knowing their hypocrisy, said to them, "Why are you testing Me? Bring Me a denarius to look at." ¹⁶ And they brought *one*. And He *said to them, "Whose image and inscription is this?" And they said to Him, "Caesar's." ¹⁷ And Jesus said to them, "Pay to Caesar the things that are Caesar's, and to God the things that are God's." And they were utterly amazed at Him.

The Greek word for Caesar is *Kaisar*, which is not specific to a Roman emperor but means generally an emperor, a ruler, or a dictator.[237] Thus, it cannot be determined by this scripture if it was referring to a Roman emperor or another ruler at the time.

There is also the mention of Romans in John 11:48, where the Pharisees say, "If we let Him go on like this, all the people will believe in Him, and the Romans will come and take over both our place and our nation." This scripture is vague as to what the Roman relationship to Yahudah was. For example, we should remember the War Scroll of the Dead Sea Scrolls, where one of the purposes of saving Yahshar-el (Israel) was to reestablish the nation so that it would defeat the Romans in a final battle. This verse could be referring to that battle against Roman dominance over Yahudah.

The only gospel that explicitly denotes a Roman colony of Yahshar-el is the gospel of Luke. Luke 2:1-7 states:

> Now in those days a decree went out from Caesar Augustus, that a census be taken of all the inhabited earth. 2 This was the first census taken while Quirinius was governor of Syria. 3 And all the people were on their way to register for the census, each to his own city. 4 Now Joseph also went up from Galilee, from the city of Nazareth, to Judea, to the city of David which is called Bethlehem, because he was

---

[237]Kaiser, Online Etymology Dictionary, https://www.etymonline.com/word/kaiser (*last visited* Jan. 18, 2024).

of the house and family of David, 5 in order to register along with Mary, who was betrothed to him, and was pregnant. 6 While they were there, the time came for her to give birth. 7 And she gave birth to her firstborn son; and she wrapped Him in cloths, and laid Him in a manger, because there was no room for them in the inn.

This passage has caused many historians to accuse Luke of a historical blunder, as no census is recorded to have happened in all of the Roman Empire under Augustus during this time, and even if it had, a Roman census would not require people to travel to their ancestors' homes. In addition, "Galilee" of Palestine was under a different district than "Judea" under Herod Antipas. However, there was a census dated to 6 CE known as the Census of Quirinius, as attested to by Josephus. It is believed this census sparked a Jewish revolt.[238]

Some Bible believers will automatically dismiss the idea this passage could contain a historical inaccuracy due to the Bible inerrancy doctrine. However, we must remember "scripture" is that which is *God-breathed*. Probably the most distinguishing aspect of the Gospel of Luke from the other three gospels is the introduction. Luke 1:1-4 states:

> Since many have undertaken to compile an account of the things accomplished among us, 2 just as they were handed down to us by those who from the beginning were eyewitnesses and servants of the word, 3 it seemed fitting to me as well, having investigated everything carefully from the beginning, to write it out for you in an orderly sequence, most excellent Theophilus; 4 so that you may know the exact truth about the things you have been taught.

Here are some essential details: Luke's writer is not identified as an eyewitness to his writing but rather as an investigator and chronicler of other's accounts. It is also important to note that this chronicling was not necessarily for outside distribution but

---

[238] N. F. Gier, Serious Problems with Luke's Census, *excerpted from* God, Reason, and the Evangelicals, University Press of America, https://www.webpages.uidaho.edu/ngier/census.htm, (1987) 145-49.

to a person named Theophilus, something that sets Luke apart from the other gospels and most other books of the Bible. The necessary question is, what sources did Luke use in chronicling this information? Most Bible scholars believe most of the materials contained in the Gospels of Luke and Matthew draw from the Gospel of Mark and another common source.[239] However, it is also possible that Luke's source for the census was Josephus.

Luke and John's gospels were written to a gentile audience and are believed to be the last two completed. The consensus in Bible academia is that Luke and Acts were written together as two parts to a series by the same author. Most Bible scholars date these books to 80-90 CE; however, a growing number have dated them to 110-120 CE. The first reason is Acts was seemingly unknown before the last half of the 2nd century. Second, the author of Luke seems to use some material from Josephus as a source, and Josephus did not complete *the Antiquities of the Jews* until 93-94 CE. Third, the author of Acts was seemingly aware of Paul's letters, or at least the letter to Galatians, due to similarities between Acts 15 and Galatians 2.[240]

If Josephus was a source of the Gospel of Luke, then the gentile author of the book who compiled this narrative may have, in good faith, drawn from a source who self-identified as a Yahudi (Judean) but was an imposter. However, acknowledging this historical detail of a census as incorrect does not negate the entirety of Luke's account, much of which details the works and teachings of the messiah, which are in fact *God-breathed*.

Other than these mentions in the Gospels, we read in the Book of Acts of the Apostle Paul being arrested in Yerushalem (Jerusalem)

---

[239] Sarah E. Rollens, Did the Authors of the Canonical Gospels Know Each Other?, Bible Odyssey, https://www.bibleodyssey.org/articles/did-the-authors-of-the-canonical-gospels-know-each-other/ (*last visited* Dec. 8, 2023).

[240] Joseph B. Tyson, When and Why Was the Acts of the Apostles Written?, Southern Methodist University, (Apr. 2011) https://bibleinterp.arizona.edu/opeds/actapo358006.

and then turned over to Roman jurisprudence once it is discovered Paul is a Roman citizen by birth.[241] This makes it clear that there was a Roman presence in Yahudah, however the nature of this presence is not established by scripture alone.

Rome in East Africa

History does not record a Roman protectorate or client territory in East Africa. However, history records a Roman presence in the region and southern Arabia that coincides with the timeline of the establishment of the Yahudah colony. Still, not much is known about the Roman's interactions within East Africa during this period, similar to the founding of Aksum which is shrouded in mystery.

There were two directions from where the Romans could have encountered Aksum: from the north through Egypt and Kush or from the south through Arabia and Yemen. Starting with the Roman presence in Kush, Queen Amanirenas of Kush, who ruled from 25-21 BCE, had ongoing clashes with the Romans who controlled Egypt. On September 2, 31 BCE, the Battle of Actium occurred, where the fleet of Mark Antony and Cleopatra was defeated by Roman Emperor Octavian Augustus, who then annexed Egypt into the Roman Empire. The Romans then set their sights on the empire of Kush and encroached on the land of Nubia. During the Nubian occupation, the Romans made Nubia a tributary and enforced high taxation on the people of Meroë. However, the Romans temporarily withdrew some troops from Nubia for a campaign in Arabia. Amanirenas' forces struck back and captured the Roman-occupied cities of Aswan, Philae and Elephantine, plundering the towns and taking Roman slaves.[242]

---

[241] Acts 21-23.
[242] Hai Mora, The Nubian Queen Who Fought Back Caesar's Army, History.com (Mar. 23, 2022) https://www.history.com/news/nubian-queen-amanirenas-roman-army.

Queen Amanirenas, who bravely defended her empire by preventing the Romans from conquering Kush, stifled Roman ambitions of gaining an East African empire and forced the Romans to the negotiation table. A peace treaty was signed between Rome and Kush from 21-29 BCE where the Meroites were exempted from paying tribute to the Emperor, and the Romans withdrew from the Second Cataract to Maharaqqa.[243]

While it is conceivable the Romans may have interacted with Aksum during their occupation of Meroe, given the Sabean presence in Aksum, it would seem more palpable that the Romans established a relationship with Aksum through their military campaign in Arabia. The Romans were actively working to extend their empire into Arabia at the same time they were campaigning to conquer Kush. Had they been successful, the result would have been the empire connecting Egypt and Arabia, which would have immensely propelled their power in the region.

The Romans first aspired to conquer the Arabian Peninsula under Emperor Octavian. According to Strabo, a Greek geographer, after the conquest of Egypt in 30 BCE, 120 Roman shops captured Eudaemon, a port city in present-day Aden, Yemen. The Romans renamed the city Arabia Felix and aspired to conquer all of Sheba, especially as the Sabeans controlled the monopoly on trade in the region and prevented merchants from Alexandra (including Romans) from entering the Bab el Mandeb Straight. [244]

Under the command of Gaius Aelius Gallus, the prefect in Egypt, from 26-24 BCE, the Romans organized an expedition along with their close allies, the northern Arabian Nabataeans, who acted as guides. The Nabateans ruled the southern levant and northern Arabia,

---

[243] Amanirenas – Fearless Queen Of Kush Who Defeated Ancient Romans, Ancient Pages, (January 30, 2019) https://www.ancientpages.com/2019/01/30/amanirenas-brave-one-eyed-queen-of-kush-defeated-ancient-romans/.
[244] Vedran Bileta, The Roman Empire and Ancient Africa: Trading with East Africa, The Collector, Jan. 10, 2023), https://www.thecollector.com/rome-trade-ancient-africa/.

including the Edomite location Ma'an in Petra, which would soon become a client-state to the Roman empire. [245]

The Romans conquered Negra, Amnestrum, Neska, Maguza, Tammakum and Labecyja during the expedition. However, at this point Gallus decided to retreat when faced with a lack of regular deliveries. This expedition ended in defeat, the invaders were driven back and Gallus moved the remnants of his troops back to Egypt. There was also later a clash between the Romans and Arabs in 1 BCE after the Roman Navy destroyed the port of Aden for failure to respect the terms of peace.[246]

We thus know the Romans were conducting military campaigns around the vicinity of Aksum before and during the time of Yahusha (Jesus). In addition to the military campaigns, there is more evidence of a Roman connection to Aksum. A significant excavation in the ancient city of Aksum revealed treasures and artifacts that go back to the 1st and 2nd century CE.[247] In addition, King Zoscales of Aksum, who ruled in the 1st century CE, was known to speak and write in Greek, along with Aksum's elite class who adopted Greek for both economic and cultural prominence. Hellenic influences on the region were so strong that until the early 4th century CE, nearly all inscriptions were made in Greek.[248]

---

[245] Imperium Romanum, Romans on the Arabian Peninsula, https://imperiumromanum.pl/en/article/romans-on-arabian-peninsula/amp/, (*last visited* Nov. 23, 2023).

[246] Imperium Romanum, Romans on the Arabian Peninsula, https://imperiumromanum.pl/en/article/romans-on-arabian-peninsula/amp/, (last visited Nov. 23, 2023).

[247] April Holloway, Amazing Jewels and Artifacts Found in 2,000-year-old Ethiopian grave reveal link to Rome, Ancient Origins, (June 8, 2015), https://www.ancient-origins.net/news-history-archaeology/amazing-jewels-and-artifacts-found-2000-year-old-ethiopian-grave-020381.

[248] http://www.madote.com/2013/08/the-ancestors-of-tigrinya-people.html, citing The Archaeology of Ancient Eritrea by Peter R. Schmidt, Mattew C. Curtis and Zelalem Teka, p.302.; Eritrea: A Pawn in World Politics by Okbazghi Yohannes, p. 24

Thus, history records Rome waging expeditions close to Aksum in Arabia and to the north in Kush around the time of the New Testament. Roman garrisons frequented the region and even held occupation in Arabia and Kush. Because the historical records on Aksum have vanished, a Roman occupation or operational posts in Aksum can only be presumed based on the Biblical texts.

The Sabeans Move into East Africa

There is another possibility on the Roman occupation in Yahudah (Judah). That is that it was not Roman at all, but was actually Sabean. While the issue may seem highly implausible, if Bible translators were willing to change the names of locations to fit Palestine, it is conceivable they would be willing to change the empire overlording Yahshar-el as well to accommodate Palestinian history.

The earliest account of Yahusha (Jesus) not in the Bible was by Thallus, a Roman historian who around 50 CE is recorded to have written about Yahusha's death. Not much is known about Thallus, including where or when he wrote this account, as the account itself is no longer in existence. Julius Africanus, a Libyan who lived from 160-240 CE is the closest reference we have to Thallus's commentary.[249] Other Roman references were a considerable time after the resurrection and thus could not have been firsthand accounts.[250] Thus, outside of the Biblical text, firsthand information on Yahusha is nonexistent.

Whether the Romans power extended to Aksum, or not, the Sabeans were the most immediate foreign hand ruling Aksum. The Saba

---

[249] Dionysius, Thallus, & others — Darkness at the crucifixion of Christ, Never Thirsty, https://www.neverthirsty.org/bible-qa/qa-archives/question/dionysius-thallus-darkness-at-the-crucifixion-of-christ/ (last visited Jan. 17, 2024)

[250] Bryan Windle, Top Ten Historical References to Jesus Outside of the Bible, Bible Archeology Report, (Nov. 18, 2022) https://biblearchaeologyreport.com/2022/11/18/top-ten-historical-references-to-jesus-outside-of-the-bible/

Empire of modern-day Yemen exuded great influence in the ancient world. However, today we can only see remnants of their dominance from their impressive agriculture, such as the Ma'rib Dam, the oldest known dam in the world. Much of Saba's prominence was obtained due to their control of trade routes over both water and land.[251]

The Sabeans supplanted the Minaeans in orchestrating trade in the region across the Red Sea and up and down the Nile River through their highly lucrative "Incense Routes." It wasn't until Egypt, under the Ptolemaic Dynasty, decided to cut out the middleman and trade directly with the coastal city of Qani that Saba lost their dominance. Saba continued to be a powerful kingdom however from 950 BCE to 275 CE.[252] Throughout this time, Sabeans were heavily present in modern-day Ethiopia, even before the establishment of Aksum. There is also evidence that the Sabeans may have established Aksum.[253]

The pre-Aksumite period of Ethiopia, from 500-300 BCE, has been characterized as one with a profound Sabean influence.[254] On the biblical timeline, this corresponds to a new people entering Yahshar-el during the captivity of the Kingdom of Assur. As stated in 2 Kings 17:24:

> Then the king of Assyria brought *people* from Babylon, Cuthah, Avva, Hamath, and Sepharvaim, and settled *them* in the cities of Samaria in place of the sons of Israel. So they took possession of Samaria and lived in its cities.

Sabaeans began migrating from the area surrounding their capital, Marib, into modern-day southeast Eritrea and the Tigray region of northern Ethiopia. They brought their South Arabian culture and technology, creating a cultural landscape known as Ethio-Sabaean,

---

[251] Kingdom of Saba Timeline, World History Encyclopedia, https://www.worldhistory.org/timeline/Kingdom_of_Saba/ (*last visited* Jan. 18, 2024).
[252] *Id.*
[253] Rodolfo Fattovich, Pre-Aksumite Civilization of Ethiopia: A Provisional Review, Proceedings of the Seminar for Arabian Studies, vol. 7, (1977), 73–78.
[254] *Id.*

which extends to areas along the trade routes from Adulis to the Tigrinian Highlands. Aspects of the South Arabian culture in Ethiopia are apparent in architecture, epigraphic documents written in the ancient South Arabian alphabet, forms of religion and rule.[255] One such example is the Yeha Temple, the modern location of an Ethiopian Orthodox Tewahedo Church monastery built in Sabean style. As archeologist Rodolfo Fattovich attested:

> The monuments at Yéha and Kāskāsé exhibit some typical South Arabian
> features, such as the podium with steps (Yéha; Marib, Hureida), the square pillars such with big rectangular bases (Yéha, Kāskāsé, Hawlti, Marib, Gebun, etc.), the pecked stone slabs (Yéha, Marib, Hureida) and building decorations. In particular, the temple at Yéha is comparable with the temple C at Hureida (which is later in time), the temple at el-Mesagid and the 'Mausoleum' at Marib; the portico of the palace at Yéha is like the ones of the oval temple at Marib and the temple of Atar at Timna. Finally, an inside wall under the floor of the third level in the 'palace' at Yéha
> is built within the same technique of the walls of the oval temple at Marib, with two layers of rectangular sterne slabs and a pebble filling.
>
> From the paleographical and linguistic point of view, the monumental inscriptions perfectly correspond to the Sabean ones, as we have already stated. The ibex frieze along the edge of the baldachin on the "throne' from Hawlti is typically, South Arabian too. The votive altars are very common in South Arabia. The offering tables with l km head spouts are frequent at Marib. Cylindrical and cubic altars have been found.[256]

The inscriptions prove that Sabean was the official language in northern Ethiopia at this time. Thus, a total assimilation took place of the indigenous population into Sabean culture. The question is, how is it possible that a foreign power could completely erase and take dominance over an indigenous population absent war? Experts have proposed three hypotheses to explain the Sabean takeover: 1) simple

---

[255] The Pre-Aksumite Site of Yeha (1st Half of 1st Millennium BC) in the Highlands of Northern Ethiopia: Studies on Ancient Water Use and Irrigation Techniques, Topoi, https://www.topoi.org/project/a-1-6/ (*last visited* Jan. 18, 2024).
[256] *Supra* note 253.

migration, 2) Sabean colonization, and 3) acculturation. Based on the Biblical account, we can ascertain the answer is a mixture of the three.

The Habasha Abyssinians

Modern-day Ethiopia and Eritrea together have tribal diversity that exists alongside a glaring ethnic line. At the root of this contentious landscape is an ancient division that originates with the induction of Sabeans into the African continent. This division drives many of the country's major conflicts, and historical suppression has caused lasting resentment that often unearths through political upheavals.

While there are strong claims made by numerous tribal groups as to which are genuinely indigenous to Ethiopia, it is primarily agreed among experts that those tribes from a group known as *Habasha*, also known as the Abyssinians (Abesha), are descendants of Sabeans. As stated by the website Africa 101 Last Tribes:

> Before the 20th century, the Sabean theory was the most common one explaining the origins of the Habesha. It was first suggested by Hiob Ludolf and revived by early 20th-century Italian scholar Conti Rossini. They said that at an early epoch, South Arabian tribes, including one called the Habashat, emigrated across the Red Sea from Yemen to Eritrea. According to this theory, the Sabaeans brought South Arabian letters and language, which gradually evolved into the Ge'ez language and Ge'ez script. Linguists have revealed, however, that although its script developed from Epigraphic South Arabian (whose oldest inscriptions are found in Yemen, Ethiopia and Eritrea) used to write the Old South Arabian languages, Ge'ez is descended from a different branch of Semitic.[257]

In addition, Bymagn Nyang of the Sudan Tribune wrote regarding this group:

> It was documented that around first century A.D., some Hamitic-Semitic peoples (Sabaean traders) from South Arabian came into

---

[257] Habesha, Africa 101 Last Tribes, https://www.101lasttribes.com/tribes/habesha.html (*last visited* Jan. 18, 2024).

contact with native people and intermarried. Their off-springs were referred to as "Habesha", which means "people of mixed blood". Their land (Tigray, Begemdir, Gojam, Northern Shewa, and Welo) was later termed Abyssinia.[258]

The earliest inscriptions mentioning the Habesha deal with wars, alliances and peace treaties among rivaling Yemeni kingdoms during wars between the rival Himyarite and Saba kingdoms. According to epigraphist and historian Dr. Eduard Glaser, Habeshas were originally from southeastern Yemen, in the modern district of Mahra, but took on a dominant role in Ethiopia in what could only be labeled as colonialism.[259] As also attested to by Asafa Jalata, professor at the Department of Sociology at the University of Tennessee:

> *Habasha* settler colonialism developed five forms of institutions in Oromia: the *katamas* (garrison cities), which were an integral component of a larger grid of towns, slavery, the *balabat*[2] system, the *nafxanya-gabbar* system, and the colonial landholding system. The *Habasha* colonial settlers hierarchically organized the *katamas* in Oromia as their main geopolitical centers for practicing political domination through various control agencies, wealth and capital accumulation, and religious and cultural dissemination. The colonialists used the *katamas* as nerve centers of the colonial system for implementing colonial political, economic, and ideological programs; they were hierarchically organized as the principal, provincial, and subdistrict towns so that chains of command would flow from the center to the local level without any interruption. These garrison towns were established in strategically and politically secured places and became centers of regional rule and trade networks connecting various parts of Oromia to Ethiopia and Europe. They constituted nodal points of a more extensive countrywide network of towns that, woven, territorially organized the relational structure of Ethiopia's political economy, including the colonialist rule and the flow of products. The garrison cities were geopolitical headquarters. The colonialists dispatched soldiers to impose colonial rule through enslavement, subjugation, and appropriation of the primary means of production, such as cattle, land, and other valuables.

---

[258] Bymagn Nyang, The difference between Ethiopian and Habesha, Sudan Tribune (Feb. 17, 2009) https://sudantribune.com/article30090/.
[259] The True Origin of Habesha, Madote, http://www.madote.com/2013/01/the-true-origin-of-habesha.html?m=1 (*last visited* Oct. 23, 2023).

Through these centers, expropriated goods flowed for local consumption and an international market.[260]

During the age of colonialism, European missionaries, explorers and merchants chose to collaborate with the Habasha elite by convincing their governments to support the Habashas against the Oromo and others they considered "pagan" and "savage."[261] Today, the Habasha people are mostly comprised of three major ethnic groups in the Eritrean and Ethiopian Highlands: the Amhara, Tigray, and Gurage peoples, about 35.5% of Ethiopia's population. Tigrayans make up 85% of Eritrea's population. [262]

The Kebra Negast

One tradition that solidified Habasha rule in the consciousness of many, not just in Ethiopia but globally through movements such as the UNIA and the Rastafari, is the legend of the imperial family's bloodline who claimed descent from Solomon and the Queen of Sheba named Makeda. In 1225 CE, a narrative was written of this story known as the *Kebra Negast* or "Glory of Kings." In this account, the famous story of the Queen of Sheba visiting Yahshar-el's (Israel's) King Solomon results in Solomon seducing Makeda and impregnating her with Menelik I, the first Emperor of Ethiopia. While this legend is believed to be indigenous to Ethiopia, the story of the Queen of Sheba ruling Ethiopia was initially told by Josephus in *Antiquities of the Jews*:

> The Ethiopians were in danger of being reduced to slavery and all sorts of destruction, and at length, they retired to Saba, which was a royal city of Ethiopia, which Cambyses afterward named Mero, after the name of his own sister. The place was to be besieged with very great difficulty, since it was both encompassed by the Nile quite round... for the city was situate in a retired place, and was inhabited

---

[260] Asafa Jalata, Review Essay: Are the Tulama and Wallo Oromo Habasha?, Scientific Research, (Oct. 2021) https://www.scirp.org/journal/paperinformation.aspx?paperid=112398.
[261] *Id.*
[262] *Supra* note 257.

after the manner of an island, being encompassed with a strong wall, and having the rivers to guard them from their enemies, and having great ramparts between the wall and the rivers, insomuch, that when the waters come with the greatest violence, it can never be drowned; which ramparts make it next to impossible for even such as are gotten over the rivers to take the city.[263]

... There was then a woman queen of Egypt and Ethiopia; she was inquisitive into philosophy, and one that on other accounts also was to be admired. When this queen heard of the virtue and prudence of Solomon, she had a great mind to see him... So when this queen of Ethiopia had obtained what we have already given an account of, and had again communicated to the king what she brought with her, she returned to her own kingdom. ...[264]

Josephus's account has no primary archaeological or textual support. The ruins at Aksum are a thousand years too late for a queen contemporary with Solomon to have ruled Ethiopia.[265] It seems more plausible that the story of the Queen of Sheba ruling Ethiopia was an attempt by Josephus to distract from Ethiopia and the other surrounding East African countries' real legacy as being the true Yahshar-el.

Beta Israel

According to the Gospels account, at some point, a pious Jewish South Arabian group settled in the region, carrying their religious system founded in Palestine. A shadow of this presence can be observed from the religious group known today as Beta Israel. Judaism may have entered Arabia and Saba using the same routes the Minaeans traveled to enter Palestine. A strong Jewish presence entered Arabia at an early stage, which is evidenced by Medina being under the control of the Ansar tribe. The two main clans of this tribe,

---

[263] Flavius Josephus, Antiquities of the Jews, Book 2 & 8, (93-94 CE).
[264] *Id.* Book 2.
[265] *Supra* note 260.

the Aws and Khazraj, along with other groups were known to be Jewish.²⁶⁶

Records referring to Judaism have been unearthed from the Himyarite Kingdom, which was established in Yemen in 110 BCE. This same Himyarite kingdom would become a significant destination of Judaism. The Christian missionary Theophilos when coming to Yemen in the mid-fourth century even complained about the great numbers of Jews he encountered.²⁶⁷

Beta Israel, known in Ge'ez as *Falasha* which means "strangers," historically inhabited the northwestern areas of the Ethiopian highlands. They practice a Pre-Talmudic Judaism and are known to have Habasha or Abyssinian origins. Interestingly, DNA testing has also shown the Falasha have origins in Sudan (ancient Edom).²⁶⁸ As genetic researcher Ibrahim Omer attests:

> the observed phenotypes of the Beta Israel-Ethiopian Jews today strongly reflect the features of the riverine Northern Sudanese populations. To a lesser proportion, they reflect the phenotypes commonly found among the mainstream Habash-Abyssinian populations of what is today northern Ethiopia." ²⁶⁹

Today, Beta Israel is only a remnant in Ethiopia, with most of the community "repatriating" to the state of Israel from the 1970s-1990s. The group, which became the subject of persecution in Ethiopia, where Abyssinian law prevented them from owning land, was at one

---

[266] John Martin, The First Arrow of Islam: The Confluence of Politics, Religion, and Culture in the Battle of Badr, Air University, (2010) https://apps.dtic.mil/sti/tr/pdf/AD1020049.pdf.
[267] Eric Maroney, The Other Zions: The Lost Histories of Jewish Nations, Rowman & Littlefield, (2010), 93.
[268] Bernard Leeman, Nubian Moses, Ethiopian Exodus, Arabian Solomon, Sheba University College, (Aug. 2, 2015), 15.
[269] Ibrahim Omer, Evidence mounts of ancient Jewish roots of Beta Israel Ethiopian Jewry, Genetic Literary Project, (June 16, 2015) https://geneticliteracyproject.org/2015/06/16/evidence-mounts-of-ancient-jewish-roots-of-beta-israel-ethiopian-jewry/.

point influential in Aksum. However, over time, the community became relatively reclusive with restricted interaction with outsiders and intermarriage strongly prohibited. According to the testimony by a Beta Israelite in the 1890s:

> Formerly we were very numerous; formerly there were 200 synagogues, now only 30 remain. In the time of the Dervishes [Sudanese- Mahadist invaders] a frightful number of people died from famine…. We are in great misery. Our books have been destroyed; the Dervishes burnt them by fire. We have no longer any schools; they are destroyed. [270]

We should undoubtedly question why the History of Beta Israel was destroyed.

While Beta Israel is most famously known as being "Ethiopian Jews," another group commonly identified as Hebrew had a close connection to this community, known as the Agaws. In fact, the Agaw word "ayhud" means Judean, which resembles the Hebrew words "Yahudah" and "Yahudi." Agaws, however, are known to practice a Hebraic form of Paganism. Another group with a close relationship to the Agaws and Beta Israel was the Qement, also identified as a Hebraic group.[271] However, ethnicity differentiates Beta Israel from the Agaw and Qemant, as Beta Israel does not share a semblance of features with the two despite a close historical relationship. While Beta Israel is Habasha, or "Ethio-Semitic," the Agaw and Qemant are considered "Cushitic."[272] We should remember, the true Hebrews who originate from south of Egypt, in modern ethnic terms, would be considered Cushitic, and not Semitic.

---

[270] *Id.*
[271] *Id.*
[272] Jason A. Hodgson, et al., Early Back-to-Africa Migration into the Horn of Africa, PLOS Genetics, (June 12, 2014)

https://journals.plos.org/plosgenetics/article/comment?id=10.1371/annotation/87e3e975-1957-4688-a945-657e1ac45694.

If other Ethiopians were known to be Hebrew, how are these people ethnically separate from Beta Israel? The Biblical account explains that Yahshar-el went into captivity in Assur, and Yahudah went into captivity in Babylon. While the general population, likely those of social stature, were undoubtedly targeted for exile, a remnant was left in the land and subjected to foreign rule. We can hypothesize the Agaw and the Qemant, who are said to have practiced a Hebraic form of Paganism, are either a part of that remnant who remained in the land or a part of the returnees. Beta Israel, however, who brought into the land the religious system of Judaism, has its roots mostly in Arabia. This explains Beta Israel's close relationship to the Agaw and Qemant while remaining a separate priesthood. Essentially, the Beta Israel community likely descend from the Pharisees and Sadducees written about in the New Testament.

Scripturally, we are given clues that at least most of the Pharisees were of a distinct ethnic origin than the Hebrews. For example, John 8:31-38 says:

> So Jesus was saying to those Jews who had believed Him, "If you continue in My word, *then* you are truly My disciples; [32] and you will know the truth, and the truth will set you free." [33] They answered Him, **"We are Abraham's descendants and have never been enslaved to anyone; how *is it that* You say, 'You will become free'?"**
> [34] Jesus answered them, "Truly, truly I say to you, everyone who commits sin is a slave of sin. [35] Now the slave does not remain in the house forever; the son does remain forever. [36] So if the Son sets you free, you really will be free. [37] I know that you are Abraham's descendants; yet you are seeking to kill Me, because My word has no place in you. [38] I speak of the things which I have seen with *My* Father; therefore you also do the things which you heard from *your* father."

Why did the Pharisees identify themselves as Abraham's descendants but not Jacobs, and as having never been enslaved when the Hebrews were enslaved in Egypt? This passage may be referencing the fact the Pharisees descended largely from Edom.

As is attested in the Dead Sea Scrolls, this group promised to help the Yahudi reestablish Yahshar-el as a great kingdom that correctly followed the laws of Yahuah (God). The problem is, as is stated by Yahusha, these converts were not teaching the pure Torah but instead taught many of their man-made traditions. When Yahusha came to take the Hebrews back to the righteous Torah, his revolutionary approach was met with disdain from the Pharisees. The Falasha community, then, descends from the Pharisees in the Bible, who conspired against Yahusha.

The Oromo Hebrews?

The Oromo, also known as the *Gallas*, are the largest ethnic group in Ethiopia today and are of "Cushitic" origins. Oromos have historically faced a unique threat from those in power who have determined their erasure to be essential to their supreme rule. This is because the Oromos are, in fact, descendants of the original Hebrews of the land.

There has been an intentional campaign to erase Oromo history from Ethiopia by depicting them as newcomers, while the Abyssinians depicted themselves as indigenous. For example, the Abyssinian court historian Alaqa Taye alleged that in the fourteenth and sixteenth centuries, the Oromo migrated from Asia and Madagascar, entered Africa from Mombasa, then spread northward and eastward. Others have advocated that the Oromo crossed the Red Sea via Bab el Mandab and spread westwards. Abyssinian clergies have even advocated that the Oromo emerged from the water. [273]

This narrative, however, conflicts with the known history of D'mt, where the Oromo tribe ruled. Oromo people have also consistently rejected this view that they were late arrivals and have an oral history that states instead they were the original inhabitants of Northern Ethiopia and Eritrea. This history has been backed up by modern scholarship, which attests that the Oromo were in North East Africa long before the arrival of the Habasha. As demonstrated by British

---

[273] The people of Oromo, Fatherland gazette (Sept.11, 2020) https://fatherlandgazette.wordpress.com/2020/09/11/the-people-of-oromo/

historian Margery Perham, "the emigrant Semites landed in a continent of which the North-East appears to have been inhabited by the eastern groups of Hamites, often called Kushites, who also include the Gallas." [274]

In an attempt to hide the Oromo's connection to the land, the Abyssinians, particularly the Amhara, worked to assimilate the conquered peoples in what has been deemed Amharaization, a way of destroying the identity of the colonized population groups.[275] As explained by Asafa Jalata:

> "Ethiopia" is the name that was eventually given to the geographic unit created when Abyssinia, a cluster of small kingdoms in northeast Africa, expanded in the mid-1800s by conquering independent nations in the region using firearms provided by European power. ... To obtain slaves and economic resources, the emerging Ethiopian state committed genocide on peoples like the Oromos. The Oromo population was reduced from 10 million to 5 million through war, slavery, massive killings, disease, and war-induced famine during the second half of the 19th century. According to Alexander Bulatovich (2000), The dreadful annihilation of more than half of the population during the conquest took away from the Gallas [Oromos] all possibilities of thinking about any sort of uprising. . . . Without a doubt, the Galla, with their at least five million population, occupying the best land, all speaking one language, could represent a tremendous force if united.
>
> The Ethiopian colonizers started to dehumanize Oromos by changing their name into Galla. ...These names were invented in the process of removing these peoples from their respective cultural and historical roots and making them the target of destruction, enslavement, colonialism, and continued subjugation. The appellation Galla was given to Oromos as a name of contempt and derogation. It has characterized them as slave, pagan, uncivilized or barbaric, inferior, and ignorant. This name was invented to destroy Oromoness and to devalue Oromo culture, history, and tradition. In Abyssinia proper,

---

[274] Id. *quoting* Margery Perham, The Government of Ethiopia. Faber and Faber Ltd., (1948).
[275] Asafa Jalata, Review Essay: Are the Tulama and Wallo Oromo Habasha?, Scientific Research, (Oct. 2021)
https://www.scirp.org/journal/paperinformation.aspx?paperid=112398.

> Galla and barya have been used interchangeably. Galla is the name of racist ridicule in academia and popular discourse. Habashas have effectively used the discourse of cultural racism in destroying or suppressing other peoples. Cultural racism can be defined as the conscious or subconscious conviction of the politically dominant population group that imposes its cultural patterns and practices through its social institutions in an attempt to destroy or suppress the cultural patterns and practices of the colonized and dominated population.[276]

An article on the Oromo website Yerooblog, a website dedicated to political, economic and social issues facing the Oromo people, gives another riveting account of this history:

> The Habasha elites tell us that Ethiopia is the only country in Africa that was not colonized by the European super powers. What the habashas elites were unable to understand was the fact that, there was no country called Ethiopia when the Europeans came to Africa in the mid 19the century. The present Ethiopia got its present map in 1900 after the Habasha king, Minlik II, completed his expansion towards the south.
>
> Before they were conquered by Minlik II peoples such as the Oromo, Sidama, Woliyta, Gamo, Gedeo and others, had their own administration; that means, they ruled themselves. They had their own culture, tradition, belief and values. They lost all these when the Habashas came and imposed their own culture on them. The Habashas always claimed that they are the civilized people and expanded the south to civilize others whom they considered backward and uncivilized.
>
> There are ample evidences that the Habashas had Semitic origin drawn from the Middle East. They are close kin of the Arabs and the Jews. However, they claim that they are indigenous people of Africa whereas according to them other nations inhabiting in the horn of Africa such as the Oromo came into Africa from Madagascar crossing the Indian Ocean. The habasha elites and priests wrote distorted history about the Oromo who are indigenous to Africa. The Oromos belong to the Cushitic origin. The Cushitic people lived in the horn of Africa as far as the present day Egypt. The Cushitic people are black people and they had their own civilization… The cushite moved southwards among them were the Oromos and the Agaws. Moreover, the

---

[276] Asafa Jalata, Being in and Out of Africa: The Impact of Duality of Ethiopianism, Sociology Publications and Other Works. (2009), https://trace.tennessee.edu/utk_socopubs/78

Semitic people such as the Amhara and the Tigres crossed the red sea and invaded the land that originally belonged to the Cushitic people. Naturally, the Semitic people like invading others land and establishing themselves. What the habashas did to the Oromos and what the Arabs did to the indigenous Africans proves this fact. In the places they settled they tried to destroy the native settlers and imposed their culture and values on them. The invaders from the Arab land built their own empire along the red sea co(a)st that later became the Axumite empire.

The Axumite Empire was started by Cushitic people such as the Oromo and the Agawa though the Tigreans claim that they were the ones who founded the empire. There are some historical facts that prove that the obelisks in Aksum were built by the Oromos and other cushite people. In the 400 A.D the king of Aksum Ezana accepted Christianity and made it a state religion. Since then the habasha kings used Christianity as an instrument for consolidating their power. The Axumite Empire weakened in the twelfth century because it lost the trade route it had been using for years to the Arabs. The external forces such as the Arab developed interest in the red sea area and threatened the Aksum Empire. Eventually the Aksum Empire declined failing to defend itself against the external forces.[277]

Waaqeffanna a Hebraic Oromo Religion?

The most convincing evidence of the Oromo's Hebraic origin is their indigenous religion, Waaqeffanna, which, much like the Agaw and Qemant religious practice, resembles a paganized Hebraic religion. Oromo traditionalists are monotheistic and believe there is one god named *Waaqa*. Waaqa existed before all things, was the world's creator, is all-powerful, omniscient, omnipotent, benevolent, pure, good, and the source of love and truth. In addition, Waaqa is intolerant of sin, injustice, crime, and all falsehood. In worshiping Waaqa, Oromo never worshipped carved statues, trees, rivers, mountains, or animals as substitutes.[278]

---

[277] We, the Oromos, Know our History!, Yeroo Blog, (July 9, 2014) https://yerooblog.wordpress.com/2014/07/09/two-days-in-arbaminch-2/.
[278] Workineh Kelbessa, Traditional Oromo Attitude Towards the Environment, Social Science Research Report Series, http://www.ossrea.net/publications/images/stories/ossrea/ssrr-19-p-3.pdf (*last visited* Jan. 18, 2024).

Some Oromo proverbs include:

- Waaqa malee, gaariin hin jiru , or" There is no one who is kind except Waaqa"
- Waan Waaqni fide lafti ba'aa hin or "Whatever Waaqa brings the Earth does not fail to carry it."
- Namni yaa Waaqijedhe Waaqarraa hindhabu, or "One who worships God will get everything."

According to the Oromo, Waaqa created the first human beings from the soil by breathing into it. Waaqa used to be present on Earth with humans, but when humans sinned, he left the Earth to go to the sky and became invisible. Sin and human error are why Waaqa allowed evil things to exist in the world, and illness and misfortune are often considered a punishment from Waaqa for the sins a person has committed. However, people living according to Waaqa's order will be happy and respected community members. There are also divinities created by Waaqa called Ayyaana, each seen as a manifestation of the one Waaqa who act as an intermediary between human beings and Waaqa. [279] Thus, the commonalities between Waaqa and Yahuah, the God of the Bible, are astounding.

---

[279] *Id.*

Chapter 10: The Dispersion

"and they will fall by the edge of the sword, and will be led captive into all the nations..."

~Luke 21:24

The dispersion of the Hebrews was a systematic campaign of oppression and assimilation, all to make the Hebrews lose knowledge of their identity. This began with the Assur and Babylonian captivity, and continues until today, as the descendants of the original Hebrew inhabitants of Yahshar-el (Israel) continue to face systemic oppression.

For this chapter, we return to the study of Esau. From what we read in the scripture of the Pharisees and Sadducees, who we associate with Beta Israel, we can observe that Edomite-Sabeans eclipsed the Hebrews as people of the book, even ruling over them. These same Sabeans, we will see, have links to numerous groups that later have a part in the Hebrew dispersion.

The Campaign for Erasure

History has not recorded what happened to the real Yahudah (Judah) settlement of returnees from the Babylonian exile after the death and resurrection of Yahusha Hamashiach (Jesus Christ). The Bible, however, records many prophecies of what will happen to the Yahudi (Judeans) following Yahushua's resurrection. The Gospel of John 16:1-4 reads:

> "These things I have spoken to you so that you will not be led into sin. 2 They will ban you from the synagogue, yet an hour is coming for everyone who kills you to think that he is offering a service to God. 3 These things they will do because they have not known the Father nor Me. 4 But these things I have spoken to you, so that when their hour comes, you may remember that I told you of them. However, I did not say these things to you at the beginning, because I was with you.

Luke 21:20-24 states:

> "But when you see Jerusalem surrounded by armies, then recognize that her desolation is near. 21 Then those who are in Judea must flee to the mountains, and those who are inside the city must leave, and those who are in the country must not enter the city; 22 because these are days of punishment, so that all things which have been written will be fulfilled. 23 Woe to those women who are pregnant, and to those who are nursing babies in those days; for there will be great distress upon the land, and wrath to this people; **24 and they will fall by the edge of the sword, and will be led captive into all the nations; and Jerusalem will be trampled underfoot by the Gentiles until the times of the Gentiles are fulfilled.**

Matthew 24:1-2 and 18-22 reads:

> Jesus left the temple area and was going on His way when His disciples came up to point out the temple buildings to Him. 2 But He responded and said to them, **"Do you not see all these things? Truly I say to you, not one stone here will be left upon another, which will not be torn down."**... 18 And whoever is in the field must not turn back to get his cloak. 19 But woe to those women who are pregnant, and to those who are nursing babies in those days! 20 Moreover, pray that when you flee, it will not be in the winter, or on a Sabbath. **21 For then there will be a great tribulation, such as has not occurred since the beginning of the world until now, nor ever will again. 22 And if those days had not been cut short, no life would have been saved; but for the sake of the elect those days will be cut short.**

What Yahusha tells his disciples is clear. 1) the Temple will be destroyed entirely; 2) the Hebrews will be led into captivity *into all nations*; 3) gentiles will overtake Yerusalem (Jerusalem); and 4) a great tribulation will occur unlike any that ever occurred before.

Yerusalem Trodden by Gentiles

As was covered in the previous chapter, the Oromo oral tradition is that Oromo were the original inhabitants of Aksum along with the Agaw and Qemant. A significant act of the dispersion of these groups occurred under the Abyssinian monarch Menelik II (1889 to 1913 CE), who enacted a brutal system of mass extermination and enslavement against the Oromo people. As described by Asafa Jalata:

Menelik unleashed a system of mass extermination and enslavement against the Oromos, Menelik subjugating the south, southeast, southwest, Oromos and other related groups. Menelik used the booties and slaves from these conquered territories as a springboard for achieving his broad colonial and imperial scheme to dominate Ethiopia [mainly] for the benefit of his Menz group. The conquest, therefore, has a special significance for all groups presently suffering under the yoke of Menz subjugation. [The foreign powers provided advice and material supplies] to Menelik's subjugation of the southern territories... A colonized man who survived the wanton and... onslaught of Menelik's army was either taken and sold as a slave or subjected to humiliation by the stationing of soldiers who had the license to rape his wife and daughters.

Jalata details that one of the ways Menelik solidified his rule was through the tale of his descent from King Solomon and the Queen of Sheba:

Using the Orthodox Christian ideology, Menelik gained access to European technology, weapons, administrative and military expertise, and other skills that allowed him to consolidate the modern Ethiopian clientele state…Menelik and Haile Selassie established settler colonialism by establishing and consolidating the Habasha political and religious institutions, Garrison, and other cities, creating and reducing an intermediary class, colonial education, the colonial landholding system, and the media… They forcefully converted some Oromo to Christianity by killing confident Oromo political and religious leaders. As one source noted, "If a Christian [would] kill… [an Oromo]… it would be considered for him … an offering to God". The Oromo communities fought against the invading Christian kingdom until the advent of Ahmed Gragn, a Muslim imam who conquered the Shawa kingdom and other independent communities between 1527 and 1543. Certain Oromo groups suffered immensely from the *jihad* war because they were involved in both sides of the Christians and the Muslims. When the Christian and the Muslim forces were contesting in the Horn of Africa for power and control of resources such as lands, northern and southern Oromo fought to liberate their territories and the conquered Oromo communities from the two invaders. When the Abyssinian Christian kingdom attacked the Tulama Oromo clans such as Gaalaan, Yaya, Waji, Abichu, and others, the Muslim empire builders also attacked the Oromo branches living in the area is currently called Somalia and other areas. Before and after the sixteenth century, the Christian empire builders from the north and the Muslim empire builders from the south attacked the Oromo.[280]

For clarity, Aksum's brand of Christianity should not be confused with "The Way," or the faithful followers of Yahusha. Aksumite leaders used Christianity as a tool for political consolidation of power and subjugation of the masses to be ruled. The scriptures clearly show that the followers of *The Way* suffered immense persecution for introducing their faith into the kingdom. This movement of organic devotion to Yahuah (God), as far as we know, was wiped out. Instead, Aksum embraced Orthodox Christianity in the 4th century (340–356 CE) under the rule of King Ezana after the king was converted by Frumentius, a former Syrian captive who was made Bishop of Aksum.[281]

After being baptized, King Ezana declared Aksum to be a Christian state. By the 6th century, the kingdom under King Kaleb was recognized as Christian by Emperor Justin I of Byzantium when Kaleb supported his military campaign in South Arabia, avenging atrocities suffered by Christians there. After this invasion, the Aksumite kingdom was recognized as part of the Roman Church for the next seven decades.[282]

Gradually, due to several factors, including environmental deterioration, economic decline, prolonged population pressure, and overexploitation, Aksum descended into obscurity, with its powerful position as a world empire today largely forgotten.[283] The Kingdom's power was eroded entirely by the 8th century, with buildings and monuments having been abandoned.[284] Political power shifted to a

---

[280] Asafa Jalata, Review Essay: Are the Tulama and Wallo Oromo Habasha?, Scientific Research, (Oct. 2021) https://www.scirp.org/journal/paperinformation.aspx?paperid=112398.

[281] The British Museum, The Kingdom of Aksum, https://smarthistory.org/the-kingdom-of-aksum/ (*last visited* Jan 18, 2024).

[282] *Id.*; David W. Phillipson, Aksumite Civilization, Its Connections and Descendants, Fritz-Hintze-Vorlesung (2009).

[283] *Id.*

[284] *Id.*

new dynasty, the Agaw Zagwe Dynasty, based in the city of Lalibela.[285] The prominent city of Aksum, the true Yerusalem, has been lost in the subconscious of the world ever since.

Gudit

Aksum's decline as a powerful nation is said to have begun during the sacking of the capital city. According to tradition, this sacking was done by a Jewish queen named Gudit (also Yodit or Judith). According to the oral history, Gudit was a rebel leader who, in 970 AD, laid the city of Aksum to waste. Her murderous campaign destroyed churches, monuments, literature; slaughtered priests and monks; and sought to destroy all members of the royal family. Because Gudit was of Jewish faith, it is assumed she was of Falasha origin, leading some to label her the Queen of Beta Israel. However, it is also possible that Gudit is the Agaw founder of the Zagwé dynasty and reigned for forty years to have been succeeded by her descendants.[286] According to the Dictionary of African Christian Biography:

> The basic theme of the legend of a rebel queen as a destructive fury bringing ruin and devastation upon Aksumite civilization is common to Ethiopian tradition, both oral and written, and to the corroborative external sources. Ethiopian tradition affirms, however, that this queen was of the Jewish faith. Some manuscripts studied recently at Aksum by the contemporary scholar Sergew Hable-Selassie provide a surprisingly detailed framework to the story. They indicate a belief that Gudit was related in some way to the royal family - she is, for example, said to have been a grand-daughter in the female line of Emperor Wedem-Asfäré. She is also said to have married a Jewish prince, a certain Zenobis, son of the King of Šam, which is an Arabic

---

[285] The Kingdom of Aksum, National Geographic, https://education.nationalgeographic.org/resource/kingdom-aksum/10th-grade/ (*last visited* Jan. 18, 2024).

[286] Michael Belaynesh, Gudit, Dictionary of African Christian Biography, https://dacb.org/stories/ethiopia/gudit/ (*last visited* Jan. 19, 2024); Mitchell Bard, Who are the Ethiopian Jews?, Jewish Virtual Library, https://www.jewishvirtuallibrary.org/who-are-the-ethiopian-jews (*last visited* Jan. 19, 2024).

form for Syria, but here appears to designate a country on the Red Sea coastal plain, perhaps to the north of Ethiopia. She set out with her husband at the head of an army he had provided to attack Aksum in vengeance for harsh treatment that she had received in the past, coming across the Samhar plain from the coast, at Arkiko, i.e. a complete change of direction from that usually postulated by modern scholars.[287]

Queen Gudit's raid is not just oral history but also confirmed from independent sources. In *the History of the Patriarchs of Alexandria*, it is recorded that during the Patriarchate of Philotheos from 979-1003 CE, that King George of Nubia received an appeal from an unnamed ruler of Aksum seeking the appointment of a new Metropolitan. The letter described how a woman laid waste to the country as well as displacing the Emperor and his followers by driving them from place to place to wipe out Christianity.[288]

It should be emphasized that Gudit's invasion was an intentional assault not just on Aksum's power, but also its culture with the destruction of historical buildings and literature. This seems to be the genesis of the violent erasure of Yahshar-el from East Africa.

The Sabeans Become the Berbers

Although the Sabean presence in Africa seems to be a relic of the past, Sabeans did not disappear from African history. Like Edom's "disappearance" was a reappearance into Arabia, Sabeans disappeared into many groups from where they reemerged, including the Berbers. Diplomat Leo Africanus, best known for his 1526 work *Cosmographia et geographic de Africa*, noted that Berbers are the Sabeans. A map of his 1st century Roman periplus even shows the Berbers around Aksum, in the horn of East Africa and on the Nile River.(See Map 14)

Moorish Science Temple researcher Sheik Way-El argues that Berbers who founded Morocco, also known as the Moors, are the

---

[287] *Id.*, Belaynesh.
[288] *Id.*

Berber descendants of the Moabites in the Bible. According to Way-El:

> the original name for Morocco is rendered Marab, obviously, a play on the word Mo'ab with the elision filled with the letter 'r'. It is without question that the Almoravids are the Moabites who are the Moors that first went into Spain. In fact, in many Christian chronicles, Moab is used in place or interchangeably with Moor.[289]

Moab, one of Yahshar-el's (Israel's) enemies who joined the Psalm 83 confederacy against Yahshar-el, bordered Yahshar-el to the south of Edom, thus modern-day Southern Sudan. This explains the prevalence of the name *Berber* in the region, with Berbera towns in both Sudan and Somalia. The Moabites became an early enemy of Yahshar-el when the King of Moab attempted to commission Balaam, the diviner, to curse Yahshar-el as the people were in the wilderness. Instead, Balaam cursed Moab and prophesied its subjugation to Yahshar-el.[290]

Moab, too, like Edom, was assigned judgment from Yahuah (God) for its acts against Yahshar-el, including its ultimate destruction.[291] Jeremiah 48:45-47 states:

> "In the shadow of Heshbon
> The fugitives stand without strength;
> For a fire has spread out from Heshbon
> And a flame from the midst of Sihon,
> **And it has devoured the forehead of Moab**
> **And the scalps of the loud revelers.**
> **46 Woe to you, Moab!**
> **The people of Chemosh have perished;**
> **For your sons have been taken away captive,**
> **And your daughters into captivity.**
> 47 Yet I will restore the fortunes of Moab

---

[289] Sheik Way-El, Moabites, and Berbers; are these names and people historically synonymous? Moorish American Research Group For the Moorish Science Society Moors, (Mar. 23, 2017).
[290] Numbers 22-24.
[291] Isaiah 15, Jeremiah 48.

In the latter days," declares the Lord.

Way El traces Moab to the Arabian Peninsula, arguing that the Moabites founded the Sabean capital city of Mar'ib.[292] That would mean the Moabites intermixed with the Sabeans, as did Edom. This conclusion is confirmed by Jeremiah 25:21-24:

> To **Edom, Moab**, and the sons of Ammon; 22 and to all the kings of Tyre, all the kings of Sidon, **and the kings of the coastlands which are beyond the sea;** 23 and to Dedan, Tema, Buz, and all who trim the corners of their hair; 24 **and to all the kings of Arabia and all the kings of the foreign people who live in the desert**;

While the Berbers existed in the Nile Region, the group later dispersed into North and West Africa over several migration periods.[293] Although Berbers today are typically much lighter in complexion than other African groups, this is due to Arab invasions. As stated by Nii Ntreh in the online newspaper Faces 2 Africa:

> The 6th-century Roman poet, Corippus, in his book *Johannis,* describes the Berbers as "facies nigroque colorus" which means "faces of the black colour".. In the same century, Procopius in Book IV of History of the Wars discussed the difference between the Vandals who had settled in North Africa and the Moors. Procopius says that the Vandals were not "black-skinned like the Maurusioi (Moors)" . The tribes he classified as Maurusioi are those now described as ancient Berbers. They include the Numidians, Masaesyle, Gaitules, Massyles, Masmuda and Mezikes. Nasr Khusrau, an 11th-century Iranian also described the Masmuda soldiers of the Fatimid dynasty as "black Africans".[294]

The Black Berbers, initially referred to as Amazigh, would move throughout the Sahel, inhabiting scattered communities across Morocco, Algeria, Tunisia, Libya, Egypt, Mali, Niger and Mauritania.

---

[292] *Supra* note 289.
[293] *Id.*
[294] Nii Ntreh, Do you know what North Africans looked like before Islam and Arabs invaded?, Faces 2 Africa, October 26, 2019, https://face2faceafrica.com/article/do-you-know-what-north-africans-looked-like-before-islam-and-arabs-invaded.

They spoke various Amazigh languages originating from an Afro-Asiatic language related to ancient Egyptian. Several Berber peoples, including the Mauri, Masaesyli, Massyli, Musulami, Gaetuli and Garamantes, would give rise to Berber kingdoms under Carthaginian and Roman influence in Numidia and Mauritania, which were formally incorporated into the Roman Empire in the late 2nd century BCE. [295]

---

[295] Berber, Britannica. https://www.britannica.com/topic/Berber (*last visited* Aug. 17, 2023).

Chapter 11: Into Captivity

"And the Lord will bring you back to Egypt[296] in ships, by the way about which I said to you, 'You will never see it again!' And there you will offer yourselves for sale to your enemies as male and female slaves, but there will be no buyer."

~ Deuteronomy 28:68

The Berbers, The "Jews" of West Africa & Negroland

After leaving East Africa, Berbers began to take up residence in the Sahel region of Africa, which extends from the Sahara to the equator. This territory was referred to by Arabs as "Bilad al-Sudan," which means "land of the blacks." The term "Negroland" has been applied to this region in English.(See Map 17) While some in the Hebrew Israelite movement believe this term has a positive connotation, it has a negative one. The name *Sūd* in Arabic, the root of black, means "denigrate."[297] Why the Arabs named this region the Land of the Blacks in a continent that was itself overwhelmingly Black likely has to

---

[296] "The Hebrew word for Egypt is Mitzraim מצרים, which is a masculine plural noun in Hebrew. It stems from a Hebraic root which means to bind (shackle or imprison), to be bound or a boundary, and lastly it means bondage, servitude, or slavery. The above descriptions align perfectly with the Torah's appellations and synonyms for Ancient Egypt or Kemet. Within the Torah, Egypt known in Hebrew as Mitzraim מצרים, is synonymous with BONDAGE and servitude (Slavery).
There are at least 13 references in the Torah to Egypt מצרים as being the House of Bondage: (Exodus:13:3, Exodus:13:14, Exodus:20:2, Deuteronomy:5:6, Deuteronomy:6:12, Deuteronomy:7:8, Deuteronomy:8:14, Deuteronomy:13:6, Deuteronomy:13:11, Joshua:24:17, Judges:6:8, Jeremiah:34:13, Micah:6:4). So, whenever Egypt or in Hebrew Mitzraim is mentioned in the Torah, it is synonymous with physical and mental Bondage (Slavery)." Egypt means bondage in Hebrew, Learn Torah, (Jan. 19, 2015) https://learntorah.blogspot.com/2015/01/egypt-means-bondage-in-hebrew.html.

[297] Sheik Way-El, Moabites, and Berbers; are these names and people historically synonymous? Moorish American Research Group For the Moorish Science Society Moors, (Mar. 23, 2017).

do with them extending their conquests, culture and influence to that particular region of Africa.[298]

While today most of these areas are Islamic, before the Muslim conquests of North Africa this area was inhabited by "Jews"[299] as Berbers took on the religion of Judaism. This creates a problem of identification. There has been an effort, particularly within the Hebrew Israelite movement, to identify Hebrews or the Yahudi (Judeans) in Africa. However, the mere presence of Jews in Africa is not an indication of Yahudi or Hebrews but of the convert religion of Judaism. Thus, we must distinguish between Jews, that is, people identifying their religious beliefs as Judaism, versus the descendants of Yahshar-el, the Hebrews, or the descendants of Yahudah (Judah), the Yahudi.

As stated by Rudolph Windsor in *From Babylon to Timbuktu*, the Jews throughout Africa were essentially collaborators with Muslims, guiding their exploits into the continent:

> The black Jews who migrated to the Sudan from the North converged with the Jews migrating from the eastern Sudan to the countries of the Niger River. It is a known fact that the Jews and Judaism were in Africa fifteen hundred years before Islam and that everywhere the Arabs went, the Jews were there. The black Jews guided the Arabs and Moors into Spain and acted as interpreters. When the Moslems came into the Sahara, they found the black Jews stationed on all trade routes, and I can positively say that where Mohammedanism is currently prevailing in Sudan, Judaism once had been dominant.[300]

Following the Arab conquest of North Africa during 642 to 711 CE, Bilad al-Sudan took on a vastly different look. Socially, ethnically,

---

[298] Nii Ntreh, How Sudan came to have its name, and why there are two Sudans, (May 09, 2020) https://face2faceafrica.com/article/how-sudan-came-to-have-its-name-and-why-there-are-two-sudans.
[299] For lack of a better term, from here on we refer to practitioners of Judaism as "Jews," despite the religion's roots being non-Hebrew.
[300] Rudolph R. Windsor From Babylon to Timbuktu, Windsor Golden Series, (2006), 120-121.

culturally and religiously the region had become Arabized, and from the Atlantic coast to Cyrenaica, the population of this area now looked closer to the Arab Muslim world. Berbers adopted Islam en masse during this period and Arab immigrants settled throughout North Africa. According to the United Nations Educational, Scientific and Cultural Organization (UNESCO):

> They came as peaceful newcomers, and were made welcome everywhere. Large Arab settlements were established in many areas in Cyrenaica and the provinces of Ifrikiya. They persisted for many years, especially in the two provincial divisions of Ifrikiya and Mzlb. A considerable proportion of these colonists belonged to the great Arab confederation of Tamïm. Later, during the Aghlabid period (184/ 800-296/909), these Arab colonies fell into decadence and were gradually absorbed into the local population. There were also small groups of Arabs, sometimes even single families or individuals, who settled among Berber tribes where they were regarded as teachers; they acted as imams or religious leaders. This spiritual leader-ship often developed into political leadership as well, the Arab imam becoming the political head of the tribe. This development involved some Berberization of the Arab colonists in turn. One characteristic example is that of the Arab family of the Banü Sälih ibn Mansür al-Yamanï. In 91/ 710, the Caliph 'Abd al-Malik offered them as a gift the region of Nakür, near what is today Alhucemas in northern Morocco. The family settled there, they intermingled with the local population, and the Berber came to recognize them as emirs.[301]

The Slave Trades

Usually, when one thinks about a global slave trade, the Trans-Atlantic Slave Trade instantly comes to mind. It is believed to be the most extensive and brutal campaign of mass slavery in the entirety of humanity. What must be understood, however, is the Trans-Atlantic Slave Trade does not stand on its own. The Arab Slave Trade carried out in Africa has direct links to the Trans-Atlantic Slave Trade as a

---

[301] UNESCO, The Conquest of North Africa and Berber resistance, International Scientific Committee for the Drafting of a General History of Africa (1988), 243.

contributor and inspiration to the barbaric system. As professor of Black Studies Kehinde Andrews explains:

> Long before Europe had the idea to turn to Africa for a slave labor force, Arabs who invaded North Africa in the seventh century had established a system of slavery on the continent. Over a span of more than 1,250 years around 6 to 7 million Africans were forcibly trafficked across the Sahara Desert. It was, in fact, the Arab system that gave Europeans the idea and early access to African flesh. When Columbus enslaved 500 indigenous Americans it was the Arab slave markets that he sold them into. Europe did not even invent the idea of Africans being inferior...Europeans essentially plagiarized Arab racial thinking.[302]

The Arab Slave Trade

While it is impossible to determine or quantify which slave trade was more destructive, at the very least, the Arab Slave Trade should be recognized as equally horrific and barbarous to Africa, with the blood of millions of innocent Africans having been spilled. The Arab Slave Trade, which commenced 700 years before the Transatlantic Slave Trade, encompassed Western Asia, North Africa, East Africa and select areas of Europe such as Iberia and Sicily. While in the early days of that slave trade Turks, Iranians, Europeans and Berbers were traded as slaves, with the emergence of the Oman sultanate, which was centered in Zanzibar, the trading of Bantu slaves from East Africa grew in the 18th and 19th centuries.[303]

During the Trans-Saharan/Arab Slave Trade, many Nilotic peoples from the lower Nile Valley were purchased as slaves and brought to work elsewhere in North Africa and Asia by Berbers and Arabs. These Africans were principally from Ethiopia, Eritrea, Kenya, Mozambique, East Tanzania and other parts of East Africa. They were taken to Iran, Iraq, Kuwait, Turkey, Somalia and other countries in

---

[302] Kehinde Andrews, The New Age of Empire: How Racism and Colonialism Still Rule the World, Bold Type Books, (Mar. 2, 2021), 79.
[303] Ayomide Akinbode, The Forgotten Arab Slave Trade of East Africa, Historyville, (Dec. 20, 2021) https://www.thehistoryville.com/arab-slave-trade/.

the Middle East or South Asia. (See Map 15) It is estimated that three out of four enslaved persons died before even reaching the market where they would be sold, having died from hunger, disease or fatigue due to the long trips, especially through the Sahara.[304]

The treatment of these enslaved Africans was brutal. As human breeding was not a goal of this slave trade, male captives were usually castrated and frequently forced into being servants, soldiers or laborers, while female captives were taken to Middle Eastern countries as concubines and maids. The horrors of slavery in these countries was documented by Scottish physician David Livingstone in 1870, who wrote:

> In less than I take to talk about it, these unfortunate creatures — 84 of them, wended their way into the village where we were. Some of them, the eldest, were women from 20 to 22 years of age, and there were youths from 18 to 19, but the majority was made up of boys and girls from 7 to 14 or 15 years of age.
>
> A more terrible scene than these men, women and children, I do not think I ever came across. To say that they were emaciated would not give you an idea of what human beings can undergo under certain circumstances. "Each of them had his neck in a large forked stick, weighing from 30 to 40 pounds, and five or six feet long, cut with a fork at the end of it where the branches of a tree spread out. "The women were tethered with bark thongs, which are, of all things, the most cruel to be tied with. Of course they are soft and supple when first striped off the trees, but a few hours in the sun make them about as hard as the iron round packing-cases. The little children were fastened by thongs to their mothers. "As we passed along the path which these slaves had travelled, I was shown a spot in the bushes where a poor woman the day before, unable to keep on the march, and likely to hinder it, was cut down by the axe of one of these slave drivers. "We went on further and were shown a place where a child lay. It had been been recently born, and its mother was unable to carry it from debility and exhaustion; so the slave trader had taken

---

[304] *Id.*

this little infant by its feet and dashed its brains out against one of the trees and thrown it in there."³⁰⁵

The Arab Slave Trade had a catastrophic impact on the continent of Africa. Between the years 650 and 1900, it is estimated that 10 to 18 million Africans were enslaved by Arab traders and taken over the Red Sea, the Indian Ocean and the Sahara.³⁰⁶ The castration of enslaved males and the concubinage of enslaved females has resulted in the descendants of enslaved Africans in Arabia being difficult to identify, as their ethnic bloodlines faded overtime. However, where racial differences are observable, descendants of the Arab Slave Trade suffer systemic brutality, stagnation and discrimination.³⁰⁷

Three things should stand out about the Arab Slave Trade. The first is where it was primarily focused. Ethiopia. It was said that the demand for Oromo slaves was greatest due to their beauty and sexual temperament. ³⁰⁸ Second, the fact that many of the victims were Bantu-speaking carries great significance, as will be discussed. Lastly, many who survived the excruciating Sahara Desert trip would have been moved to different parts of Africa, notably North and West Africa.

The Arab Slave Trade ended in 1463 during the Ottoman Turks' rise to power, right before the Trans-Atlantic Slave Trade began. As author Duncan Clarke states, "the effective closure of the last major source of slaves on the European continent… thus co-incidentally took place at the same time as the Portuguese explorations of the West African coast, which were to open up the second and most devastating route for the exploitation of Africans as slaves."³⁰⁹ However, this is no coincidence.

---

[305] Recalling Africa's harrowing tale of its first slavers – The Arabs – as UK Slave Trade Abolition is commemorated, New African, (Mar. 27, 2018) https://newafricanmagazine.com/16616/.
[306] *Supra* note 303.
[307] *Supra* note 305.
[308] *Id.*
[309] *Id.*

The Fulani

While some Berbers intermixed with Arabs and Europeans, it is important to note some remained noticeably African. One notable tribe is the *Fulani*, who are believed to have their origins in interactions between West Africans and the Berbers.[310] The *Fulani* (*Fula*), also known as the *Toroobe*, may have originally been Jewish, as they are believed to have "Judeo-Syrian" origins. Their history seems to begin around the 8th century CE when North African Berbers migrated south and mixed with peoples in the Senegal region of West Africa.[311]

The Fulani are among the first group of Africans to convert to Islam, and today, 99% of Fulani are Muslims. It is even said that to be a Fulani is to be a Muslim.[312] Fulani became instrumental in upholding Islamic teachings and ideologies in centers such as Timbuktu, as well as working with Berber and Arabian Islamic clerics to chart the spread of Islam in West Africa. Because of this, the Fula led many jihads, or holy wars, which spread Islam in West Africa, establishing them as a political and economic power.[313] Today, Fulanis are spread over many countries, predominantly in West Africa, but also found in Central Africa and East Africa, including Mauritania, Senegal, Guinea, the Gambia, Mali, Nigeria, Sierra Leone, Benin, Burkina Faso, Guinea

---

[310] Pat Ikechukwu Ndukwe, Fulani, The Rosen Publishing Group, (1996), 9–17; "Fulani oral traditions suggest an origin in Egypt or the Middle East, a common theme in West African Muslim traditions," Carl Skutsch, Encyclopedia of the World's Minorities, Routledge, (2005), 474.

[311] Tarig Anter, Who Are the Fulani People & Their Origins?, Modern Ghana, (Sept. 9, 2011) https://www.modernghana.com/news/349849/who-are-the-fulani-people-their-origins.html.

[312] *Id.*

[313] Knut Vikor, Leif Manger, Muslim Diversity: Local Islam in Global Contexts. Routledge,(2013) 92–93; Marion Johnson, The Economic Foundations of an Islamic Theocracy – The Case of Masina, The Journal of African History ,Cambridge University Press (1976), 481–495; Walter van Beek. Purity and statecraft: The Fulani Jihad, The Quest for Purity: Dynamics of Puritan Movements, Walter de Gruyter, (1988),149–177.

Bissau, Cameroon, Ivory Coast, Niger, Togo, the Central African Republic, Ghana, Liberia and Sudan in the east.[314]

The Moorish Slavers

Before discussing the Trans-Atlantic Slave Trade, it is worth discussing the travels of Berbers at this time. The Berbers participated in the Trans-Sahara Slave Trade, or Arab Slave Trade, along with the Arabs. As stated previously, Berbers occupied Bilad al-Sudan. Jewish Berbers, in particular, created prominent settlements from Morocco to Angola.[315]

Jewish Berbers are the ancestors of the group we know today as the Sephardic Jews, who later made their way into Portugal and Spain. American-born Israeli linguist Paul Wexler, who is also known for arguing Ashkenazi Jews are non-Mediterranean, and are actually of Turkic, Slavic and Iranian origin, detailed in his book *The Non-Jewish Origins of the Sephardic Jews* these Berber origins. Wexler concluded using linguistic, ethnographic and historical analysis, that Sephardic Jews are in fact of non-Hebrew origin, and instead originate from Berber and Arab proselytes. Using Linguistic analysis, he found that Sephardi Jews were "predominantly speakers of Judeo Arabic or possibly even (Judeo-) Berber."[316]

In addition, studying Iberian Jewish culture prior to 1492, Wexler found that "Comparison of Jewish folkways and religious practices with those of the co-territorial non-Jews in North Africa and Spain suggests that the Berbers and Arabs were the major suppliers of Sephardic Jewish practices."[317] Wexler goes on to say:

> The Sephardic Jewish population had the same constellation of geographical origins as the Arabs and Berbers. Historical,

---

[314] *Supra* note 311.

[315] Joseph J. Williams, The Vail Ballou Press, Hebrewisms of West Africa, (1930), 122.

[316] *Id.* at 179

[317] *Id.* at 180.

ethnographical and onomastic evidence shows that, in addition to a North African component in the Iberian Jewish community, Jews from Syria, Iraq, and the Arabian Peninsula also accompanied the Arabs to North Africa and Spain (on the westward march of Jews and Bedouins).[318]

This conclusion has been corroborated by DNA evidence. Harry Ostrer of the Albert Einstein College of Medicine in New York led a study demonstrating a shared genetic history between Berbers and Sephardic Jews, with the Sephardic Jews who settled in Africa being shown to have originated in North Africa more than 1,000 years earlier.[319]

The Moors entered Spain and Portugal bringing their culture and technology, thus contributing immensely to those countries' achievements. However, the "Christian" country of Spain undertook an effort to rid itself of non-Christian religions through a compulsory cultural and religious conversion known as the Spanish Inquisition. North African Muslims were forced to become Christians and became known as *Moriscos*, meaning "Little Moors," while the Sephardic Jews were given the name *Marranos* meaning "pigs." The tension between Christian Spain and its Muslim and Jewish communities resulted in several decrees, most notably in 1492, when all Jews and Muslims who had not yet converted were expelled from the country. However, those who had converted were allowed to remain.[320]

Portugal received the vast majority of Spain's exiled Jews. However, when King Manuel of Portugal sought to marry the daughter of Spanish Monarchs Ferdinand and Isabella, the Spanish monarchs demanded that Portugal expel its Jews. Manuel agreed, and on the 5th of December 1496, he issued a decree giving Jews eleven

---

[318] Paul Wexler, The Non-Jewish Origins of the Sephardic Jews, State University of New York Press, (Feb. 15, 1996), 25-26.
[319] Sharon Begley, Reuters, Genetic study offers clues to the history of North Africa's Jews (Aug. 6, 2012), https://www.reuters.com/article/idUSBRE8751EJ/.
[320] Ali Mazrui, When Spain Expelled the Jews and the Moors... A Lesson in History. Africa Today, vol. 20, no. 1, (1973), 73–75.

months to leave the country, a delayed time likely to allow the Jews time to convert to Christianity. When October 1497 arrived, thousands of Jews who assembled in Portugal were converted in a mass baptism.[321]

The Trans-Atlantic Slave Trade

It is not a coincidence that many Sephardic Jews and Moors took up residence in Portugal, the same country that started the Trans-Atlantic Slave Trade. Again, the Jews in Portugal were forcibly converted in 1497. The Trans-Atlantic Slave Trade was launched from Portugal in the early 1500s. The evidence of their involvement is overwhelming.

The Sephardic Jews who decided to remain in Spain took on the title "New Christians" after the expulsions. These New Christians prospered as merchants and professionals, took on public offices and became tax collectors, which led to them becoming targets of vilification.[322] Many New Christians left Spain and resided in new lands where they reclaimed their Jewish faith and founded European communities, including Amsterdam, Venice, Leghorn, London, Bordeaux, Bayonne, and Hamburg. Others left the continent altogether to return to North Africa or other locations, including Central and South America, Zimbabwe, South Africa and the Belgian Congo.[323] Amsterdam, in particular, became a central enclave for Jewish refugees. According to the World Jewish Congress:

> The city of Amsterdam became one of the most favored destinations for Sephardic Jews exiled from the Iberian Peninsula, and because most of the refugees were traders and merchants, Amsterdam

---

[321] Jews, Expulsion Of (Spain; Portugal), Encyclopedia.com, https://www.encyclopedia.com/history/encyclopedias-almanacs-transcripts-and-maps/jews-expulsion-spain-portugal (*last visited* Jan. 20, 2024).
[322] Eli Faber, Jews, Slaves, and the Slave Trade, New York University, (1998) https://www.washingtonpost.com/wp-srv/style/longterm/books/chap1/jewsslavesandtheslavetrade.htm.
[323] Rebecca Weiner, Judaism: Sephardim, Jewish Virtual Library, https://www.jewishvirtuallibrary.org/sephardim (*last visited* Nov. 30, 2023).

profited substantially from their arrival. The flux of Sephardic Jews played an important role in Amsterdam's growing status as a world leader in trade... The Jews of Amsterdam built an international trading network that mirrored the Jewish Diaspora. Ashkenazic Jews began settling in the Netherlands in 1620, and by 1635 had established a separate community in Amsterdam.[324]

These "traders and merchants" were traders of slaves. In the Netherlands, some Jews brought with them African slaves from Portugal slaving and tried to sell them locally, although they were unsuccessful as the slave market had been barred there. Then, between 1608 and 1621, several ships chartered by Jewish merchants in Amsterdam transported slaves from West Africa to the Americas. By the second half of the seventeenth century, Sephardic Jewish merchants in the Netherlands had a role in the transit of African slaves to Spanish colonies in the Western Hemisphere. However, the scope of their involvement is unknown.[325]

This is worth emphasizing. The two countries that had become a haven for European Jews, Portugal and the Netherlands, not only participated, but dominated the Trans-Atlantic Slave Trade in the seventeenth century. Portugal was so instrumental in the slave trade that the largest number of enslaved Africans anywhere were found on Brazilian plantations, where 38 percent of those taken from Africa were sent. The Dutch, through the Dutch West Indian Company, worked collaboratively to engage multiple European powers, encouraging the French and Danes to incorporate similar slave trading companies for collective expeditions. They were also central in soliciting the British to engage in the slave trade, with whom they worked collaboratively in supplying slaves and assisting the British in breaking Spain's monopoly in the Caribbean.[326]

---

[324] Netherlands, World Jewish Congress, https://www.worldjewishcongress.org/en/about/communities/NL (*last visited* Jan. 20, 2024).
[325] *Supra* note 322.
[326] *Supra* note 302 at 70-71.

England, too, wanted in on the international trafficking ring, and at almost the same time Jews received permission to resettle in England, the English government began to carve out a lane in the Trans-Atlantic Slave Trade. England built numerous forts along the West African coasts to challenge the Dutch presence in Africa from 1660 to1663, dispatching military forces to capture fortifications held by the Netherlands. The Dutch counter-attacked, leading to the Second Anglo-Dutch War.[327]

The advent of the Dutch West Indian Company furthered Jewish involvement in the Trans-Atlantic Slave Trade. Jewish settlers became involved in slavery in Braziland and attracted an extensive number of Jewish settlers. These settlers in Brazil between 1630-1654 acquired sugar plantations and mills, provided the capital for exporting sugar and advanced the credit for slaves. According to professor of history Eli Faber:

> As creditors, according to the historian of the Brazilian Jewish community, "they dominated the slave trade." To be sure, all slave imports from Africa were in the hands of the Dutch West India Company, which under the terms of its charter held the monopoly to the slave trade. But the Company sold the slaves it transported to Brazil at auctions where Jewish purchasers predominated, purchasing slaves and then selling them to plantation owners and others on credit. For the brief time that they resided in Brazil, therefore, Jewish settlers were an essential part of the fabric of the slave trade, although the actual number of slaves they might have purchased and then sold as middlemen amounted to a minute fraction of the huge number of Africans brought to Brazil over the course of more than three centuries.[328]

The Jewish relationship with the Dutch West Indian Company was so influential that when Portugal sought to expel Jews in Brazil after retaking some of the Netherlands' colonies, the Jews were able to remain by appealing to the Company. As reported by Jose Lev Alvarez Gomez in the Times of Israel:

---

[327] *Supra* note 322.
[328] *Id.*

> As result of the pressure made by the Dutch Jewish Community, the Dutch West India Company rejected Governor Stuyvesant's petition of forbidding Jews from entering and staying in New Amsterdam, and asked for equal treatment and freedom of religion (and worship). They considered "unreasonable and unfair" to not let Jews stay in New Amsterdam because of the considerable loss of the colonial Jewry in Recife during the taking of Brazil. Nonetheless, the three main reasons of why the Dutch West India Company decided to support the Jews were because: they held large amounts of capital invested in the Dutch West India Company, appreciation of the Jews allegiance in Brazil and the necessity of mercantilism to fulfill with its provisions.[329]

Jews also had a leading role in the Dutch *East* Indian Company, the first multinational corporation and the first to issue stock in the world. It is also the wealthiest corporation in history, with an estimated worth of $7.9 trillion today, more than Facebook, Apple and Google combined.[330] Between 1602 and 1796, the company sent nearly a million Europeans on 5,000 ships to Indonesia, Japan, India and other Asian lands to pursue trade and colonization. This included the trade of enslaved Africans.[331]

The company's main financiers were Jews, such as Isaac le Maire or Joseph Salvador, and the majority of the executives were Jews.[332] In 1748, Isaac De Pinto, a Jew of Portuguese origin, became the

---

[329] Jose Lev Alvarez Gomez, Petition to Expel the Jews from New Amsterdam and the Dutch West India Company response, Times of Israel, (Sep. 19, 2017) https://blogs.timesofisrael.com/petition-to-expel-the-jews-from-new-amsterdam-and-the-dutch-west-india-company-response/.

[330] Bobby Salomons, The Dutch East India Company was richer than Apple, Google, and Facebook combined, (Mar. 30, 2023), https://dutchreview.com/culture/history/how-rich-was-the-dutch-east-india-company/.

[331] Lawrence Bush, August 14: Isaac De Pinto and the Dutch East India Company, Jewish Currents, (Aug. 16, 2016) https://jewishcurrents.org/august-14-isaac-de-pinto-and-the-dutch-east-india-company,

[332] Indonesia's Jews, The Jewish Community of the Dutch East Indies, (Jun. 20, 2011) http://www.insideindonesia.org/indonesia-s-jews

director of the Dutch East India Company.[333] David Ezekiel Rahabi, from 1726 on, was the chief merchant of the Company who negotiated on their behalf with local rulers.[334]

The Trans-Atlantic Slave Trade was particularly harsh and violent, reducing human beings to commodities. The arduous journey made it the most deadly long-distance global human migration of all time. The boat ride to America, known as the Middle Passage, had horrendous conditions with African men, women and children being kept naked, packed closely together, and chained for much of the day. Twelve percent of Africans did not survive this trip.[335]

After their arrival, Africans suffered brutal and dehumanizing treatment under a totalitarian ruling white regime. Africans in Haiti were frequently worked to death, with the French having calculated slaves were cheaper to replace than to provide for. In the Caribbean, Dutch Guiana and Brazil overall, the death rate of slaves was so high and the birthrate so low that new Africans were constantly needed to replace the population. American slavery was no less brutal. The death rate for slaves in America was about the same as that in the Caribbean, however the birthrate in the United States was more than 80 percent higher.[336]

European participants in the Trans-Atlantic Slave Trade included the Portuguese, Spaniards, Dutch, Italians, Germans, Swedes, French, English and Danes, among others. Also involved were Arabs, Berbers and certain African tribes.[337] Some of the most notable African

---

[333] *Supra* note 331.
[334] David Ezekiel Rahabi, Britannica, https://www.britannica.com/biography/David-Ezekiel-Rahabi (*last visited* Jan. 20, 2024).
[335] Steven Mintz, Historical Context: Facts about the Slave Trade and Slavery, The Gilder Lehrman Institute of American History, https://www.gilderlehrman.org/history-resources/teacher-resources/historical-context-facts-about-slave-trade-and-slavery (*last visited* Jan. 20, 2024).
[336] *Supra* note 302 at 75.
[337] David Brion Davis, The Slave Trade and the Jews, The New York Review, (Dec. 22, 1994) https://www.nybooks.com/articles/1994/12/22/the-slave-trade-and-the-jews/ .

participants in the Trans-Atlantic Slave Trade were the Kingdom of Dahomey, Morocco, Algeria, Egypt, the Kingdom of Allada, the Aro Confederacy, the Ashanti Empire, the Songhai Empire and the Mali Empire. Five of these nine nations are associated with the Berbers of Bilad al-Sudan, including Morocco, Algeria, Egypt, Songhai and Mali Empires.[338]

---

[338] 10 African nations involved in the slave trade, Think Africa, (Mar. 14, 2021) https://thinkafrica.net/african-nations-involved-in-the-slave-trade/.

Chapter 12: Where the Children of Yahshar-el Went

"Furthermore, the Lord will scatter you among all the peoples, from one end of the earth to the other; and there you will serve other gods, made of wood and stone, which you and your fathers have not known."

~ Deuteronomy 28:64

As stated in the previous chapter, Berber Jews dispersed throughout North Africa, into Spain and Portugal, then throughout Europe and other places throughout the world. This makes identifying the children of Yahshar-el (Israel) much more difficult. We cannot simply look for Jewish migrations; in fact, the fact those migrations are identified as Jewish denotes that they are practitioners of Judaism. Because of this, the search for Yahshar-el requires more nuance.

The most effective way to trace the dispersion of Hebrews from East Africa is not to look for traces of people who call themselves Jews or are identified as Jews but to follow Hebraic peoples who were a part of the dispersion. Among tribes and peoples, there is one identifier that stands out as a target of the dispersion, that is the Bantu.

The Hebrew Dispersion into the Bantu

Bantu is not an ethnic identification but rather a language identification that relates to several hundred ethnic groups. Bantu languages constitute a subdivision of the Benue-Niger sector of the Niger-Congo division of the Niger-Kordofanian language family.[339] The Kordofanian language is geographically separate from the rest of the

---

[339] Bantu Languages, Encyclopedia.com, https://www.encyclopedia.com/reference/encyclopedias-almanacs-transcripts-and-maps/bantu-languages (*last visited* Jan. 20, 2024).

Niger-Congo languages, originating in the Nuba Hills of southern Sudan.[340] Among the Niger-Congo languages, Bantu is considered the youngest.[341]

The Bantu were among the top targets of the Arab Slave Trade, and then again, many Bantu and related groups became victims of the Trans-Atlantic Slave Trade. Today, the Bantu live in sub-Saharan Africa and are spread over a vast area from Central Africa across the African Great Lakes to Southern Africa. While the origins of the Bantu remain uncertain, most scholars subscribe to the hypothesis that the group originated from West Africa around 4,000 years ago between Cameroon and Nigeria, where they expanded towards eastern and southern Africa.[342]

There is also a "late split theory" of the Bantu's expansion. Using genomic data, scientists Etienne Patin and Lluis Quintana revealed that Bantu speakers from eastern and southern African populations are genetically more similar to populations based south of the equatorial forest than those to the north. This data supports the late split theory, suggesting that the Bantu first crossed the equatorial forest before branching into two groups following migratory routes towards eastern and southern Sub-Saharan Africa.[343]

As of 2010, the total number of Bantu people was estimated at roughly 350 million, approximately 30% of the population of

---

[340] John Bendor-Samuel, Kordofanian languages, Britannica, https://www.britannica.com/topic/Kordofanian-languages (*last updated* Mar. 15, 2012).
[341] Roger Blench, Mallam Dendo, Kordofanian and Niger-Congo: New and Revised Lexical Evidence, Overseas Development Institute, https://www.rogerblench.info/Language/Niger-Congo/Kordofanian/Kordofanian%20unity.pdf, (*last visited* Jan. 24, 2024), 3.
[342] Eugenia D'Atanasio1, et al., Y Haplogroup Diversity of the Dominican Republic: Reconstructing the Effect of the European Colonization and the Trans-Atlantic Slave Trades, Advance Access (Aug. 24, 2020).
[343] Special Report, Who are the Fulani People and their Origins, Point Blank News, (Jun. 8, 2013) https://pointblanknews.com/pbn/exclusive/special-report-who-are-the-fulani-people-and-their-origins/.

Africa.[344] Today numerous Bantu groups live in East Africa, such as the Gosha, Shabelle, Shidle and Boni (collectively known as Wa) who live in the Lower Juba Valley. In contrast, others live in the Shebelle Valley in Somalia.[345]

Contemporary Bantu society in Africa is primarily a result of the influx of hundreds of thousands of Bantus in the late 19th century due to the Arab Slave Trade, which has also led to scattered Bantu communities throughout Asia.[346] Scattered Bantu communities in India, Sri Lanka and nearby Islands are known today as Sidi or Shidi in Pakistan and Kaffir. While these groups initially spoke their African languages and practiced their culture, they have become Indianized and Arabized over time.[347]

Are the Bantu related to the Hebrews who originated in East Africa? While some African Hebrew Israelites would contend that Bantu are themselves the original Hebrews, pointing to the many Hebrewisms in Bantu languages,[348] evidence for this explicit link is scarce. However, at minimum, we can observe a systematic campaign to target Bantu-speaking peoples and a correlation of numerous Hebraic tribes who intermixed with Bantu speakers. What seems more plausible is that scattered Hebrews found refuge among Bantu tribes, spreading their culture and intermixing. This mixture seems to have occurred during the intercourse of the Bantu with Central Sudanic-speaking populations, some of whom Hebrew, who pushed into parts of Central Africa.

---

[344] People, Locations, Episodes, The Bantu People of Africa, a story, African American Registry, https://aaregistry.org/story/the-bantu-people-a-brief-story/ (*last visited* Jan. 20, 2024).
[345] Somalia, Bantu, Minority Rights Group, https://minorityrights.org/minorities/bantu/, (*last visited* Oct. 21, 2023).
[346] *Id.*
[347] Abdulaziz Lodhi, Bantu origins of the Sidis of India, Pambazuka News, (Oct. 29, 2008) https://www.pambazuka.org/global-south/bantu-origins-sidis-india.
[348] Bantu is Hebrew, Hebrew Readers Church, https://www.hebrewreaders.com/hebrew (*last visited* Jan. 20, 2024).

Sudanic languages are spoken from Cape Verde to the Great Lakes and further north to the Red Sea. If one were to compare the vocabulary roots of Bantu with those of monosyllabic and affixes of the Sudanic group, more than one-third of vocabulary are familiar to Bantu and Sudanese speakers alike.[349] Today, Central Sudanic languages are found in the Central African Republic, Chad, Sudan, South Sudan, Uganda and the Democratic Republic of the Congo.[350] As Christopher Ehret wrote for the Transafrican Journal of History, an interaction of these groups is likely to have happened as Bantu carries several terms of Central Sudanic origin:

> Taken together with the evidence of cattle terminology… data could be explained by hypothesizing an initial interaction between the earliest Eastern Bantu groups and Central Sudanic-speakers in an undetermined location and several subsequent periods of interaction between particular later Bantu peoples and different Central Sudanic communities in several regions of central and southern Africa. A detailed investigation of this hypothesis has since been undertaken. The results strongly support the general view of history offered in the hypothesis and, as well, add considerable elaboration to that picture. The basic evidence for this history consists of a number of Central Sudanic loanword sets variously distributed among Bantu languages. Since whole sets of loanwords, in the absence of an evolved scholarly tradition, are adopted only in situations of direct social interaction between the people adopting the words and the people from whose languages the words come, these borrowing sets define various periods of contact between Bantu and Central Sudanic-speaking communities.[351]

This language dispersion is compounded with the fact the Ethiopian gnome is shared with groups throughout Africa. For example, a study published by NIH found close Y chromosomes among Ethiopians, the

---

[349] N. W. Thomas, The Sudanic Languages, Bulletin of the School of Oriental Studies, University of London, vol. 1, no. 4, (1920), 107–24.
[350] Gerrit Dimmendaal, Central Sudanic languages, Britannica, https://www.britannica.com/place/Central-African-Republic#ref40683 (*last visited* Dec. 13, 2023).
[351] Christopher Ehret, Patterns of Bantu and Central Sudanic Settlement in Central and Southern Africa (CA. 1000 B.C. - 500 A.D.), Transafrican Journal of History, vol. 3, no. 1/2, (1973), 1–71.

Khoisan people in South Africa, and Senegalese people.³⁵² This gives us a window into the possible routes taken by the Hebrew people as they fled their Arab and Berber oppressors.

East & Southern African Dispersed Hebrews

There are many groups who claim Hebrew ancestry throughout Africa. The next two sections will cover only a handful of tribes who, based on the information available, display obvious Hebrew heritage. However, this list is not meant to be exhaustive. The author strongly suspects a strong Hebrew heritage in the Luba, Kongo and Mmundu tribes, which were among the most targeted in the Trans-Atlantic Slave Trade by the Portuguese.³⁵³ It is even estimated 30% of African American DNA traces to around Angola, where these tribes originate.³⁵⁴ However, without sufficient information available on Hebraic oral history or customs, these and other tribes should be further investigated.

Again, it is not sufficient to rely on a mere identification of people claiming they are Jews, but rather oral history, language similarities and cultural practices give the greatest indication of a group's Hebrew lineage. Something remarkable is most of these Hebraic tribes have an oral history tracing their lineage to Ethiopia or to the East African region, despite the common belief that Palestine is Yahshar-el (Israel).

---

³⁵² Ornella Semino, et al., Ethiopians and Khoisan share the deepest clades of the human Y-chromosome phylogeny, Science Direct, (Jan. 7, 2002) https://www.sciencedirect.com/science/article/pii/S0002929707613019.
³⁵³ The 5 African Tribes Affected by the Slave Trade, Black Excellence, (Dec. 22, 2021) https://www.blackexcellence.com/5-african-tribes-affected-the-most-by-the-trans-atlantic-slave-trade/; Democratic Republic of the Congo, Kulanu, https://kulanu.org/communities/democratic-republic-of-the-congo/ (*last visited* Jan. 20, 2024).
³⁵⁴ John Timmer, How the Bantu people surged across two-thirds of Africa, Ars Technica, (May 6, 2017) https://arstechnica.com/science/2017/05/how-the-bantu-people-surged-across-two-thirds-of-africa/.

The Lemba

We begin with the Lemba. The Lemba are one of the few African tribes that mainstream Judaism has recognized for their Hebrew identity. However, the methodology from which this conclusion was reached should be scrutinized. Using DNA testing, British researchers reached an odd conclusion, that Jews share a common ancestor with the Lemba and that the Lemba descend from the Tribe of Levi.[355] However, it is in no way possible for British scientist to have the capacity to identify and possess DNA from this actual tribe from over two thousand years ago, who we know were in East Africa. However, the British researcher's overall conclusion of the Lemba having Hebraic roots does carry legitimacy.

The Lemba are Bantu, specifically Karanga-speaking Shona people living in Zimbabwe and South Africa. Some Lemba claim to have migrated to Zimbabwe from north of Zimbabwe, others claim to have migrated from outside of Africa, through Southern Arabia. However, a recent study by the Senior Curator of Ethnography at the Museum of Human Sciences in Harare categorically denied the suggestion that the Lemba migrated from outside of Africa, stating emphatically that the Lemba are purely African and the idea that they came from abroad was invented by outsiders.[356]

In actuality, the religious traditions of the Lemba share elements with the Qemant of Ethiopia.[357] The Lembas historically have practiced an ancient monotheistic religion where God made the first man from stones and then told them to multiply themselves. They also believe in a global flood where all people upon earth were killed at once. The Lemba have strict laws of purity and a specific diet,

---

[355] JTA, African tribe descended from Jews, DNA tests show, Jerusalem Post, (Mar. 8, 2010), https://www.jpost.com/Jewish-World/Jewish-News/African-tribe-descended-from-Jews-DNA-tests-show.
[356] Tutor Parfitt, The Construction of Jewish Identities in Africa, Jews of Ethiopia, Routledge, (2005), 25-31.
[357] Bernard Leeman, Nubian Moses, Ethiopian Exodus, Arabian Solomon, Sheba University College, (Aug. 2, 2015), 12.

where eating pork was traditionally punished by death. Lemba also did not intermarry nor interdine outside of their community, and they practice circumcision. The meat they did eat had to be ritually slaughtered by a Lemba. [358] All of these traditions mirror the practice of Torah.

The Tutsi

The Tutsi, also called the Watusi, are a Bantu speaking tribe located in Rwanda and Burundi. The tribe has a history of immense suffering and oppression, having been victims of grave persecution, including two genocides; one genocide in Burundi in 1993 where 25,000-50,000 Tutsi were killed, and another in Rwanda in 1994 where as many as 800,000 Tutsi were killed.[359]

According to their oral history, the Tutsi were disaffected royal family members from the remnants of Yahshar-el who migrated to the Great Lakes region from Ethiopia in ancient times to protect holy sites on Mt. Kilimanjaro, and secret gold mines for the kingdom.[360] As noted by Yochannan Bwejeri of the organization Havila, which studies the Hebrew diaspora:

> Some clans among Batutsi are contemporary with the time of Moses, people who moved from Egypt, judging by the exact knowledge they display about the laws of Moses. Others joined their brothers after the different misfortunes that affected the Israelite people, such as the destruction of the Holy Temple of Yerusalem. The
> Batutsi *Halakhah* has kept encoded references to these events, such as the annual Festival of *Sukkot,* called *Umuganuro* (literally "the festival of return").

---

[358] *Supra* note 356; African Lemba Tribe, Encyclopedia.com, https://encyclopedia.com/science/encyclopedias-almanacs-transcripts-and-maps/african-lemba-tribe (*last visited* Nov. 1, 2023).
[359] Tom Bundervoet, Livestock, Land and Political Power: The 1993 Killings in Burundi. Journal of Peace Research. (May 2009), 357–376; Rwandan Genocide, History.com, https://www.history.com/topics/africa/rwandan-genocide (*last updated* May 19, 2023).
[360] *Supra* note 356.

The cultural and religious references of Batutsi allude to either the pharaonic monotheism of the 18th Dynasty of Egypt or Moses's laws in the Hebraic Torah.

The Havila Institute has concentrated its efforts on the description and analysis of the biblical culture as carried by the ancient Batutsi. The parallelism of pharaonic practices and symbols with the Batutsi standards refers to the culture of the 18th Dynasty of Egypt and explains the Mosaic faith of the Batutsi. The antiquity of Batutsi monotheism has always been astonishing to the European witnesses, including those who reached the land of Havila in the early 19th century.

The political organization of the Batutsi kingdoms (from the Kush Kingdom until post-Zaagwe Kingdoms — 1270-1960) are strictly related to the Solomonic system. The Hebraic *kashrut* under the Levitic law is the staple of Batutsi feeding. The Batutsi system of law is the exact copy of the Deuteronomic Code, and none can attest that such a system is of recent import.[361]

Yibir/Ibro of Somalia & Ibire

The tribe Yibir/Ibro of Somalia are Muslims religiously, but commonly held in Somali society to be descended from Hebrews. The greatest showing of their Hebrew ancestry is their name, *Yibir*, very similar to the Hebrew word for "Hebrew," which is *Ibri*.[362] Their customs and beliefs reflect First Temple Hebrew practices.[363] Unlike other groups of Hebrew descent who have explored their Hebrew ancestry, the Yibir have largely rejected embracing this identify due to persecution. As detailed by a New York Times article, "Somalia's 'Hebrews' See a Better Day:"

> The sultan of the Jews in Somalia is a handsome, silver-haired man named Ahmed Jama Hersi who does not know the first thing about

---

[361] Yochannan Bwejeri, Hebraic Traditions of the Batutsi, Kulanu, https://kulanu.org/communities/tutsi/hebraic-traditions-batutsi/ (*last visited* Jan. 20, 2024).
[362] 5680. Ibri, Bible Hub, https://biblehub.com/hebrew/5680.htm (*last visited* Jan. 20, 2024).
[363] *Supra* note 357 at 12.

Judaism. He is a Muslim, as were his ancestors back at least 800 years. But he and his people are treated badly, cursed as descendants of Israelites. The name of the tribe is Yibir, or Hebrew.

"Even our young people," he said, "they are ashamed when you ask them what tribe they belong to. They will not say Yibir."[364]

Today, the Yibir are known in their society as ritual specialists with magical powers, which has led to suspicion and resentment against them. Similarly, the libire clan of the Rendille in North-East Kenya, are close cousins of the Somalis, and are also ritual specialists with alleged powerful curses. "libire" and "Yibir" belong to the same etymological root.[365]

West African Hebrews

For many, the West African connection is harder to imagine, principally because of distance. However, the dispersion did indeed go west, likely as a collective force. Four of the major coastal tribes of Western Africa, the Yoruba, Igbo, Akan and the Gaa-Adangbe, are very closely related. Several studies have been commissioned over the years on linkages of genetic similarity between these ethnic groups. One study in particular, conducted by the National Human Genome Centre, Howard University and Charles Rotimi of the University of Ibadan revealed that there was 99.9 percent within-population variance among the tribes, and the between-population variance was less than 0.1 percent, meaning that Yorubas, Igbos, Gaa-Adangbe and Akan are 99.9 percent similar.[366] As detailed in the article on News Rescue "Yoruba Are 99.9% Genetically Identical To Igbos, Akan And Gaa-Adangbe – Study:"

---

[364] Ian Fisher, Djibouti Journal; Somalia's 'Hebrews' See a Better Day, New York Times, (Aug. 15, 2000), https://www.nytimes.com/2000/08/15/world/djibouti-journal-somalia-s-hebrews-see-a-better-day.html.
[365] Aweis A. Ali, A Brief History of Judaism in the Somali Peninsula, Somali Bible Journal (Jun. 2, 2021), 31.
[366] Owolabi Oluwasegun, Yoruba Are Genetically 99.9 Percent Igbo – Study Reveals, the Herald, https://www.herald.ng/yoruba-genetically-99-9-percent-igbo-study-reveals/ (last updated Jul. 2, 2016).

Adebowale et al made the shocking discovery that whereas there was 99.9% within-population variance, the between-population variance was less than 0.1%. This means that Yorubas, Igbos, Gaa and Akan are 99.9% similar as populations, while within each of the groups there are differences/variations between individuals as high as 99%, i.e. One Igbo may be 99% variant to another Igbo, or one Yoruba to another Yoruba... "In addition, these four ethnic groups have a long history of trade and other interactions and they all speak languages belonging to the Niger-Kordofanian group. As noted by Cavalli-Sforza et al the genetic relationships observed in West Africa indicate that major migrations and admixtures occurred within the region in earlier times It is important to point out that despite the small amount of genetic differentiation in the sample as a whole, it was possible to distinguish between the groups from each country using a hierarchical AMOVA model and a dendrogram algorithm.[367]

The genetic semblances and the Niger-Kordofanian languages attest that these tribes likely came to the region from East Africa in a singular migration, before branching off and dispersing.

The Ashanti

The Ashanti (or Asante) are a tribe with over 5 million members primarily based in Ghana, the Ivory Coast and Togo.[368] There is overwhelming evidence that the Ashanti tribe descends from Yahshar-el (Israel). The name Ashanti in itself is Hebrew; there was even a town named Ashan in Yahudah (Judah).[369] The "ti" or "tie" in West African names tends to mean "the race of," "the men of," or "the children of." Thus, the word Ashanti means "the children of Ashan"[370]

---

[367] Dr. Brimah, Yoruba Are 99.9% Genetically Identical To Igbos, Akan And Gaa-Adangbe – Study, News Rescue, (Nov. 20, 2015) https://newsrescue.com/yoruba-are-99-adangbe-study/.

[368] Ashanti / Asante, Africa 101 Last Tribes, https://www.101lasttribes.com/tribes/ashanti.html (*last visited* Jan. 20, 2024).

[369] Joshua 15:42.

[370] Joseph J. Williams, The Vail Ballou Press, Hebrewisms of West Africa, (1930), 66.

The Hebrew identity of the Ashanti has long been a topic of conversation. Joseph J. Williams in *Hebrewisms of West Africa* documents historians such as Andre Arcin and his assertion that "from Ethiopia, Middle Egypt and Central Sudan, descended the Ashanti and the tribes known as Bantu." Similarly, Sir Harry Johnson was of the opinion, that "according to their language relations the Ashanti group of Negros once came from Niger north of Yorubaland, in Borgu country." Lieut. Col. Mockler-Ferryman insisted that "that Borgus claim relationship with the Bornus, and the Bornus are located to the south of Lake Chad, there is a far-reaching indication of the possible origin of the Ashanti," providing verification of a collective journey from the Nile Valley. [371]

Genetic evidence also points to an East African origin of the Ashanti. Professor Roland B. Dixon of Harvard found that:

> the oldest strata in Africa are represented by the Mongoloid—that is round-headed)brachycephalic) low-skulled (chamaecephalic) broad-nosed (platyrrhine) and the Proto-Australoid—that is long headed (dolichocephalic) low skulled (chamaecephalic) broad-nosed (platyrrhine) – types. Speaking of the later classification, Professor Dixon calls attention to the fact this type "appears as a not inconsiderable element in the Abyssinian plateau and among the Ashanti of West Africa." Professor Dixon concluded that the Ashanti "seem to be quite comparable to the Chad group in the Sudan." This Negro immigration he added "was in part a westerly drift from the Chad-Nile area, and in part a direct southward movement from the western Sudan and the Sahara borders, forced by the expansion in the Sahara region of the Caspian peoples who have poured into north Africa since very early times. [372]

Steven Jacobs, a Jewish historian in his work *The Hebrew Heritage of Black Africa* made the following observations on the Ashanti:

1. The Ashanti are an ethnic mixture of the peoples of West Africa, the ancestral home of most Black Americans

---

[371] *Id.* at 31-34.
[372] *Id.* at, 34-35.

2. The Ashanti are closely related to the Fanti, Yoruba, Sudanese, and more distantly to the Bantu, whose combined population stretches fully across sub-Saharan Africa.
3. The Ashanti tribe appear to have migrated and later been pushed westward by alien White invaders of European origin known as Berbers and Arabs. The Ashanti appear to have spread from Chad-Nile region of Northeast Africa.
4. The Ashanti and related peoples live in the very region near the West Coast of Africa from which most Black African slaves were captured and transported. Hence they are the ancestors of most African Americans of today.[373]

The general belief is that Fantis, Ashantis, Wassawa, and all the Twi-speaking or Akan peoples were originally one tribe. They were a pastoral community and inhabited the open country beyond before being pushed into the forest belt and farther north. A northern and lighter skinned people, commonly believed to have been the Fulani, began encroaching on their territory, seizing their cattle and young women, and enslaving their people. Fleeing these oppressive forces, the Akans began to migrate into the forest where they lived in hiding. When the population grew numerous their oppressors sought after them, but were unable to fight in the dense forest. The people living in peace continued to thrive, and gradually extended further south populating the forest belt and eventually reaching the coast.[374]

Culturally, the Ashanti have many Hebraic traditions as well. Similar to the Hebrew word for the Law of Moses, *Torah*, in Ashanti culture the Law-giver is referred to as *Toro*.[375] The name of the god of the Ashantis is a supreme being known as *Nyame*, to whom Saturday is dedicated.[376] In addition, Williams list a number of Hebrew feats of Ashanti culture, including religious dances, the use of "Amen," vowel value, a patriarchal system, the authority in a stool or chair, endogamy, cross-cousin marriages, familial names, exogamy, marriage

---

[373] Steven Jacobs, Moses Farrar, The Hebrew Heritage of Black Africa, African Tree Press, (2016) 20-21.
[374] *Supra* note 370 at 37.
[375] *Id.*
[376] *Id.* at 81

rites, uncleanness after child birth, the purification ceremony, menstrual seclusion, ceremonial ablutions and loan words of Hebrew origin. [377]

Williams also noted Ashanti customs which are Abyssinian. Citing T Edward Bowditch, "The Ashanti is never presumed to speak but through his ministers or interpreters, who invariably repeat his ordinary observations, however audible, with the Abyssinian exordium, 'Hear what the King says!'" [378] In addition, with the prefix Sai or Zai, the names of Ashanti kings are a vestige of the Abyssinian Za or Zo prefix of shepherd kings, or the original Ethiopians. He also discusses that the Ashantis, like the Abyssinians and ancient Egyptians, never fight at night, not even after sunset, whatever advantage they may lose. The Ashanti also never fight on Saturday. This is even closer to Hebrew tradition than the Gallas of Ethiopia, who never fight on a Friday.[379]

Jacobs also notes the Ashanti and Bantu connection:

> scholars believe there is a common origin for the Ashanti and Bantu peoples. They both came, it is thought, from the northeastern part of the African continent. The Ashanti eventually migrated to the west coast roughly parallel to the southern edge of the Sahara Desert. The Bantu, by contrast, moved mainly to the south so that today they occupy nearly the entire southern half of the continent from the Congo Republic and Zaire on the west to Mozambique on the east and southward to the very southernmost tip called the Cape of Good Hope.[380] The Ashantis are far from the only Bantu culture with a plentitude of Hebrewisms, however what makes their case study different is the fact Islam never gain influence over the Ashanti either socially or politically.[381]

---

[377] *Id.* at 72
[378] *Id.* at 42
[379] *Id.* at 42-43.
[380] *Id.* at 51.
[381] *Id.* at 47.

The Yoruba

When the United Monarchy of Yahshar-el first split, 11 of the 12 tribes decided to be governed apart from the Davidic dynasty. An Ephramite was chosen by Yahuah (God) to lead Yahshar-el, becoming the first king of the southern kingdom. His name was *Yarobam* (Jeroboam), pronounced Yaw-rob-awm.[382] The name Yoruba clearly derives from Yarobam, meaning the Yoruba likely originate from the southern kingdom of Yahshar-el.[383]

The Yoruba people are a tribe of over 44 million people who inhabit parts of Nigeria, Benin and Togo. [384]According to the Yoruba's origin story, the tribe originally migrated from the Nile Valley. This is confirmed as Yoruba culture has many similarities to ancient Egyptian culture. In addition, Yoruba religious tradition of Oduduwa teaches that the ancestors of the Yorubas emerged from Egypt, not Arabia as it has been speculated, leading some scholars to conclude Yorubas were Coptic Christians from Egypt.[385]

The Hebrewisms in Yoruba culture include circumcision, the division of tribes into separate families, and very frequently into the number twelve; sacrifices with the sprinkling of blood upon the altars and door-posts (similar to Passover); a specified time for mourning for the dead, during which time they shave their heads and wear soiled or tattered clothes; belief in demon possessions, purifications rituals, among other cultural feats. [386]

---

[382] 1 Kings 12; 3379. Yarobam, Bible Hub, https://biblehub.com/hebrew/3379.htm (*last visited* Jan. 22, 2024).
[383] Dierk Lange, Origin of the Yoruba and "The Lost Tribes of Israel", Anthropos 106(2):579-595 (2011).
[384] Yoruba, Africa 101 Last Tribes, http://www.101lasttribes.com/tribes/yoruba.html (*last visited* an. 24, 2024).
[385] Jock Matthew Agai, Rethinking Yoruba Culture in Light of Yoruba Origins, Journal for Semitics, (2015) 427–450 , 430.
[386] Agai M. Jock, The Coptic Origins of the Yoruba, AOSIS. (Oct. 18, 2021), https://theologiaviatorum.org/index.php/tv/article/view/124/266.

The Ewe & Gbe

The Ewe are a tribe of over six million people inhabiting Togo, Benin, southwest Nigeria and the Volta region of Ghana. Their language *Ewegbe* is a part of the Gbe language cluster which comes from Ethiopia along with Gen of Togo, the Aja of Togo and Benin, the Fon of Togo and Benin, and the Phla-Phera of Togo and Benin. They belong to a member of the Kwa family of Sudanic languages, a sub-family of the Niger-Congo family of the Congo-Kordofanian language family of Africa. The Ewe are said to have left Ethiopia due to slave raids where their community members were being sold as far as India.[387]

The Ewe, along with other Gbe, including the Aja, Fon and Ga-Dangme descend from the Yoruba. It is said all groups lived in harmony until Yoruba people pushed the related groups westward. The Ewe thus migrated from Ketu, a Yoruba town in modern Benin. Some Gbe returned and founded the Aja kingdom of Allada, Whydah, Popo and Jakin, and later the Fon kingdom of Dahomey in the early eighteenth century that became a central location of the Trans-Atlantic Slave Trade.[388] The Whydah, or Ouidah kingdom is notable for being a variation of Yahudah, and is even labeled "Kingdom of Juda" in a 1747 map published in England.[389] (See Map 19)

---

[387] United Volta Association, The Origins and Brief History of the Ewe People, ,https://www.uvainc.org/history-of-the-ewe-people/ (*last visited* Dec. 13, 2023); Sudanic languages, Britannica, https://www.britannica.com/topic/Sudanic-languages, (*last visited* Jan. 20, 2024).
[388] Michael Eli Dokosi, The fascinating history and culture of the Ewe in Ghana, Togo, Benin and Nigeria, Face2Face Africa, (July 4, 2020) https://face2faceafrica.com/article/the-fascinating-history-and-culture-of-the-ewe-in-ghana-togo-benin-and-nigeria.
[389] Emanuel Bowen, New & Accurate Map of Negroland, 1693 or 1694-1767, 1747, https://digital.library.illinois.edu/items/338af630-e946-0133-1d3d-0050569601ca-8#?c=0&m=0&s=0&cv=0&r=0&xywh=-1824%2C-126%2C7646%2C3463 (*last visited* Jan. 20, 2024).

The Ga-Dangme

The Ga-Dangme are an ethnic group in Ghana, Benin and Togo numbering about 2 million people that is made up of the Ga and Dangbe people grouped respectively as part of the Ga–Dangme ethnolinguistic group.[390] The Ga-Dangme have an oral history that they are originally Hebrew, from the tribes of Gad and Dan, thus the name Ga-Dangme has Hebrew origin.

According to Ga-Dangme oral history, the group migrated to Ethiopia's Gonder Province where the Blue Nile originates. The Ga-Dangme word for high priest *Nai Wulomo* even means "High Priest of the Nile."[391] Dr. Joseph Nii Abekar Mensah gives a further oral history of this tribe:

> In 640 B.C, the Assyrians attacked the Ga-Dangmes again while they were in Ethiopia. From Ethiopia, they travelled through Southern Sudan and settled for a period of time at Sameh in Niger and then to Ileife in Nigeria. They migrated again in 1100 A.D and settled at Dahome and later, travelled to Huatsi in Togo where they stayed briefly.
>
> From Huatsi, the Ga-Dangmes travelled to the eastern banks of River Volta (know as JOR). From there, they crossed the Volta River at a place between the Old Kpong and Akuse and established settlements on the plains of Tag-logo where they lived till 1200 A.D. Later, the Ga-Dangmes migrated to the plains of Lorlorvor between Lorlorvor and Osudoku Hills. The Shai occupied a settlement in Shai highlands…. The descendant of Eri, son of Gad are believed to have founded the Nri Kingdom around 900 A.D of the South Eastern and parts of the mid-western Igboland in Nigeria with other tribes of Levi, Zebulon, Ephraim and possibly more. In the Book of numbers, the

---

[390] Ga, Joshua Project, (May 26, 2013), https://joshuaproject.net/languages/gaa; Ga-Adangbe, Ghana Web, https://www.ghanaweb.com/GhanaHomePage/tribes/adangbe.php (*last visited* Jan. 20, 2024).
[391] Dr. Joseph Nii Abekar Mensah
HEBREW ISRAELITES ORIGINS OF GA-DANGMES OF GHANA IN BRIEF, http://ghanadot.com/Review.mensah.gahebrew.032111.html, (*last visited* Jan. 20, 2024).

Bible had made extensive references to the children of Israel, which includes Gad and Dan and their children (Numbers 1:1-54).

Ga-Dangmes have Hebrew customs of circumcision, the *Homowo* Festival which is similar to the Passover festival, GaDangme Proverbs which are similar to Hebrew proverbs, as well as Hebrew names as documented by Mensah:

> Ga-Dangme names are found throughout the OLD TESTAMENT. Examples are: NIIKOILAI (Rev:2, 6, 15); AMASA (2 Samuel 17, 25; 1 Chronicle 33 20-21 DJAANI/JANNE, 2 Timothy 3: 8; AMON, 2 Chronicle 33: 20-21; ASHALE (ASAHEL), 1 Chronicle 2:16, 2 Samuel 2: 18-19."[392]

The Igbo

Similar to the Yibir, the name *Igbo* is the first indication of the Igbo tribe's Hebrew origins, as *Igbo* draws great semblance to *Ibri*. However, the greatest confirmation of their Hebrew lineage is Igbo culture.[393] Traditional Igbo religion Odinani has a supreme being called *Chukwu*. Chukwu is the source of all things, is invisible, genderless although referred to with male pronouns, and is benevolent. He also punishes evil doers and evil deeds but rewards good deeds. There are also lesser spirits called *agbara* who similar to angels can be approached. There is also *Igu Aro*, the Igbo festival that is very similar to Passover, where animals are sacrificed and blood is smeared on doorposts, trees, roadways, feet, hands and earlobe as a seal to ward off evil spirits. [394]

In addition, Igbo's eating patterns resemble those of the Hebrews. Eating pig is forbidden and considered filthy. Though male infidelity is frowned upon, it is considered an abomination when a woman

---

[392] Dr. Joseph Nii Abekar Mensah, Hebrew Israelites Origins of Ga-Dangmes of Ghana in Brief, http://ghanadot.com/Review.mensah.gahebrew.032111.html.
[393] Culture Of Ibi Ukwu (circumcision) in Igbo Land, Olalekan Oduntan, (Mar. 31, 2017) http://www.olaleone.org/2017/03/culture-of-ibi-ukwu-circumcision-in.html.
[394] Igbo Jews, Kalanu, https://kulanu.org/wp-content/uploads/nigeria/Igbo-Jews-Senior-Project.pdf (*last visited* Nov. 20, 2023).

commits adultery. Women who are accused of adultery are taken to the community central place of worship where she is administered an oath, similar to the oath of drinking bitter waters of the Hebrews,[395] however, the woman was to eat a kola nut from the ground that was prayed over. In addition, premarital sex, homosexual acts, and bestiality are all considered abominations.[396]

The Diaspora

The Trans-Atlantic Slave trade rocked West Africa unlike any event, creating a disconnected diaspora with little knowledge of their heritage. It is difficult to parse out how much of the slave trade was an extension of the age long struggle of Yahshar-el with Esau, and how much was motivated by pure economic greed. Probably the most diabolical aspect of the slave trade is the love of money, which motivated Hebrew descended tribes into engaging in the mass selling of other Africans as commodities. However, West African tribes that were early collaborators of the slave trade would become later victims themselves.

The Portuguese, the first European nation to engage in the Trans-Atlantic Slave Trade, acquired slaves for labor on the Atlantic African island plantations, and later for plantations in Brazil and the Caribbean, as well as sending a small number to Europe. Initially, the Portuguese attempted to capture Africans through direct raids along the coast, however, they found these raids to be too costly and ineffective against West and Central African militaries. Instead, the Portuguese traders established commercial relations with African chiefs who agreed to sell them slaves taken from wars or domestic trading in exchange for European and North African goods.[397]

---

[395] Numbers 5:11–31.
[396] *Supra* note 394.
[397] African Passages, Lowcountry Adaptations, The Trans-Atlantic Slave Trade, LDHI, https://ldhi.library.cofc.edu/exhibits/show/africanpassageslowcountryadapt/introductionatlanticworld/trans_atlantic_slave_trade (*last visited* Jan. 2024).

The Ashanti, the Fon kingdom of Dahomey and the Yoruba empire of Oyo were all solicited to supply slaves to the slave trade. Slavery was a common feat of most African societies, although not as dehumanizing as chattel slavery as people enslaved still had rights. Initially the pool of Africans were war captives, people from rival tribes, or people who were indebted.[398]

While African collaborators in the slave trade should not escape condemnation for their participation, what should not be minimized is the overall scheme was a work of European manipulation. According to Kehinde Andrews:

> the disparaged groups did not feel a particular affinity to each other. Europeans exploited these differences and rivalries to the fullest extent… Europeans used the lack of an organized African polity to exploit the continent, something that, as we will see, became a common tactic for Western domination of the globe.[399]

As demand and pressure from Europeans grew, raids and warfare would be specifically conducted to meet that demand.[400] Thus, the system of slavery encouraged warfare to produce captives for trading and stimulated an increase in slavery in Africa.[401] Ninety percent of the enslaved were sent to forcibly work in the Caribbean and South

---

[398] Angela Thompsell, African Traders of Enslaved People, ThoughtCo. (Jun. 15, 2020) https://www.thoughtco.com/african-slave-traders-44538.
[399] Kehinde Andrews, The New Age of Empire: How Racism and Colonialism Still Rule the World, Bold Type Books, (Mar. 2, 2021), 78.
[400] Hakim Adi, Africa and the Transatlantic Slave Trade, BBC, (Oct. 5, 2012) https://www.bbc.co.uk/history/british/abolition/africa_article_01.shtml.
[401] The Colonial Williamsburg Foundation, The Slave Hunt – Capture and Captives, BlackHistoryMonth.org, (May 20, 2021) https://www.blackhistorymonth.org.uk/article/section/history-of-slavery/the-slave-hunt-capture-and-captives/; *Supra* note 398.

America. Only six percent were sent to work in the United States.[402] The Yoruba, Igbo and Fon were among those most enslaved.[403]

The Fon people of Dahomey made up a large proportion of slaves sent to sugar plantations in the French West Indies, particularity Haiti and Trinidad. The Igbo were primarily taken to Barbados, Haiti, Jamaica and the United States. From the mid 1600s to 1830s, the United States brought a large number of Igbos to Virginia and Maryland for tobacco plantations. It has been hypothesized that about 60% of all African Americans have at least one Igbo ancestor.[404] (See Map 18)

The Ashanti also make up a significant number of enslaved Africans in the slave trade, particularly in Caribbean nations, namely Jamaica. Even today, Jamaican day names given to children, Adinkra symbols used on houses, Anansi stories and the dialect of Jamaican Patois all have roots in the Ashanti. There was also an early wave of Akan-Ashanti people brought to South Carolina in the seventeenth century by colonists from Barbados.[405] Both Marcus Garvey and his first wife, Amy Ashwood Garvey are of Ashanti descent.[406] In addition, famed abolitionist Harriet Tubman was of Ashanti descent.[407]

---

[402] Steven Mintz, Historical Context: Facts about the Slave Trade and Slavery, The Gilder Lehrman Institute of American History, https://www.gilderlehrman.org/history-resources/teacher-resources/historical-context-facts-about-slave-trade-and-slavery (*last visited* Jan. 20, 2024).
[403] 10 Most Enslaved African Tribes, Africa is Woke, (Oct. 3, 2022) https://www.afrikaiswoke.com/most-enslaved-african-tribes/.
[404] The 5 African Tribes Affected by the Slave Trade, Black Excellence, (Dec. 22, 2021) https://www.blackexcellence.com/5-african-tribes-affected-the-most-by-the-trans-atlantic-slave-trade/.
[405] Annette Kashif, Notes on the Origins and Evolution of African American Language, Park Ethnography Program, https://www.nps.gov/ethnography/aah/aaheritage/sysMeaning_furthRdg1.htm (*last visited* Jan. 22, 2024).
[406] The Ashanti People, a story, African American Registry, https://aaregistry.org/story/the-ashanti-people-a-short-story/ (*last visited* Jan. 20, 2024).
[407] Allison Keyes, Ghana Welcomes Tubman Family Members, NPR, (Aug. 15, 2005), https://www.npr.org/templates/story/story.php?storyId=4797502.

Both Garvey and Tubman have been lauded as Moses figures by their followers.

Where Did Slaves In The United States Originate From?[408]		
Ethnic Groups	**Origins (Modern Countries)**	**Percent of American Slaves**
Kongo and Mbundu	Angola, DR Congo, Republic of the Congo	25%
Bamileke, Bubi, Ibibio, Igbo, and Tikar	Equatorial Guinea, Cameroon, and Nigeria	22%
Mende and Temne	Guinea, Liberia, and Sierra Leone	15%
Fula, Mandinka, and Wolof	Gambia, Mauritania, and Senegal	14%
Akan and Fon	Benin, Ghana, and Ivory Coast	13%
Kru and Mande	Ivory Coast, Liberia, and Sierra Leone	5%
Allada, Ewe, Mahi, and Yoruba	Benin, Ghana, Nigeria, and Togo	4%
Makua and Malagasy	Madagascar, Mozambique, and Tanzania	2%

In 1773 the First African Baptist Church was built under the leadership of Reverend George Leile in Savannah Georgia. Located in the church are pews that were installed during the early 1900's and had been made by enslaved Africans. On the outside of some pews, enslaved Africans engraved cursive Hebrew, Ethiopian Amharic Ge'ez and Ancient Aramaic, a testimony to origins that have long since been forgotten.[409]

---

[408] Ancestral Homelands Of Slaves In The United States, World Atlas, https://www.worldatlas.com/articles/ancestral-homelands-of-slaves-in-the-united-states.html (*last visited* Jan. 20, 2024).
[409] First African Baptist Church, https://firstafricanbc.com/history.php, (*last visited* Jan. 20, 2024).

Africa all together was completely devastated by the massive and unprecedented population loss of *at least* 11 million Africans from the Trans-Atlantic, and 25 million from both together.[410] Those tribal persons spared by the Trans-Atlantic Slave Trade were not spared for long. While the Trans-Atlantic slave trade came to an end in the early 1800s, not long after European colonist began their encroachment and colonization of the African continent. By the 1880s the Scramble for Africa was in full swing. [411] Former kingdoms that had traded slaves with Europeans were now forced into being slaves on their own land. No one would escape.

---

[410] *Supra* note 400.
[411] Claims of territorial boundaries, Britannica, https://www.britannica.com/place/western-Africa/Claims-of-territorial-boundaries (*last visited* Jan. 20, 2024).

Conclusion: Rebel

"All these died in faith, without receiving the promises, but having seen them and having welcomed them from a distance, and having confessed that they were strangers and exiles on the earth. For those who say such things make it clear that they are seeking a country of their own. And indeed if they had been thinking of that country from which they went out, they would have had opportunity to return. But as it is, they desire a better country, that is, a heavenly one. Therefore God is not ashamed to be called their God; for He has prepared a city for them."

~ Hebrews 11:13-16

This work was not meant to be comprehensive. Further research is necessary to firmly grasp what has been done to systematically deprive the children of Yahshar-el of their knowledge of themselves, knowledge of their homeland and knowledge of their Elohim and savoir Yahusha Hamashiach. This savoir, who was been mimicked and recreated into a docile being with no sense of justice for the oppressed in actually will be the one to destroy this wicked system, bringing the reign of Esau and his collaborators to an end. Thus, in preparation for him, we must avail ourselves of the knowledge that has been artfully hidden from us. This cannot be done by one person, nor should it. It is on those devoted to learning and spreading truth to take up their mantle and wake up the masses of Yahshar-el, the natural branches and those grafted in,[412] to who they are, and the work that must be done.

We also cannot expect the systems of this world to entertain truthful dialogue on this question, especially dialogue that exposes Esau and the people who descend from his physical and spiritual bloodline. The entire world system is implicated in this conspiracy. That includes the churches, synagogues, mosques, universities, corporations, secret societies and governments, all collaborating to not only hide the truth but cover their tracks. For that reason, we must lean totally on

---

[412] Romans 11:17

Yahuah for His instruction and not on the knowledge authorized by the Babylon System.

Shem's Lot Splitting from the Continent— Sign of the Return & Regathering

Isaiah 11:11-16 the passage to the ressurection

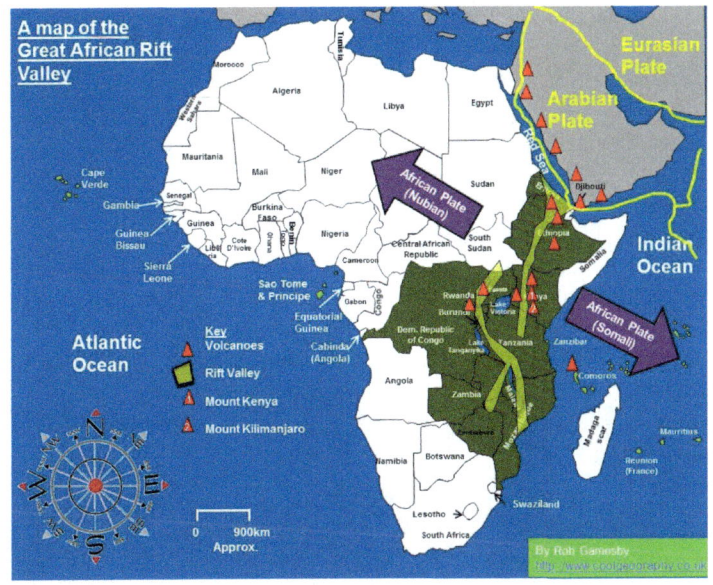

Shocking photos show Africa splitting apart as new ocean forms

Callum Jones
Published 13:19, 23 October 2023 BST| Last updated 13:19, 23 October 2023 BST

Featured Image Credit: Julie Rowland, University of Auckland / BBC

Our world is an ever-changing place, and perhaps our best indication as to how much it's changing is by looking at pictures.

Earlier this year, shocking photographs showed Africa splitting apart as a new ocean began to form.
The photographs have shown just how deep the damage is, as parts of Africa are physically splitting apart and a new ocean is forming between them.

A volcanic vent has opened in the Afar desert in Ethiopia. Credit: Julie Rowland, University of Auckland

Two parts of land in Kenya have began to split apart over recent years, with the two masses now so far apart that a whole new ocean will run through the divide in the future.

If the separation continues, it's thought that the African countries of Zambia and Uganda could one day have their own coastlines.

Expert research has also confirmed that a new ocean will one day run through the gap, named the East African Rift, millions of years from now.

According to the peer-reviewed journal Geophysical Research Letters, experts know the exact spot where the crack began as the borders of three tectonic plates have been gradually moving away from each other.

The international effort has discovered that the crack currently runs 35 miles long, after first appearing back in 2005 in the Ethiopian deserts.

Christopher Moore, a Ph.D. doctoral student at the University of Leeds, told NBC News: "This is the only place on Earth where you can study how continental rift becomes an oceanic rift."

Moore utilised satellite radar technology to monitor volcanic activity in the East African region, most commonly associated with the continent's gradual breakup.

The crack resides on the borders of the boundaries of the African, Arabian and Somali tectonic plates.

For the past 30 million years, the Arabian plate has been slowly moving away from the African continent.
The gap is growing, but not so quickly that you'll see it by looking at it, as the Arabian plate is moving away from Africa at a rate of approximately one inch per year.

The crack is certainly evident.

It's slower for both the African and Somali plate though, as they are reported to be breaking away at an even slower rate, at round half an inch to 0.2 inches every year.

It's thought that the gap will continue to widen in the future, to the point where East Africa could form its own separate continent.

Ken Macdonald, a marine geophysicist and professor emeritus based at the University of California, explained: "With GPS measurements, you can measure rates of movement down to a few millimetres per year.

"As we get more and more measurements from GPS, we can get a much greater sense of what's going on.

"The Gulf of Aden and the Red Sea will flood in over the Afar region and into the East African Rift Valley and become a new ocean, and that part of East Africa will become its own separate small continent."[413]

---

[413] Callum Jones, Shocking photos show Africa splitting apart as new ocean forms, UNILAD (Oct. 13, 2023,) https://www.unilad.com/news/world-news/east-african-rift-new-ocean-502323-20231023.

Photo Gallery

Chapter 1: Finding Eden

The Borders of Yahshar-el in Palestine, According to the Bible (Map 1)

Map of Ancient Israel According to Mainstream Bible Scholars (Map 2)

The Blue Nile River, the River Perath

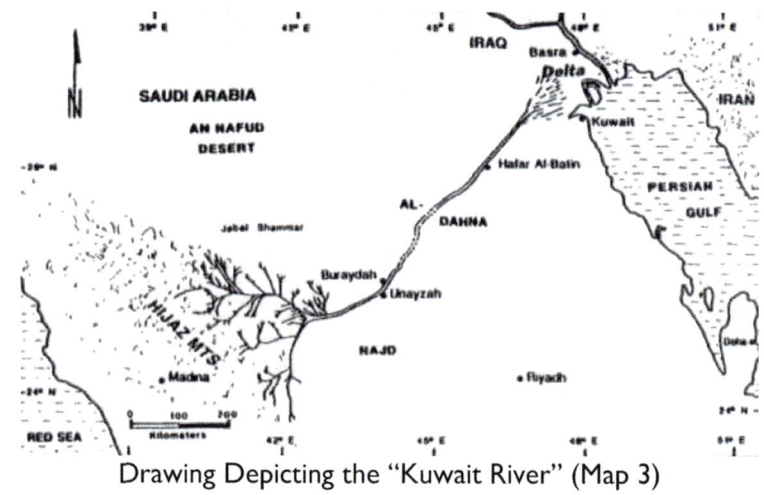

Drawing Depicting the "Kuwait River" (Map 3)

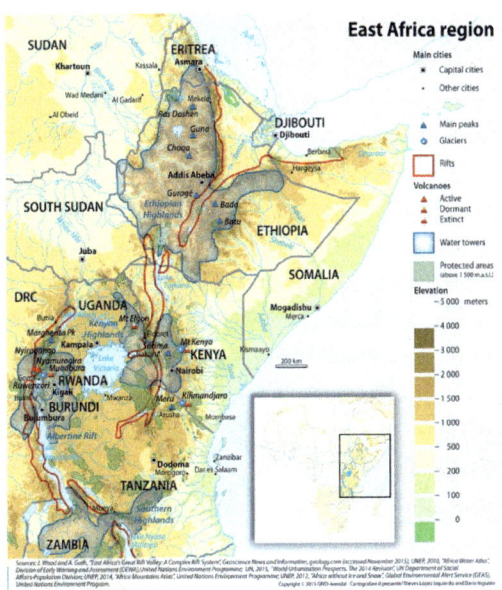

East Africa Region where Shem's Lot Fell

Chapter 2: Finding Yahshar-el

Images of Aksum City, the Real Yerusalem

Images of the Tekeze River, the Gihon that flows through Yerusalem

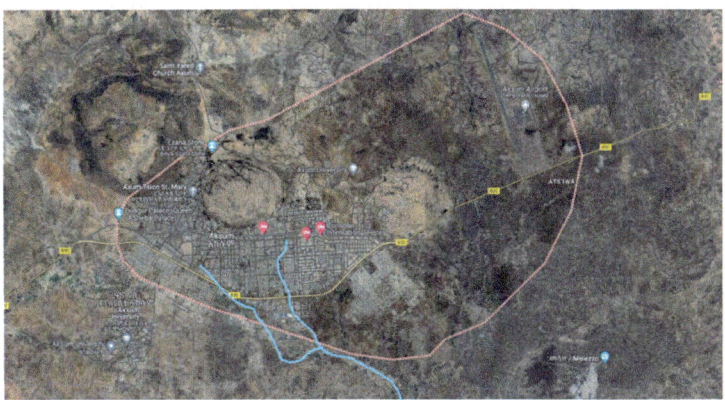
Satellite image of the Tekeze River, the Gihon that flows through Yerusalem (Map 4)

Map of the Horn of Africa, where Biblical Tyre and Sidon are located (Map 5)

Recreations of the Temple of Solomon

Recreation of Dungur, or the Aksum Palace

Chapter 3: The Palestine Lie

Hieroglyph of Nubians and "Semitic" Egyptian slaves making bricks.

Map of Egyptian Gold Mining (Map 6)

Chapter 4: Evidence From Hidden Scriptures

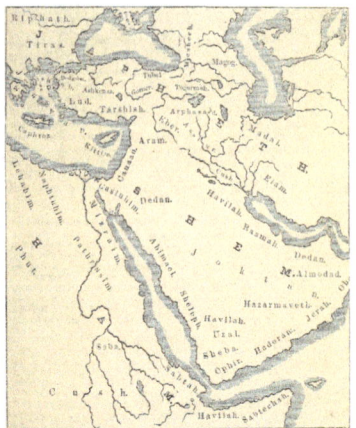

Commonly Held View of Division of the World by Noah's Sons (Map 7)

The Actual Division of the World by Noah's Sons (Map 8)

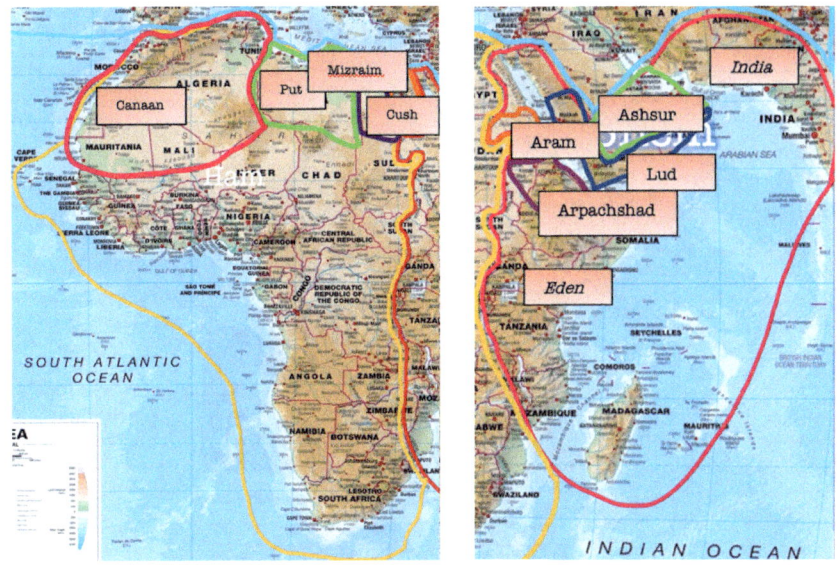

Division of Ham's Lot (Map 9)   Division of Shem's Lot (Map 10)

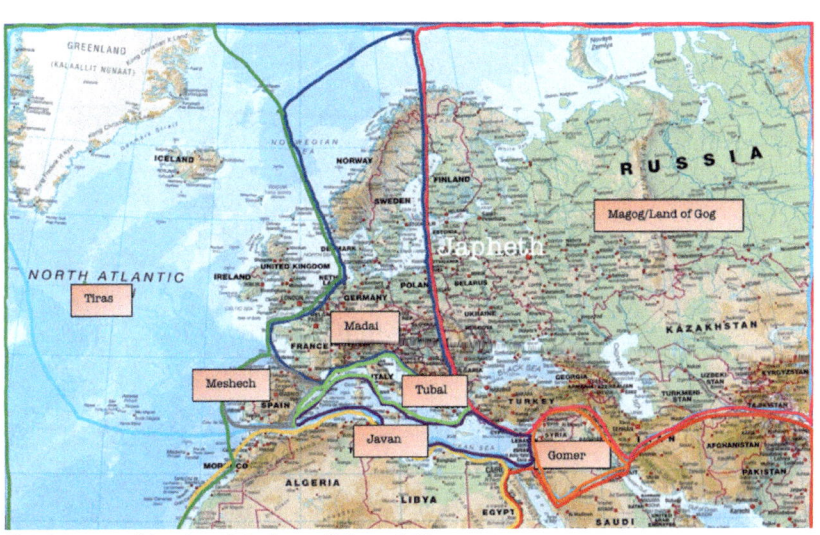

Division of Japheth's Lot (Map 11)

Chapter 8: The Real Yahshar-el

Land of Punt (Map 12)

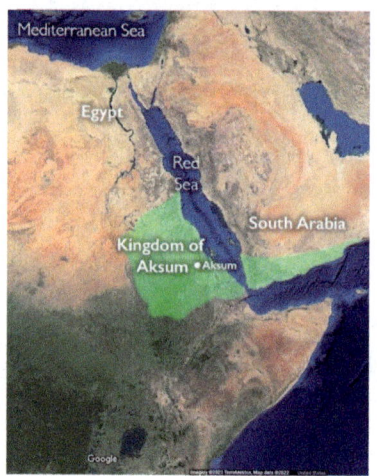

Map of Aksum (Map 13.1)

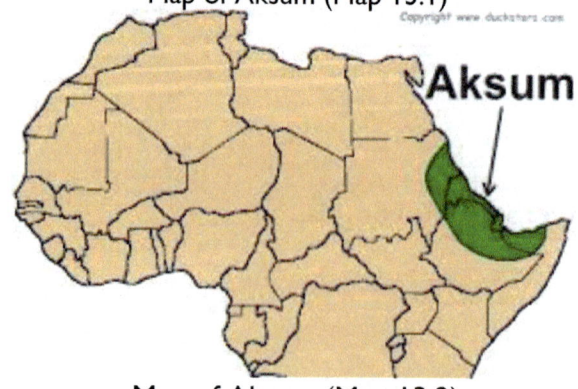

Map of Aksum (Map 13.2)

Chapter 10: The Dispersion

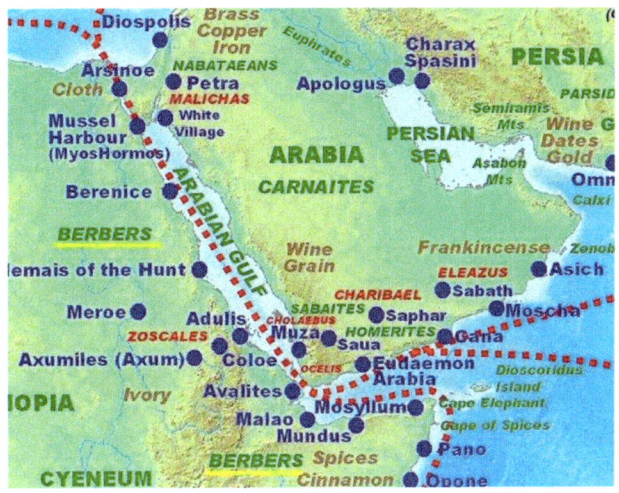

Redrawn Leo Africanus Map Showing Berbers in East Africa (Map 14)

Chapter 11: Into Captivity

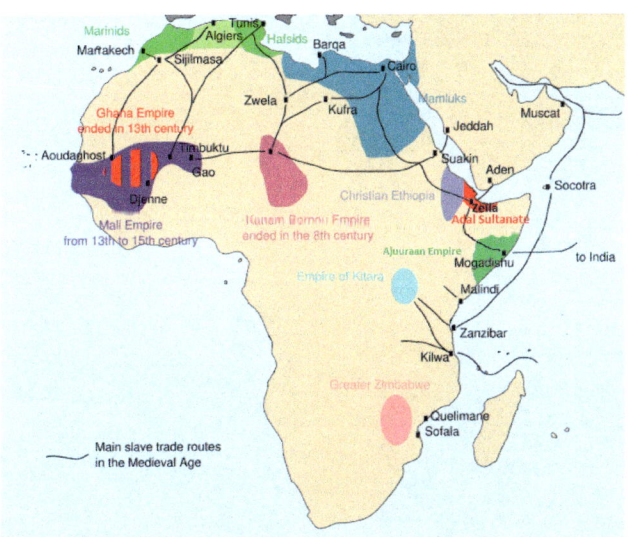

Map Aliesin, La traite arabe en Afrique au moyen-âge, showing Arab Slave Trade in Africa. (Map 15)

The Global African Slave Trade (Map 16)

Bilad al-Sudan or "Land of the Blacks" (Negroland) (Map 17)

Berber Jew Rabbi Mordechai Aby Serour from 1870s -1880s.
He was the Last Rabbi of Timbuktu.

Chapter 12: Where the Children of Yahshar-el Went

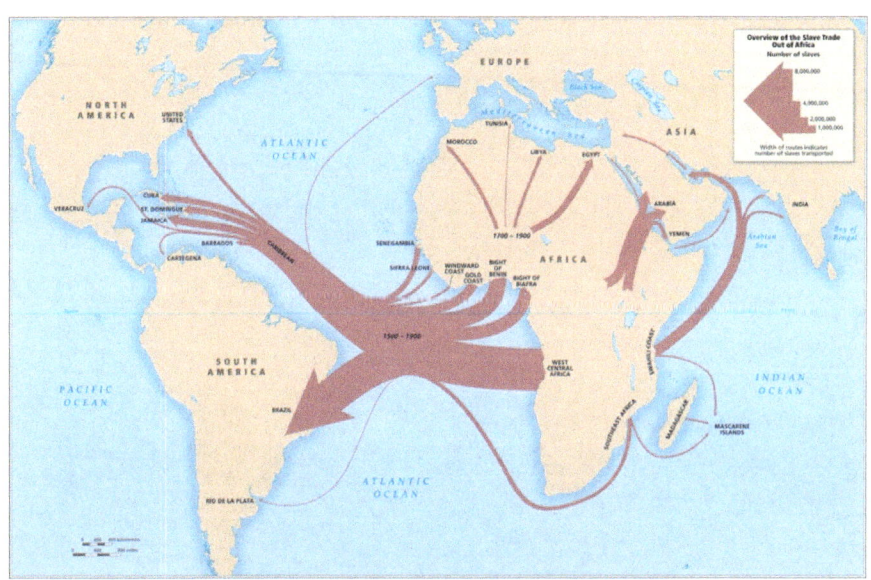

Map of Global Dispersion (Map 18)

Emanuel Bowen 1747 Map of Negroland and Whidah (Map 19)

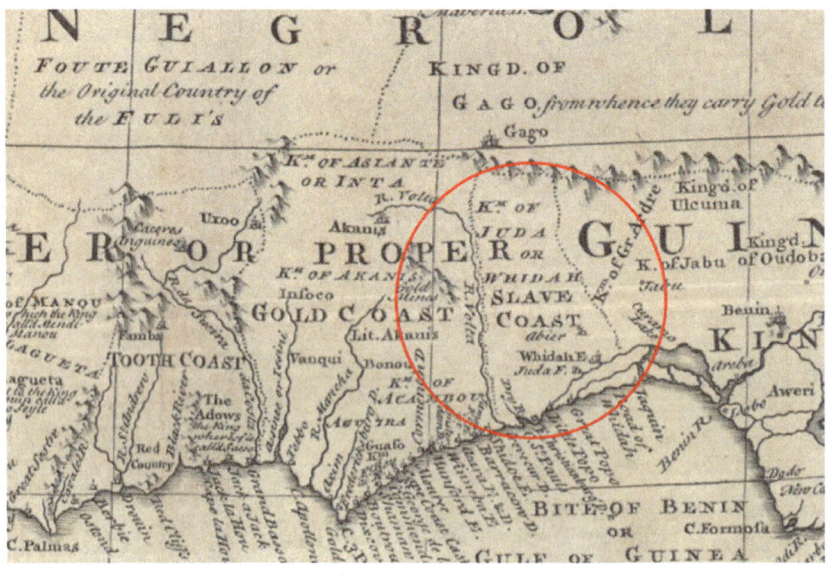

Close up of Whidah Slave Coast's, "Kingdom of Juda"

Addendum Chapter 4: The Dispersion

Gulf of Tadjoura – the Real Sea of Gallile

Map A

Map B

Satellite view of Galile

KML Export for Google Earth
Google maps view of Galile
Google links for Galile

Map C

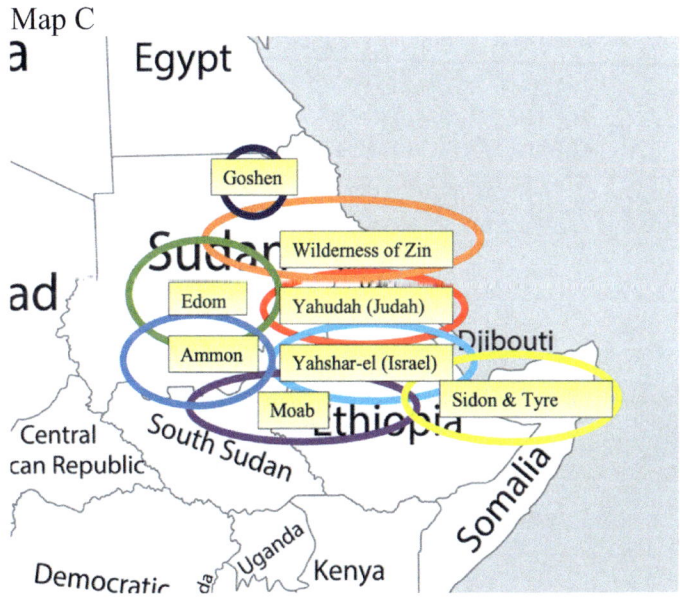

Map D

Printed in Great Britain
by Amazon